THE WHITENESS OF DESTRUCTION

The Whiteness of Destruction

THE ORIGINS AND
CONSEQUENCES OF
WHITE AGGRESSION

Dr. Mauray L. Tolbert

Acknowledgements

I would like to express my gratitude to those without whom this work would not have been possible. First, I must thank the Universe and the Ancestors. I pour libations and give thanks to the elders mentioned in this work who have transitioned. To my beautiful and intelligent counterpart, Yvonne: thank you for being my supportive rock. I also give thanks for the undying and selfless acts of every author in this work, for their willingness, drive, and desire to spread truth, impart wisdom, and teach about white supremacy and racism. This effort aims to better our families, neighborhoods, communities, and the world as a whole. Thank you to Michelle Alexander, Dr. Claud Anderson, Marimba Ani, Dr. Yosef Ben-Jochannan, John Henrik Clarke, Tommy J. Curry, Cheikh Anta Diop, Thomas A. Foster, Neely Fuller Jr., George G.M. James, Stephanie E. Jones-Rogers, Harriet A. Washington, Dr. Frances Cress Welsing, Chancellor Williams, Amos Wilson, Vincent Woodard, Carter G. Woodson, Bobby E. Wright, Ivan Van Sertima, The C.O.W.S, (Gus T. Renegade), The New Black Media, the B1 family, Victor of RWS, and "ALL" the other writers, content creators, and frontline soldiers in the war for freedom, justice, and reciprocity—the state of being reciprocal in action, speech, mental understanding, and/or influence.

Table of Contents

Chapter 8: Race War/Civil War 193

Chapter 9 Modern-Day Lynchings   207

Chapter 10   230

Chapter 11 Get Ready and Stay Ready   246

Author's Note

The language used to describe melanated Black people in America has evolved over time, with changes influenced by social and political attitudes towards race as well as historical and cultural contexts, indicating shifting attitudes towards race and identity. The language used in referenced materials mirrors that of the original author.

I paraphrase and quote other writers works as a vital resource in this work to communicate ideas in my own distinct way while making sure that the original source material is properly acknowledged (last name of the author, page number, if applicable; if not, n.p. (no page) will follow within the in-text citation) and can be located in the work cited section. This is more complex than just changing words or phrases around; it requires a thorough comprehension, careful consideration, and interpretation of the information being communicated.

This approach is used to pay tribute to the work of my predecessors and contribute to the ongoing discourse in their field. It also gives the work a fresh perspective on concepts that are already well known in order to spark conversations on the topic. Readers are encouraged to study and research the referenced authors' works thoroughly.

Foreword

Over the past 400 years, African history has been marked by deeply entrenched adversities, including slavery, colonialism, and systemic racism. These injustices have had a lasting impact on the Black Diaspora and continental Africans, leaving behind trauma and persistent obstacles in fighting poverty reduction, equality, and human rights. Black descendants of enslaved people continue to grapple with the legacy of the transatlantic slave trade and the Jim Crow era. At the same time, continental Africans face ongoing challenges such as economic inequality and political corruption. Despite these challenges, the legacy of African history is a powerful reminder of the strength and resilience of the Black Indigenous People. This legacy includes countless examples of resistance, innovation, and cultural richness that continue to shape contemporary society.

The impact of white supremacy on Black Indigenous people worldwide is profound, leading to confusion, internal conflict, and systemic oppression. To address these issues, non-white Black people must educate themselves on the effects of white supremacy and how it operates. This involves studying the history of racial oppression, listening to Black Indigenous People's experiences, and examining how institutional racism continues to perpetuate inequality to this day. By fostering a shared understanding of these issues and developing a shared understanding, Black Indigenous people can more effectively resist systemic racism and oppression.

Melanated people face an ongoing struggle against mistreatment and systemic oppression. In the United States, this is evident in the pushback against critical race theory in classrooms, the lack of an anti-black hate crime bill, and the denial of reparations for the harm inflicted on Black communities. Globally, the list of challenges facing Black people is extensive and includes cultural appropriation, racial injustice, police brutality, environmental hazards in Black communities, political suppression tactics, the annihilation of Black communities, media propaganda, theft of resources, and the co-opting of Black agendas by external interest groups. Each of these issues is a serious concern that must be addressed.

White supremacy in Africa remains evident through neo-colonialism, alien land ownership, environmental exploitation, discrimination, and violence against Black people. Multinational corporations exploit natural resources with little regard for black people, environmental sustainability, or local communities, and white landowners hold significant amounts of land in many African countries. Meanwhile, human trafficking, child labor, stripping minerals and resources from the land, and predatory loans reinforce white supremacy.

Whatsmore is the inability of the average Black Indigenous Person to actually acknowledge that this isn't a problem of yesteryear but a real-time lived experience right this very moment. We have all been brainwashed to accept the system of white supremacy as normalcy. Taking this a step further, Stockholm syndrome is a psychological phenomenon in which hostages or abuse victims develop feelings of affection, loyalty, or empathy towards their captors or abusers. This emotional attachment is a coping mechanism in response to the traumatic experience and the power imbalance between the victim and the captor. Cognitive dissonance is a psychological concept that refers to the mental discomfort or tension experienced by an individual when they simultaneously hold two or more contradictory beliefs, values, or attitudes.

A combination of Stockholm syndrome and cognitive dissonance occurs when a victim of white supremacy abuse feels affection or loyalty towards their abuser while simultaneously experiencing mental discomfort due to the contradictory nature of their feelings and the reality of their situation. For instance, a non-white victim might experience cognitive dissonance if they believe that white supremacists are inherently evil or dangerous, but the white supremacist _____________ (fill in the blank: doctor, teacher, politician, colleague, supervisor, lover, etc.) behaves in ways that contradicts this belief, such as showing moments of kindness or compassion. To reduce the discomfort of this contradiction, the victim might rationalize or justify the white supremacist's behavior, convincing themselves that white people are not as bad as they initially believed or that their actions are justified in some way. For example, if George Floyd hadn't used a counterfeit $20 bill, Officer Derek Chauvin, would not have knelt on Floyd's neck for over nine minutes while Floyd was handcuffed and lying face down on the street.

Many of our people remain unaware, focused on petty things, and fail to see the extent of what there is. The truth is, globally, black people are victims of white supremacy and are experiencing a combination of Stockholm syndrome and cognitive dissonance as we navigate our lives within societies dominated by systemic racism and oppression. We remain confused about the system of white supremacy because the system is complex and deeply ingrained in the fabric of society, masked in a cloak, too often operating subtly in the name of equality and proximity. Infighting continues to undermine real progress. Our inability to get on code (unite and work together) leaves us vulnerable to outside forces.

The title of this book is borrowed from Ayi Kwei Armah's "2000 Seasons." This story tells of the Black struggle against European colonization and its devastating impact on culture, spirituality, and way of life. Throughout the novel, the characters face numerous challenges, from the arrival of European colonizers to the introduction of Christianity and other western ideologies. The theme emphasizes the significance of opposing oppression and the power of collective action. The characters in the book refuse to give up their traditions and unite to fight against the forces of colonization, recognizing the interconnections of their struggles with the broader fight for African liberation.

Sankofa, a term from the Akan language of Ghana, means "go back and get it" and is associated with the symbol of a bird carrying an egg in its mouth while looking backward. In Black American culture, Sankofa represents the importance of learning from and honoring the past. It encourages Black people and communities to draw on the wisdom and experiences of their ancestors to navigate present challenges and build a brighter future. Sankofa is frequently used in the context of the African diaspora as a reminder of the significance of acknowledging and honoring African history and culture, fostering a sense of pride in one's heritage, and gaining a deeper understanding of the forces that have shaped our lives.

Ma'at is the Kemetic (ancient Egyptian) concept and goddess who represents truth, balance, order, harmony, law, morality, and justice. Ma'at is integral to the cosmic order, as is reciprocity, which stresses the importance of mutual, proportional responses in social interactions, balancing personal actions with the actions of others, and maintaining equity and justice in relationships and societies.

This is a call to action for my brothers and sisters and our cousins in the diaspora and on the continent; by embracing our history, culture, and spirituality, our people can create a better future for ourselves and future generations. This book highlights the importance of Ma'at (resisting oppression), Sankofa (preserving culture and traditions and recognizing the power of community and collective action) in combating western modes of thinking (the Whiteness of Destruction).

YFD

1

200,000 years of Hyper-aggression

What is the definition of hyper-aggression? Behavior that is extremely and unusually angry, violent, or determined" ("Hyper-Aggressiveness"). In this chapter, I will attempt to describe the psychological behavior of the world's natural enemy, the white supremacist, and how the Caucasoid came to have their aggression, their warlike mentality, their need to control and dominate people with melanin in their skin, their evil behavior, and explore their moral compass—the driving force behind their actions. This analysis seeks to decode the complex psychological framework that characterizes white supremacists.

European culture and thought have been used to dominate and exploit non-European cultures, and I argue that developing our own African-centered cultural thought and practice is the way forward to better understand and counteract these barbaric cultures. The conclusion is that European culture and thought are characterized by a lack of balance, harmony, and holistic thinking. European cultural thought is based on a separation between mind and body, nature and culture, subject and object, which has led to a history of domination, exploitation, and destruction of non-European cultures. This separation has created a culture of domination and control that has been perpetuated through various institutions and practices, including education, religion, and governance.

The prehistory of the white race alone is the source of our interlocking contemporary difficulties, one of which is anti-black racism. I purposefully and defensively portray "white supremacy anti-Black racism" as wickedness and ignorance in order to defend a number of threats to our survival. The main threats to our survival, such as resource rape, environmental pollution, and nuclear war, are all the outcomes of distinctly Caucasoid behavior, attitudes, as well as their mentality.

The book "The Iceman Inheritance: Prehistoric Sources of Western Man's Racism, Sexism, and Aggression" by Michael Bradley traces the roots of Western racism, sexism, and aggression to prehistoric times, argues that these traits are deeply ingrained in the genetic heritage of Western man, and suggests that they can be traced back to the last Ice Age. Bradley uses a variety of sources, including anthropology, archaeology, mythology, and genetics, to support his argument. He argues that Western man's genetic heritage includes a predisposition towards violence, aggression, and dominance, which has been exacerbated by cultural and environmental factors.

I concur with Bradly when he said, "There is no way to avoid the truth. The problem with the world is white men" (Bradley 3).

It is our purpose to turn the Caucasoid prejudice back onto itself once we have seen that the Caucasoid does tend to differ from other kinds of men in at least one behavioral parameter: aggression. However, I also realize and will attempt to show that Caucasoid aggression is innate and immutable and is 'racial' in the sense that it is based on historical evidence, proof, and facts. This worldwide problem results from evolutionary and cultural experiences; their predisposition for aggression is genetic, for the simple fact that an extremely harsh environment created a culture of extreme jealousy and envy, along with hyper-aggression, and the necessity to survive and fight against nature in order to preserve white life.

Native to Europe, Neanderthal man and his cultural group are known as the alleged morphological genesis of modern white people.

The possibility exists that the likeness between the Neanderthals and Eastern Europeans in terms of skull structure, wormian bones, and teeth is only superficial and does not indicate any evolutionary tie, according to the findings of Italian paleontologist Alberto Carlo Blanc. Blanc's research indicates that there may have been two separate strains of mankind in Europe—'sapiens" and 'Neanderthal'—as early as 200,000 years ago. Whatever their origins, it suffices to know that the so-called "Neanderthals" represent a distinctive subset of modern white people who were clearly adapted to cold climates because they lived during glacial periods. Between 100,000 and 40,000 years ago, they ruled Europe and resided in what would later be known as the Caucasoid racial domain (Bradley 74-75).

Van Sertima adds that other archeological discoveries, including Gobekli Tepe, in the Natufian towns, and other settlements that date back to 12,000 B.C.E These findings have severely accelerated the pace of mankind's growth and cast doubt on preconceived ideas about [hu]man civilization.

According to Bradley, the roots of Western racism can be traced back to the ancient Indo-European cultures of Europe and Asia, which were characterized by a patriarchal social order and a belief in the superiority of light-skinned or non-melanated people. He argues that these cultural beliefs were carried with the Indo-Europeans as they migrated westward into Europe and that they contributed to the development of Western racism and white supremacy.

According to Bradley, the Neanderthals already had a high degree of sexual dimorphism, and the patchwork sexual adaptations only accentuated it. I'm inclined to believe that the sexes differed enough that each considered the other to be a separate species. I think that there may have been grave difficulties in each sex recognizing the other to be completely different species. Among the Neanderthals, there could not have been as much sexual solidarity as among other races of men. Even a lesser Caucasoid degree of sexual dimorphism has resulted in a noticeable amount of sexual conflict. Long before Lysistrata and Aristophanes, Caucasoid's must have been aware of a low-level sex war. Caucasoid sexes have never really gotten used to each other and have never truly trusted each other. A high degree of sexual dimorphism would tend to amplify the very aggression and frustration that sexual adaptations were meant to absorb, given the delicate balance of approach-avoidance generated by temporal territorial behavior and the aggression associated with sexual encounters. (Bradley 123).

These are a few instances that allude to typical Western aggression and anger. A fundamental dislike of nature is reflected in the urge to boost productivity and power. There is a strong desire to manage it, make the most of it, and enhance it. The psyche of Caucasoid's is treacherous and self-defense-oriented (Bradley 162).

"Symptomatic Western Aggression and Frustration" is Bradley's concept that implies that Western behavior exhibits both violent and hostile tendencies. This observation suggests a pattern where the Western world often adopts an aggressively destructive attitude in its interactions with various [hu]man groups, particularly as part of its pursuit of global dominance.

The word "symptomatic" suggests that there is a larger range of underlying problems or frustrations in Western society that are reflected in these aggressive behaviors. The phrase captures the idea that acts of violence and hostility are not isolated incidents but rather symptomatic of a deeper set of dynamics at play. The use of "symptomatic" suggests a connection between these behaviors and broader sociopolitical or cultural factors within Western societies. It proposes that the aggressive and destructive tendencies observed in Western interactions may be rooted in a complex interplay of historical, political, economic, and cultural factors.

In an effort to boost productivity and power, this is related to Western culture, which places a strong focus on economic expansion and technical improvement. Western societies have always been known for having a strong desire for advancement in order to dominate and control. Frustration with nature: the Caucasoid's quest to increase power and output is rooted in a basic frustration with nature. This implies that Western societies often view nature as an obstacle to be overcome or harnessed for mankind's benefit and never for the [hu]man's benefit. It reflects a perception of the Caucasoid as separate from and in conflict with the natural world and all that's in it.

A Darker Picture of Neanderthal Violence

Biology and paleontology paint a completely different picture. Neanderthals were definitely quite skilled fighters; their skill was probably only surpassed by contemporary man. They were anything but kind. Due to their fierce competition for scarce resources, including food, water, and territory, mankind engages in daily battles. Imagine the savagery and animalistic hunger of a place where there are no laws and "only the strongest survive." In the early stages of troglodyte history, conflicts were an inherent aspect of societal dynamics, driven by the imperative need for resources, territorial control, and overall survival (Longrich n.p.).

As hunter-gatherers, early pre-mankind communities engaged in deadly battles over crucial resources like water and any meat they could find, leading to territorial violent disputes and deadly confrontations between neanderthal clan groups. According to the article "War in the Time of Neanderthals: How Our Species Battled for Supremacy for Over 100,000 Years," Chimpanzees, their nearest cousins, also engage in fierce territorial disputes. Male chimpanzees frequently form groups to hunt down and kill other males in opposing bands—a behavior that seems like it could mimic neanderthal warfare. This suggests that cooperative aggressiveness originated in their seven million-year-old common ancestor, the chimpanzee. In that case, "Neanderthals will have inherited these same tendencies towards cooperative aggression" (Longrich n.p.).

Within these small social units, conflicts could also emerge from internal issues such as brawling over control of the clan, mating rights, or any disagreements. The inability to control violent impulsive urges, combined with no consequences, resulted in violent actions without any forethought. Archaeological findings, particularly in skeletal remains, offer glimpses into the nature of early mankind's conflicts and the types of injuries sustained. Evidence of blunt force trauma, puncture wounds from projectiles, and signs of crude weapon usage indicate a variety of violent encounters.

The evidence from archaeology indicates that "Neanderthals lives were anything but peaceful" (Longrich n.p.). Weapons such as clubs, rocks, and bones. Despite the prevalence of violence, the presence of healed injuries in skeletal remains suggests that some individuals managed to survive these conflicts and received care within their communities. Healed and unhealed bone damage found on Neanderthals themselves suggests Homosapien societies demonstrated a high level of conflict and aggression. During early mankind history, fights among different groups were inevitable, primarily driven by the fundamental need for resources, territory, and survival. Being a warmonger is inherently part of being "mankind" (kind of a [hu]man). Instead of being a recent invention, war is an ingrained, basic aspect of troglodyte nature. Caucasoid culture in history has waged war in one way or another. War myths abound in our oldest manuscripts. Ancient fortifications, combat arenas, and the locations of millennia-old prehistoric murders are all revealed by archaeology.

Mankind is prone to battle; the descendants of Neanderthals were not unlike us [hu]mans. Non-Africans share 99.7% of [hu]man DNA and have extremely similar skeletons and skulls. Neanderthals and [hu]mans behaved quite similarly. They created stone shrines, fashioned jewelry out of animal teeth and shells from the ocean, manufactured fire, and buried their dead. Given how many of their destructive inclinations they shared with modern man, Neanderthals most certainly also possessed many of the violent urges of their Caucasoid descendants. (Longrich n.p.).

The historical tendency of Caucasoid's—generally speaking, those descended from Europe—seeking to use science and technology to alter and control nature. This trend is said to be representative of a larger pattern in Western history, where the quest for dominance over nature is frequently motivated by territorial expansion and economic considerations, ultimately resulting in warfare.

Although it's important to remember that race is a socially constructed concept rather than a biological one, the term "Caucasoid" is used here to refer to a particular racial type. This alludes to a particular set of individuals who have traditionally possessed authority and sway in Western society. Caucasoid's have a mindset that is marked by deception and self-preservation. White people's actions and behaviors, especially those that support white supremacist ideology and practice anti-black racism, are driven by a desire to hold onto their privilege and power at the expense of other people.

Temporal aggression refers to the idea that Caucasoid's exhibit an extremely high propensity for aggressive actions directed towards both nature and other [hu]man beings. This aggression is portrayed as a defining characteristic of Caucasoid psychology, driving their efforts to dominate and control not only the environment but also other groups of people. Bradley, who is classified as white, serves to underscore the idea that these observations are not limited to outsiders or critics of Caucasoid culture but may also be acknowledged by individuals within the group itself. Bradley's acknowledgment of Caucasoid aggression towards nature and other [hu]mans suggests a recognition of the destructive tendencies that can arise from the pursuit of dominance and control.

Bradley says, "We Caucasoid's have a greater degree of temporal aggression, as reflected in our wars against nature and man (Bradley 174)." The Caucasoid's geographical environment was extremely harsh. Glacial adaptations robbed the Caucasoid's of sexual adaptations, which would have made it easier to come to terms with reproduction. Their sexual-sensual behavior resembles that of primates, but for completely opposite reasons. The Caucasoid's racial and physical characteristics have posed a psychological limitation comparable to the environmental limitations experienced by primitive troglodyte Caucasoid's. Due to their level of racial dimorphism and less developed sexual adaptations for pleasure, they have also been unable to accept reproduction and sex in a mature manner (Bradley 191).

Bradley argues that both the Caucasoid's aggressive mainstream society and those who oppose it incorporate elements of the 'spiritual-material' dichotomy, the sexual dichotomy, dictated long ago by Caucasoid sexual maladaptations that hampered their adjustment to the temporal, spiritual territory of time and human continuity. Both their society and those who oppose it are two sides of the same racial coin of sexual maladaptation leading to abnormal aggression. To elaborate further on this statement, here are some examples.

- *Spiritual-Material Dichotomy*: introduces the idea of a "spiritual-material" dichotomy. This suggests a division between two opposing aspects of mankind's experience or values. The spiritual aspect may represent matters of the soul, morality, or higher consciousness, while the material aspect could relate to physical desires, worldly possessions, and materialism. The implication is that both Caucasoid society and its opposition are influenced by this division.
  - *Sexual-Ascetic Dichotomy*: This also introduces a "sexual-ascetic" dichotomy. This implies a contrast between sexual indulgence and asceticism, which is a lifestyle characterized by self-denial and abstaining from worldly pleasures. It's suggested that this dichotomy is influenced by past sexual maladaptations among Caucasoid's, leading to difficulties in adjusting to the "temporal, spiritual territory of time and [hu]man continuity."
  - *Caucasoid Sexual Maladaptations:* This seems to argue that historical sexual maladaptations among Caucasian populations have resulted in difficulties in adapting to the concept of time and [hu]man continuity.
  - *Abnormal Aggression:* Asserts that both mainstream Caucasoid society and those who oppose it share a common

racial characteristic of sexual maladaptation, which in turn leads to "abnormal aggression." This suggests that the aggression displayed by both sides can be traced back to this shared sexual maladaptation, further reinforcing the idea of a fundamental commonality between the two.

Bradley's original and unconventional work tells the truth about the true culture and nature of the Caucasoid, as well as his destiny. For instance, "Western man (Caucasoid's) will succeed in destroying only his own creations of Western culture and industrialism, and the rest of mankind will eventually establish something similar to the social constructs of the ancient Egyptians." (Bradley 196). I argue that these traits are deeply ingrained in the genetic heritage of Western man/ Caucasoid's and that they can be traced back to the last Ice Age.

Bradley's describes the true nature of Neanderthals and how modern-day Caucasians mimic their forefathers and even says, "Caucasoid's are the most 'primitive' of [hu]man races and not the most evolved if you choose to regard human refinement as man's distance from ape-like physical traits. It seems reasonable to suppose that. Caucasoid's are an identifiable group because of the 'primitive' and 'bestial' physical characteristics inherited through Neanderthal genetic input." Bradley even elaborates further by saying, "our Eurasian fossil hominid history clearly shows that 'Caucasoid's' were probably the most mixed and least pure of any [hu]man group." (Bradley 105)

According to Colon Wilson's book "From Atlantis to the Sphinx: Recovering the Lost Wisdom of the Ancient World," in Makapansgat, 42 baboon skulls were discovered in 1924 by Dr. Raymond Dart, an autonomy professor at the University of Witwatersrand. Of these, 27 of the skulls bore evidence of having been struck by a club. He came to the conclusion that the club, which left two indentations, was the humerus (upper leg bone) of an antelope. As a result, he came to the shocking conclusion that Australopithecus, the earliest known progenitor of modern mankind, had been a murderer. He continued by expanding on his theory that the sole reason the southern ape-man separated from the other apes was because he had mastered the use of weapons for murder. The theory gained widespread acceptance in 1961 when playwright-turned-anthropologist Robert Ardrey contended that mankind evolved into man in a book titled African Genesis. Because he acquired the ability to kill, he will wipe out the [hu]man race if he doesn't quickly unlearn it (Wilson 196-197).

Oscar Maerth, a Hungarian anthropologist, once put forth the intriguing possibility that cannibalism might contain the solution to the Caucasoid's evolutionary development. A paleontologist named Pie Wen-Chung discovered something in the caves close to Chou-kou-tien in 1929. One of the earliest Caucasoid,s ancestors' petrified skulls was discovered by him. His colleague Teilhard de Chardin thought the teeth on this ancient creature belonged to a predatory animal because it resembled a chimpanzee more than a [hu]man. The thing had a receding chin, significant brow ridges, and a sloping forehead. But its brain, at 800 cc instead of 400 cc, was twice as big as a chimpanzee's. The discovery of additional limbs, skulls, and teeth revealed that this predator was an upright walker. At first, it appeared to be the long-awaited "Missing Link," but more data refuted this notion.

This ancient creature, who was the progenitor of modern-day Europeans and was known as "Peking Man," enjoyed venison and was proficient with fire. He was a living example of early mankind and lived about 500,000 years ago. But he also had a grisly side to him: cannibalism. Every one of the forty skulls found at Chou-kou-tien had evidence of base mutilation, which made it possible to remove the brains through a breach. The scientist in charge of the research, Franz Weidenreich, was certain that these animals were slain in groups, hauled into caves, cooked, and eaten (Wilson 222-223).

We currently have evidence indicating that Neanderthal man engaged in cannibalism. Maerth himself reports experiencing heightened vitality, including a strong sexual desire, and a warm feeling in his head the day after consuming raw ape brains in an Asian restaurant. Ritual cannibalism, which Maerth studied in Borneo, Sumatra, and New Guinea, is based on the belief that the strength of the dead enemy passes into the person who eats him, and this could well be based on the experience of heightened vitality described by Maerth, who believes that "intelligence can be eaten'.

It is evident that Maerth's theory was that if eating [hu]man brains increased intelligence, then the few tribes in southeast Asia that continue to do it should be significantly smarter than Westerners, whose ancestors gave up the practice thousands of years ago. However, this does not seem to be the case.

Further evidence that current mankind and Neanderthals are the same as they were hundreds of thousands of years ago can be found in the web article "Neanderthals Were Just As Violent As Early Humans" ("Neanderthals Were Just As Violent As Early Humans" n.p.). A recent corpus of studies describes an early hominid that resembles current humans. Based primarily on studies comparing the levels of injury across both Neanderthal and early Homo sapiens populations, experts previously thought that Neanderthal lives were noticeably rougher, more cruel, and shorter than those of early Homo sapiens.

However, following a far more extensive analysis, a team of researchers from the University of Tübingen (UIT) found that during the Ice Age, both Neanderthals and modern man retained similar levels of head trauma. The new research may help dispel some Neanderthal stereotypes that still persist in popular culture and the science community. Previous studies of Neanderthal trauma have inferred that inferior, close-range hunting methods and a violent social culture made the species more prone to injury. Instead, the study suggests that Ice Age Eurasia probably was a difficult and harsh environment for all ("Neanderthals Were Just As Violent As Early Humans" n.p.).

The proportion of Neanderthal genetic material in contemporary humans is negligible or close to zero among Black people from African populations, while it averages from 1 to 2 percent, but has been found to be as high as 5% in those of European and Asian descent. In contrast, the proportion of Denisovan DNA is most pronounced in the Melanesian population, ranging from 4 to 6 percent, and is lower in other

Southeast Asian and Pacific Islander populations, often being barely detectable elsewhere in the world.

Neanderthals, who were ancient mankind living in Europe and Western Asia approximately 400,000 years ago until their extinction about 40,000 years ago, represent one part of this genetic heritage. Denisovans, another early human population from Asia with distant connections to Neanderthals, remain less understood due to the scarcity of fossil discoveries. The exact nature of the relationship between modern mankind, Neanderthals, and Denisovans is an ongoing subject of study. Nevertheless, studies show that Neanderthals and Denisovans coexisted and interbred with modern [hu]mans for a brief period of time, leading to a small fraction of Neanderthals and Denisovans possessing genetic material from their distant ancient Black grandparents, the true [hu]man being. (What does it mean to have Neanderthal or Denisovan DNA? n.p).

"For man, two-legged anthropoids of many forms were there, but increasingly developing hominid traits. Practically everyone agrees that until the 4th glacier Epoch, flat nose negroids were the only humans. A South African scientist has recently discovered that the first men were black, strongly pigmented, according to the proofs of his disposal. it was probably not until the fourth glaciation, which lasted 100,000 years, that the differentiation of the negroid race into distinct races occurred, following a long period of adaptation by the fractions isolated and imprisoned by Ice; narrowing the nostrils depigmentation of the skin and of the pupils of the eyes." (Diop 68)

DNA From Two Distinct Troglodyte Species

In the article titled "Scientists Uncover a Girl Possessing DNA from Two Distinct Species," researchers reveal the existence of a recently discovered troglodyte girl whose parents were related to two different species who were not [hu]man, one of which was a freshly discovered species and the other was the Neanderthals. Notably, there is historical evidence of many [hu]man and mankind species dating back thousands of years. A third extinct mankind species has been discovered recently, indicating more ancestors in the Caucasoid's family tree lineage.

In the vicinity of the Altai Mountains in southern Siberia, Russia, lies the Denisova Cave, named after an 18th-century hermit who once inhabited its depths. In 2008, bone fragments excavated by archaeologists from the Russian Academy of Sciences revealed an intriguing discovery. The oldest bones, dating back at least 51,000 years, did not belong to Neanderthals or homo sapiens; instead, scientists from the Max Planck Institute identified them as a distinct species, the Denisovans. Despite limited knowledge beyond their DNA sequencing, it is established that Denisovans existed as far back as 217,000 years ago. Notably, a particular Denisovan individual was not solely of that lineage but rather the result of interbreeding between two different mankind species, challenging prior notions in Caucasoid evolution ("Scientists Discover A Girl With DNA From Two Different Species" n.p.).

Logically, different mankind species interbred; this is clear because there are modern-day Europeans and Asians. So how did Neanderthals and Homo sapiens successfully interbreed, in contrast to mules hybrids between horses and donkeys—being infertile? In order to naturally reproduce, the male and female must have the same chromosome count. A horse possesses 64 chromosomes, while a donkey has 62. The offspring, a mule, ends up with an odd number of 63 chromosomes, creating a "defective" genetic code.

In 2018, researchers uncovered compelling evidence of first-generation interbreeding between Neanderthals and Denisovans in the Denisova Cave near the Altai Mountains. The subject of this discovery, named Denny, was a 13-year-old girl who lived around 90,000 years ago. Through genome analysis, paleo geneticists Viviane Slon and Svante Pääbo determined that Denny's parents were fully Neanderthal and fully Denisovan, marking an exceptionally rare find in the study of troglodytes evolution. Denny belonged to a Neanderthal-Denisovan colony, exhibiting high heterozygosity in her DNA, suggesting diverse parental origins. Computational biologist Richard E. Green noted that Denny's parents likely came from distinct areas and were frequently interbred. Surprisingly, Denny's genetic sequence revealed a closer relation to a 55,000-year-old Neanderthal in Croatia than to the 33,000-year-old Neanderthals near the Denisova Cave, raising intriguing possibilities about the geographic interactions of Neanderthals and Denisovans.

These scientists claim that current Caucasoid's and non-Africans are descended from Denisovans. An extinct species of hominid known as denisovans lived in Siberia's Denisova Cave and were troglodytes. Based on genetic data, Denisovans may have interbred with early modern [hu]mans as well as Neanderthals. Due to this interbreeding, modern man—classified as European and Asian populations—have Denisovan DNA in their genomes. According to genomic studies, Denisovan DNA may be present in the genomes of modern Asian populations ("Scientists Discover A Girl With DNA From Two Different Species"n.p.).

This would explain how Denisovan hominids would have had sexual access to acquire modern [hu]man DNA. Scientists suggest, possibly from indigenous peoples in Papua New Guinea, Australia, and other Southeast Asian countries with modern [hu]man DNA, that these were melanated [hu]men. This interbreeding of Denisovans and modern [hu]mans likely occurred tens of thousands of years ago, and the legacy of Denisovan DNA is still present in European and Asian people today. This mixing of hominid populations is an interesting aspect of Caucasoid's evolutionary history.

The discovery of Denny, a first-generation Neanderthal-Denisovan hybrid, has sparked a reevaluation of the interbreeding frequency between these ancient species. Svante Pääbo, a prominent researcher, suggests that encounters between Neanderthals and Denisovans likely involved more frequent interbreeding than previously thought. This revelation prompted a reassessment of other specimens, such as the 42,000-year-old Homo sapien jawbone known as Oase 1, which, upon closer analysis, exhibited a small amount of Neanderthal DNA. These findings challenge the conventional belief that interbreeding was rare, indicating a more prevalent occurrence than previously assumed ("Scientists Discover A Girl With DNA From Two Different Species"n.p.).

In addition to laying out the framework for this book, which aims to inspire the reader to comprehend the seriousness of the enemy that the world faces in the form of white supremacy and how it was founded based on the psychological trauma that primitive creatures would have experienced over the course of time, this will also provide a solid foundation for the brutal oppression and sexual deviance that Neanderthals were subjected to. It will also describe the mentality and psychological behaviors of the descendants of troglodyte culture with regard to their interactions with [hu]man beings and all life on this planet.

Troglodyte Cultural Thought of European Ancestry

European thinking was shaped to promote the idea of white supremacy. This chapter talks about how European thought included treating things as if they were objects, dividing ideas into opposing categories, and valuing science above all else. It also introduces the idea that the way people think is influenced by their culture's values and beliefs, which drive how they act in concert with a unified code system.

In the book "Yurugu: An African Centered Critique of European Thought and Behavior," Dr. Marimba Ani suggests that in European culture, the most satisfying thing is to control others. They argue that European culture is all about death. Everything in its history, methods, and symbols revolves around death, using it as a way to justify actions and ideas (Yurugu).

Dr. Ani starts her dissertation by analyzing the Dogon creation story and how this ancient African culture describes the coming of Caucasoid people from antiquity, thousands of years before the melting of the ice glaciers that held Homoerectus captive. This will better help us to think from an African perspective on why white people act and behave the way they do. According to the creation story, the conflict in the universe's early history is between Amma, the creator of ([hu]mans), and one of her creations, the Ogo the creator of (mankind).

In the beginning, there was only Amma in the form of an egg. This egg had its four collar bones fused, dividing it into air, earth, fire, and water, as well as establishing the four cardinal directions. Inside this cosmic egg, the very essence and structure of the universe resided, including 266 signs representing all things. However, Amma's first attempt at creating the world was a failure. The second creation began when Amma planted a seed within herself, resulting in the form of a [hu]man. During the gestation of this being, a flaw emerged, introducing the potential for incompleteness in the universe. The egg split into two placentas, each holding a pair of twins, one male and one female.

After sixty years, one of the males, Ogo, broke free from the placenta and tried to create his own universe, opposing the one formed by Amma. However, he couldn't utter the words needed to bring his universe into existence. As Amma transformed the fragment of placenta that went with Ogo into the void, Ogo interfered with the creative potential of the earth through incestuous relations. Amma killed Ogo's counterpart, Nommo, who had participated in the rebellion, scattering his body parts in all directions to restore order to the world.

Five days later, Amma gathered Nommo's body parts, reviving him as the ruler of the universe. Nommo created four spirits, the ancestors of the Dogon people. Amma sent Nommo and the spirits to earth in an ark, thus restoring the earth. Along the way, Nommo spoke Amma's words, making the sacred words of creation available to humans. Meanwhile, Amma transformed Ogo into Yuguru, the Pale Fox, who would forever remain alone and incomplete in eternal rebellion, perpetually wandering the earth in search of his female soul.

Ani's book cover is that of the "Yurugu" and is depicted as a scrawny, skeletal, emaciated, feral, pale malnutrition of a human-like mutant with ferocious human-consuming teeth and piercing blue eyes. In the hand of this mutant human-like creature, it holds a face that resembles humanity, and when this creature puts the face of humanity on its grotesque mutated face, which is incomplete and not fully human, it tricks and is able to destroy the world.

Ani uses Swahili words to describe culture, cultural structured thought, as well as the vital force that drives the culture that motivates and inspires all who are related to the culture to practice the structured thought. Terms like Asili, which is the "trademark" of a culture, are like the core idea that holds all the different parts of that culture together. It's the fundamental concept or seed from which the culture grows. Think of it as the heart and soul of a culture—the central idea that shapes everything people in that culture create. To understand a culture's creations, you need to figure out this central concept.

The word Utamawazo means "culturally structured thought," meaning the way people think is influenced by their culture and how that culture is organized. It also means that people in a culture need to behave in a certain way for their society to work well.

"Utamaroho" is like the life force of a culture. It gets started by the driving force, which is called "Asili." It's what gives a culture its emotional vibe and gets people in that culture to act together. Both Utamaroho and Utamawazo come from Asili, so don't think of them as separate things but as different ways that Asili shows itself.

Analyzing what Ani describes as European culture and Michael Bradley's depiction of caucasoid harsh living environments living behind the ice glacier walls, which formed the culture of the Caucasoid's innate hyper-aggression and sexual frustrations, we can start to paint a picture and get an idea of the driving force that makes up "The Whiteness of Destruction."

It is important to stress the level of violence and anger, along with extreme savagery, that breeds and fuels the culture in which modern terms would be called the systematic practice of white supremacy, lacking any compassion for any living organic being on Earth in order to control and dominate the "said object."

African and non-European worldviews regard the universe as inherently sacred, with its origins steeped in spirituality. It's seen as an organic, living entity, a true "cosmos," where everything is interconnected. In these worldviews, nature and the cosmos are revered and considered integral to [hu]man existence. This worldview offers an explanation of the universe from the perspective of some cultural viewpoints, especially non-European and melanated people's home regions. Think of it as inherently sacred, with roots in mysticism. This point of view holds that the universe is a living, connected organism and that everything in it is a part of a larger whole. These viewpoints hold that the natural world and the cosmos are sacred and fundamental to human existence.

Understanding the universe, in these worldviews, is not achieved through detached analysis but through a personal relationship with it. It involves perceiving the spiritual essence within the material world. Knowledge is gained through experiencing the spirit within all things. The universe is viewed as a single, unified entity where different spheres or aspects are interconnected by a unifying force that permeates all existence. This unifying force is believed to be the source of meaningful reality. These world-views are considered reasonable, meaning they make sense to those who hold them, but they are not rigidly rationalistic. They are complex and deeply intertwined with daily life, often expressed through metaphor and intricate symbols, which convey their intricate beliefs (Yurugu 31).

Just like the extreme harsh living conditions that shaped and cultivated Neanderthals/early mankind's worldviews, that allowed them to become uncivilized barbarians who were determined to control, dominate, and preserve themselves in order to avoid genetic annihilation. Modern Europeans and their complex ideology oppose nature rather than working in harmony with it. The ancient Kemetic (Egyptian) word for God is "NETER" which the modern-day term for nature was derived from.

The Greek influence on Western Thought and Religion

Plato's writings played a monolithic role in the shaping of western thought. What Plato shows is a kind of mental trick where you learn to detach yourself from what you already know. This separation is like a key; it opens the door to what Europeans consider "knowledge," but it also locks you out of understanding the spiritual and natural world.

Two mind-changing events take place. First, your mind changes, and you start to see yourself in a new way. Second, the world you thought you knew also looks different because your relationship with it has changed. You no longer see yourself as part of the entire universe; instead, you start seeing yourself as a thinking individual, separate and apart from nature.

The Greek word "psyche" suggests the idea of an independent self that's separate from everything around it. In this view, the main job of this self is to engage in scientific thinking and knowing, which is different from relying on intuition. According to Plato, the highest and most valuable pursuit is philosophy, and the most esteemed person is the philosopher, who seeks and loves "truth" and thinks deeply. Other activities and functions are considered less important. This new sense of self becomes very disconnected from its surroundings. Why independent, separate, and isolated? Because this "thinking being," to be effective in scientific thought, needs to be primarily self-reliant (Yurugu 31).

The ideas that Plato and his ancestors had to put into action regarding European civilization and worldview also stem from a profound conflict with the natural order of things and the world. Ani notes that European culture values the individual above the community, reason over instinct, and treating things as objects over forming personal relationships. She argues that focusing so much on individualism and reason has caused Caucasoid's to feel disconnected from nature, others, and even themselves. Essentially, in Western culture, the emphasis on individualism has led to separation from the community, the environment, history, and the greater universe.

I am attempting to illustrate how Europeans tend to simplify and narrow down the complexity of the world. They do this by undervaluing the importance of symbols, making complex things seem simple, and seeking clear and measurable knowledge about everything. This method is known as the "barbaric way of understanding the world."

This prompts us to consider what happened during the early stages of Caucasoid development that led to this particular way of thinking. It also questions how the ideas of the ancient Greek philosopher Plato might have influenced this perspective for those who came after him and his fellow colleagues.

Civilizations ascribed to Europeans are inevitably situated in regions inhabited by people of African descent in the southern part of the northern hemisphere, encompassing Egypt, Arabia, Phoenicia, Mesopotamia, Elam, and India. As Cheikh Anta Diop eloquently asserts, "In all those lands, there were already negro civilizations when the Europeans arrived as rough nomads during the second millennium" (Diop 152).

The conventional approach involves illustrating that these populations, who were perceived as savage, carried with them all the essential elements of domination in the form of civilization wherever they journeyed. This begs a relevant inquiry. Instead of at their initial cradle in the Eurasian steppes, why did the many creative, non-melanated aptitudes of the erstwhile troglodytes only manifest when there was contact with Black/African civilizations? Why did these populations not initiate the development of civilization and settlements before embarking on migrations?

Ani suggests that the Platonic Influence on European culture is based on a fundamental opposition to the natural order of life and the universe. She points out that European culture prioritizes the self over the group, reason over instinct, and objectification over interpersonal connections. She asserts that placing so much emphasis on individualism and reason has caused the self to become fragmented and alienated from nature and other people. "Individualism is the basic premise upon which Western culture is built. The individual is separated from the community, from the environment, from history, and from the cosmos" (Ani 81).

Religion and ideology in the West, ideology has sprung inextricably from religion. She says it is crucial to define what she means by "religion" because of this and the distinctiveness of European culture. This is crucial because what is formally recognized as religion in the European experience frequently relates little to what is popularly thought to be "the religious" in a phenomenological sense. In contrast to "religion" as the expression of beliefs about the supernatural world and the foundation for ethical behavior or as a determinant of value, this discussion focuses on the European experience of religion as a formalized existence concerning the other institutions of European culture (Ani 109).

In the Western world, "beliefs" and ideology have always been closely connected to their religious rule, government, sovereignty, and controlling "beliefs." This is important to understand because the way Europeans define and practice religion is quite different from the original indigenous people's culture, thought, and ancestral practices. The founders of this new white supremacist "religion" use it as a form of subjugation in order to control and possess said "material possession" and/or object.

Definition from Oxford Languages 2023 belief (/bi'li:f/) noun

1. an acceptance that something exists or is true, especially one without proof.

"his belief in extraterrestrial life." 2. trust, faith, or confidence in (someone or something).

Similar: faith, trust

("Be·Lief /Bə'Lēf/"Oxford Languages n.p.)

The traditional and powerful ideas associated with Christianity, for example, actually came from older cultures that existed long before Christianity, which was founded in modern-day (so-called) Egypt. So, we're going to focus on what Europeans believed were the key elements of their formal religious beliefs. The early Greeks claimed to have learned about origins from teachers in what is now known as Egypt.I'll use the term "Christianity" to talk specifically about how Europeans interpreted and used religious ideas from earlier pre-European traditions. European Christianity, in this sense, was a new and unique way of understanding a new method to colonize, control, and dominate, creating a new way of thinking while simultaneously putting into practice a worldwide "religion" that would perpetually, in concert, support and mask their true intentions, which would be a genocidal worldview for people who contain melanin, are dark-skinned, and are Indigenous people of the Earth.

Now, when it comes to how European Christians perceive the natural world, they tend to see it as entirely separate, including the universal consciousness manifested in other living beings (animals, plant life, etc.). They often regard this as a wild and uncontrollable force, much like Plato did. To steer people's conduct and morality, European Christians rely on this "pattern" or "design." In a historical context, during the 16th century, when Europeans were colonizing new lands, they considered civilization, particularly the ancient Greco-Roman variety, as an essential framework imposed on the unpredictability of nature. They believed that without civilization, much like nature without guidance, things would descend into disorder.

This emphasizes that a European's perception of themselves reveals the nature of their inner being, known as "utamaroho," or the vital force of European culture, and is closely connected to how they perceive other people. Essentially, it suggests that how Europeans view themselves and others is interlinked. Dr. Frances Cress Welsing explains why this may be:

"Melanin is the black pigment which permits skins to appear other than white. Melanin is a superior absorber of all energy. The fact that the whites lack melanin may also help to explain why they have quite a different concept and understanding of God...and why, in the view of many non-white people,

they (whites) lack "spirituality" and the capacity to tune in and thereby establish harmony and justice in the universe. Because they lack the melanin sensory system, they cannot intuit that ALL is ONE." (Welsing 171), "The Concept and the Color of God"

The idea is that one of the most accurate ways to understand how Europeans see themselves is by examining how they view others. This is because the nature of their self-perception and their perception of others are intertwined and influence each other.

By breaking down the components of this self-image, it becomes clear that the European "cultural ego" is made up of traits that can be traced back to the early and formative stages of Caucasoid culture. These traits evolved and developed in tandem with European culture's growth and development. This highlights the relationship between how Europeans view themselves and others, with a focus on the origins of their self-image in a cultural and historical context. It also suggests that this self-image plays a significant role in shaping European behavior and white supremacist norms. (Ani 237-238)

European perception of themselves, their "utamaroho," relies on the way they view people who are different from them, or their "opposites." In essence, Europeans create a self-image by contrasting it with what they see as the opposite, which typically involves perceiving these others as having negative qualities. According to Caucasoid cultural beliefs, it's foundation was formed behind Ice Glacier, which developed their hyper aggression.

This unfavorable perception of "the other" serves a specific purpose for Europeans. It allows them to emphasize what they consider "good" or positive about their own culture and behavior. They create a conceptual framework that depends on their cultural values, and then they fill it with vivid images that represent these differences.

Essentially, Europeans shape their perception of other people based on this idea of "the other," who possesses characteristics they view as negative. They use the concept of the opposite to act out and support their positive self-image.

It's crucial to understand that, according to the author, if Europeans were to treat everyone as if they were just like themselves, they couldn't maintain their Caucasoid identity. This is why concepts like "universal brotherhood of man" may sound good in rhetoric, but they don't align with the core values and definitions of European culture. European culture inherently requires the existence of people who are considered different or "other," as this idea is built into the culture itself (Ani 279-280).

How Europeans treat people outside their own culture shows a lot about European culture itself, according to Dr. Ani. To understand European imperialism, we need to understand the beliefs that support this kind of behavior and the cultural ideas that form its foundation.

There have been many terrible events during the roughly two hundred years of European imperialism. For example, the U.S. Congressional Record has a long list of United States interventions from 1798 to 1845, and this is just a small part of the larger picture. There are many books and resources about this, with more being created all the time. "The West and the Rest of Us" by Chinweizu is a great historical account of European aggression from an African-centered viewpoint. Chinweizu's writings provide a strong critique of how Europeans have treated others (Ani 401).

The premise of separation—between the mind and body, spirit and matter, man and nature, reason and emotion, self, and community—lays the groundwork for Eurocentrism, which led the Europeans to develop a psychopathic racial personality.

Racially Psychotic Personality

"Blacks are now a threat and a liability to the White race".
(Bobby E. Wright 1)

"Psychopath: a mentally unstable person especially: a person having an egocentric and antisocial personality marked by a lack of remorse for one's actions, an absence of empathy for others, and often criminal tendencies".
("Psychopath." Merriam-Webster n.p.)

The term "psychopath" pertains to Black people who deviate from the ethical standards of their society, showing a deficiency in empathy and remorse. Those exhibiting psychopathic tendencies are typically marked by their callous, manipulative, and deceitful behavior, frequently resorting to acts of violence, theft, or fraud to achieve their objectives. While psychopathy is not formally recognized as a mental health diagnosis, certain psychopathic attributes coincide with the characteristics of antisocial personality disorder (ASPD), which involves an ongoing disregard for the rights, emotions, and well-being of others (Dorwart, 2023 n.p.)

This describes the nature of our created enemy, which has grafted itself to "humankind," Through the process of genetic maladaptation that evolved into "mankind" in the form of non-melanated people who were trapped behind ice glacier walls for more than 400,000 years to develop a personality and put forth into action that has been displayed throughout history and can be proven as accredited, accurate historical facts. he psychopathic personality is characterized by a lack of empathy, guilt, and remorse, as well as a tendency towards impulsive and destructive behavior. This applies these characteristics to the white supremacist ideology and argues that it too lacks empathy, is not capable of feeling guilt, and is prone to impulsive and destructive behavior.

In the essay "The Psychopathic Racial Personality," Bobby E. Wright explains, that Black people's experiences around the globe are comparable in this regard. For hundreds of years, Black people have actually been attempting to rush at the banners that were held by European (White) matadors. These banners have been symbolized by ideas like democracy, capitalism, Marxism, religion, and education. The flags never changed as long as Black people were assets. However, as global industry and technology advance, resource exploitation in Africa is escalating, leading to a surge in national consciousness among Africans (Blacks). "Blacks are now a threat and a liability to the White race." Therefore, their pride, honor, and duty, is to do, practice, and master the art of white supremacy, which champions only one concept: "Black genocide." As a result, the majority of the research conducted by white scientists today is genocidal in nature at best. (nuclear warfare, population control (warfare), environmental warfare, medical warfare, genetic engineering warfare, sex, and gender warfare, psychosurgery warfare, electrical stimulation of the brain warfare, i.e., "Smart T.V. 's" and "smartphones," and the highly complex science of behavioral technology, ect.) (Wright 1).

Wright claims (with which I concur) that it is indeed the moment of truth for Blacks; it is time for Black people to look at the white supremacist's actions and be aware. Based on the available data, I have come to the conclusion that people who identify as white and engage in white supremacist behavior are psychopaths who manipulate the environment, Black people, and all other life on Earth. They also tamper with the ionosphere, and their actions are a reflection of a basic biological tendency that has its roots in their evolutionary past. A psychopath is someone who consistently feels conflicted with other individuals or groups. "He (White male) is unable to experience guilt, is completely selfish and callous, and has a total disregard for the rights of others" (Wright 2). Observing and analyzing their universal overt behaviors and attitudes toward Blacks is one of the best methods for measuring the psychopathic traits of the White race.

Wright uses what he called a "functional definition" of racism, "the oppression and exploitation of people because of their race." Wright also claims that using this definition, it is clear that Blacks cannot be racists at this time due to their lack of power to oppress anyone (Whites, Indians, Chinese, etc.).

Wright explains why "Blacks kill Blacks because they have never been trained to kill Whites, therefore, it is outside their experience. Historically, the European system has encouraged the killing of Blacks. Because Blacks have been led to believe that they are part of the psychopath's system, they simply follow the practice" (Wright 2-5).

"Behavioral scientists generally agree that the outstanding characteristics of the psychopathic personality are the almost complete absence of ethical or moral development and an almost total disregard for appropriate patterns of behavior. This characteristic has led to a misunderstanding of the psychopath as someone who does not know the difference between right and wrong. This belief is not true; Psychopaths simply ignore the concept of right and wrong." By ignoring this lethal trait in the White race (a lack of ethical and moral development), Blacks have made and continue to make a tragic mistake in basing the global Black liberation movement on moral suasion." It is pathological for Blacks to continue attempting to persuade a people who lack morality where race is a variable (Wright 5).

We must never lose focus on how psychopaths, Black people with an almost complete absence of ethical or moral development and a total disregard for appropriate behavior, can mistreat powerless Black people in various ways. Here are some examples of how this mistreatment occurs:

- Manipulation: Psychopaths are skilled manipulators who prey on a person's vulnerabilities, emotions, or trust. They can deceive and manipulate powerless Black people into doing their bidding or making decisions that are against their best interests. For example, a psychopath might manipulate a financially vulnerable person into giving them money or assets.
- Exploitation: Psychopaths are opportunistic and often take advantage of others for personal gain. They may exploit someone who is in a weaker position, such as a Black person, by making them do extra work, taking credit for their ideas, or exploiting their resources.

- Emotional abuse: Psychopaths may engage in emotional abuse, including gaslighting, to undermine the self-esteem and mental well-being of powerless Black people. They might constantly criticize, belittle, or demean them, causing emotional distress and making them feel helpless.
- Isolation: Psychopaths can isolate Black people from their support networks, such as friends and family, to gain more control over them. They may use tactics to create dependency, making the powerless person believe they have no one else to turn to.
- Blackmail: Psychopaths may collect information about a powerless person's secrets, weaknesses, or wrongdoings and then use that information as leverage to manipulate or control them. This can involve threats of exposure or other negative consequences.
- Physical abuse: In most cases, psychopaths may resort to physical abuse when dealing with powerless Black people. This includes physical violence, intimidation, or threats to physically harm them or their loved ones.
- Financial exploitation: Psychopaths may target vulnerable Black people for financial gain. They may defraud them, steal their money, or coerce them into signing over assets or properties.
- Emotional manipulation: Psychopaths are adept at using guilt, fear, and other emotional manipulation techniques to control powerless Black people. They may make the person feel responsible for the psychopath's well-being or happiness, (Stockholm Syndrome) even when it's detrimental to the victim.

It's important to note That there are different degrees or levels of psychotic behavior and action, ranging from subtle to extreme or raw to refined. all psychopaths engage in these behaviors openly or secretly, and not all Black people who mistreat others are psychopaths. Psychopathy is a complex personality disorder, and not everyone with psychopathic traits will engage in harmful behavior but will have the ability to practice psychopathic behavior when and if triggered. However, Black people with psychopathic tendencies are more likely to engage in manipulative and exploitative behaviors when dealing with powerless Black people due to their lack of moral and ethical constraints.

Wright says, "Because of their lack of ethical or moral development, there is no conflict between the Whites' religion and racial oppression. The white race has historically oppressed, exploited, and killed Black people, all in the name of their God Jesus Christ, and with the sanction of their churches. It is generally overlooked that the Ku Klux Klan is primarily a religious organization." Additionally, Black people should never forget the image of the Pope blessing Italian aircraft and pilots as they were en route to bombing men, women, and children in Ethiopia who had no other means of defense than spears. Since Whites use the writings to defend how they treat Black people, this behavior is not at all surprising. Genesis claims that Noah cursed his son Ham, consigning all of his descendants to a lifetime of servitude to God's servants. Naturally, whites believed that Blacks were descended from Ham and that they were God's servants. (Wright 5)

Psychopathic sexual Warfare

"The Illuminati are the willing terrestrial servants of the Lord Archon, who demands everything from pedophilia and child sacrifice to war and chaos as offerings that create loosh."
— Sol Luckman, Cali the Destroyer (Luckman)

In relationships involving a psychopath, various manipulative and abusive tactics can be employed, particularly in the realm of sex and intimacy. One common strategy is "love-bombing and idealization," where the psychopath initially inundates the powerless person with an overwhelming display of affection, compliments, and intense desire, making them feel exceptionally cherished and significant. This phase, often referred to as "love-bombing," is designed to foster a deep emotional attachment and dependency on the psychopath.

Psychopaths are skilled at identifying and "Exploiting vulnerabilities." They pinpoint the insecurities and weaknesses of the powerless person and then proceed to exploit these vulnerabilities to establish control, using sex as a tool for manipulation and emotional tethering. In some cases, psychopaths resort to "Withholding sex" as a form of control. By dictating when and how sexual intimacy occurs, they create a sense of insecurity and dependence in the powerless person, leaving them feeling emotionally trapped. "Promising commitment" is another method used by psychopaths to maintain the powerless person's engagement. False assurances of commitment or a shared future can serve as a means to guarantee ongoing access to sex while exercising emotional control.

Psychopaths are also known for "Gaslighting," a form of manipulation where they distort the victim's perception of reality. In the context of sexual interactions, this can be used to confuse the powerless person and make them doubt their own experiences and feelings. The psychopath may introduce "Infidelity and triangulation" into the relationship, involving third parties to create jealousy and emotional turmoil for the powerless person. This tactic helps maintain control and sows emotional chaos.

"Emotional manipulation" during sexual encounters is another avenue for psychopaths to control the powerless person. This manipulation can involve guilt, shame, or emotional coercion, making the person feel responsible for the psychopath's happiness or well-being. More extreme forms of abuse can include "Sexual coercion," where the psychopath uses physical or emotional pressure to compel the powerless person into engaging in sexual acts they are uncomfortable with or have not consented to.

Additionally, psychopaths may engage in "Degrading and dehumanizing behavior" during sexual acts, leaving the powerless person feeling objectified, humiliated, or diminished. These actions can further erode the victim's self-esteem and self-worth. "The psychopath is usually sexually inadequate and has a very limited capacity to form close interpersonal relationships. The European's sexual inadequacy psychologically explains the constant projection of Blacks as supersexual beings and as lacking in sexual inhibitions. Yet, Europeans "streak," "mate swap," participate in orgies, etc (Wright 6)." Due to their psychopathic nature, they constantly fail in their desperate attempts to establish meaningful relationships, which is the driving force behind all of their sexual behavior Tragic events have resulted from white's sexual dysfunction in the Black community.

By raping Black women, for example, they have tried to satisfy their sexual appetite. Castrating black men in the past was justified because their "animal passions" needed to be restrained. The castration of Black men was justified by the need to control their "animal passions." Black men historically were and still are the psychopath's "animal passions" that needed to be subdued. Other atrocities committed by the White race against the Black race have no precedent in history, and there is no scientific explanation other than psychopathology. The "Psychopaths' inability to accept blame or learn from previous experience can be easily proven. They never accept blame for Black people's environmental conditions, which are clearly the result of white oppression. On the contrary, Blacks are held responsible for the deterioration of their communities, even though all of the property is White controlled. In addition, municipal services are withdrawn from Black communities and most of these communities have been "used-up" before Blacks are allowed to move into them." (Wright 7).

The Subtle Tactics of Psychological Manipulation

Psychopaths are adept at employing subtle, nonviolent methods to mistreat Black people, leaving deep emotional and psychological scars. These tactics often serve to maintain control and dominance over the powerless person, all without resorting to physical violence. Such subtle forms of mistreatment can be insidious, gradually undermining the victim's self-esteem, confidence, and sense of agency.

One common strategy utilized by psychopaths is gaslighting, a manipulative technique where the perpetrator subtly distorts the victim's perception of reality. Through selective omission, misrepresentation, or subtle manipulation, the psychopath undermines the victim's confidence in their own memory and emotions. This insidious tactic can lead the victim to doubt their own experiences and perceptions of events, fostering a deep sense of confusion and self-doubt.

In addition to gaslighting, psychopaths often employ the silent treatment as a means of emotional manipulation. By withdrawing communication and affection, they leave the powerless person feeling isolated and ignored. This subtle form of emotional abuse can lead to a profound sense of anxiety and emotional distress, with the victim constantly striving to regain the psychopath's attention and approval.

Financial control is another subtle method utilized by psychopaths to maintain dominance over the powerless. Through seemingly innocuous actions such as scrutinizing expenses, limiting access to funds, or making unilateral financial decisions, the psychopath can establish a sense of dependence and vulnerability in the victim. This financial manipulation subtly reinforces the power dynamic within the relationship, leaving the victim feeling economically and emotionally trapped.

Furthermore, psychopaths may subtly undermine the victim's self-esteem through consistent criticism, subtle put-downs, and undermining comments. By chipping away at the victim's self-worth over time, the psychopath fosters a sense of inadequacy and powerlessness, making the victim increasingly reliant on the perpetrator for validation and approval.

Psychopaths are skilled at leveraging subtle forms of manipulation and mistreatment to maintain control over Black people. These non-violent tactics can have profound and long-lasting effects on the victim's mental and emotional well-being. Recognizing the signs of subtle abuse is essential in breaking free from the cycle of manipulation and seeking support to restore one's sense of self-worth and agency.

The psychopathic personality presents a provocative argument about the psychological roots of worldwide anti-black racism. The

Whiteness of Destruction central thesis is that white supremacy is not simply the result of socialization or ignorance, but rather a manifestation of a psychopathological disorder in the dominant white population. And argue that white people's pathological need to dominate and control non-white people is rooted in a long history of imperialistic and colonialist practices, as well as a desire to maintain a hierarchical racial order.

Obviously, white supremacist thought is not a matter of individual prejudices or biases, but rather a systemic (codified) and institutionalized phenomenon that has been intentionally created and maintained by those in power. By tracing the roots of racism and the history of colonization, slavery, and segregation/apartheid, This ideology demonstrates that racism is not just an attitude, but rather a deeply embedded aspect of European culture, thought, and action to be manifested in all "things/objects" including the lives of all people on Earth.

Another strength of Wright's argument is his ability to connect the psychological and historical dimensions of racism. He argues that the need to control and dominate non-white people is a symptom of a psychopathological disorder that is rooted in a long history of colonialism and imperialism, i.e., white supremacy. He further argues that white people have used a variety of social, economic, and political mechanisms to maintain their power, including slavery, segregation, discrimination, and murder (Wright 32)

"Mendelian Autosomal Dominant Inheritance"

According to the National Human Genome Research Definition of Autosomal Dominant Disorder, "Autosomal dominant is a pattern of inheritance characteristic of some genetic disorders. "Autosomal" means that the gene in question is located on one of the numbered, or non-sex, chromosomes. "Dominant" means that a single copy of the mutated gene (from one parent) is enough to cause the disorder." A child of a person affected by an autosomal dominant condition has a 50% chance of being affected by that condition via inheritance of a dominant allele. By contrast, an autosomal recessive disorder requires two copies of the mutated gene (one from each parent) to cause the disorder. Huntington's disease is an example of an autosomal dominant genetic disorder" (Hanchard).

Dominant Allele: Each gene in an organism has two copies, one inherited from each parent. In autosomal dominant inheritance, there is a dominant allele and a recessive allele for a specific trait. The dominant allele, denoted by an uppercase letter, masks the effect of the recessive allele when present. Heterozygous Black people: Black people who inherit one copy of the dominant allele and one copy of the recessive allele (denoted as "Aa") will express the dominant trait because the dominant allele is sufficient to determine the trait's expression.

Homozygous Dominant Black People: Black people who inherit two copies of the dominant allele (denoted as "AA") will also express the dominant trait.

- Recessive Allele: The recessive allele, denoted by a lowercase letter, only determines the trait when an individual has two copies of the recessive allele (denoted as "aa"). In this case, the recessive trait is expressed. Traits and Disorders: Autosomal dominant inheritance can apply to a wide range of traits and genetic disorders. For example, Huntington's disease is a well-known genetic disorder that follows autosomal dominant inheritance. 50% Probability: When two heterozygous (Aa) Black people have children, there is a 50% chance that their offspring will inherit the dominant allele (Aa) and express the dominant trait, and a 50% chance that they will inherit the recessive allele (aa) and express the recessive trait. Mendelian autosomal dominant inheritance is one of several patterns of inheritance described by Gregor Mendel also known as "Mendel's Law" ("Autosomal Dominant Inheritance")

Do Neanderthal Fossils Contain Rhesus Monkey Gene/Rh factor?

The Rh factor, or Rhesus factor, is a hereditary genetic trait. It is determined by specific genes, and whether an individual has the Rh factor or not is inherited from their parents.

Neanderthals around 40,000 years ago, resulting in the exchange of genetic material through a process known as introgression. Neanderthals finally became extinct, but humans kept having babies only with other humans. While the amount of Neanderthal DNA in our genomes has declined over time. According to the National Library of Medicine (NLM) "approximately 2–4% of genetic material in human populations outside Africa is derived from Neanderthals who interbred with anatomically modern humans" (Harris and Nielsen 881-891).

Because these Neanderthal genes are advantageous to us, they have persisted. They support human physiology in several ways, including the immune system (living with diseases), digestive system (eating raw meat), and brain (psychopath). A portion of these genes might have contributed to the development of human intellect and helped us adjust to cooked meats and non-cannibalistic diets. When we look back, it seems that our species profited from interbreeding with Neanderthals since it provided genetic benefits that let us survive to this day.

A liger is the result of crossing a tiger and a lion. These large creatures are typically sterile, meaning they are unable to procreate. Scientists believed for a very long time that hybrids, or offspring from crosses between different species, were invariably sterile. Yet, hybrids are of two distinct species.

Studies have shown that certain hybrids are capable of producing their own offspring. For instance, a liger and a lion at the German Hellabrunn Zoo produced cubs in 1943. DNA can cross-pollinate between species when hybrids mate with one of its parent species, as is the case in Germany with ligers and lions. Introgression is the term for this process.

When examining the evidence and understanding the warfare of disinformation and the benefit of glorifying all things "white," we can read between the lines to expose that Africans are not the same as descendants of the Neanderthals. I have also concluded that the quote-unquote so-called "modern [hu]man," which was from sub-Saharan Africa, is the missing link that modern-day scientists have been puzzled about (lying) that science cannot find or approve. And it is clear that those who possess Neanderthal genes are most hostile to those who do not, which are melanated Indigenous people all over the Earth, which also explains why they created a system of white supremacy in order to dominate and control Wales, who are [hu]man.

Firstly, describe how species exchange DNA through a process called hybridization. How some human DNA descended from Neanderthals is explained in the introduction. For a very long time, humans were limited to the savannahs of Africa. About 45,000 years ago, they left Africa and came to Europe, where they met with the Neanderthals, a different species that resembled humans (Homo neanderthalensis). The Neanderthals bore little resemblance to contemporary people. They featured a conspicuous brow ridge over their eyes, longer arms, and were somewhat more robust. These Neanderthals were the parents of certain humans. Those children grew up and had children of their own. And onwards. Introgression, or the exchange of DNA, was the outcome of these two species coming together ([hu]man and mankind). Given that Neanderthals and humans exclusively had children outside of Africa. Scientists are unable to detect Neanderthal DNA in living Africans. Nonetheless, approximately 3% of people worldwide are descended from Neanderthals (Ottenburghs 4).

Which favorable characteristics for adaptation did these Neanderthal genes offer? A list of all the advantageous genes that Neanderthals inherited is being compiled by scientists. For example, the microcephalin (MCPH1) gene guarantees appropriate brain development. This

Neanderthal gene may have improved human intelligence and allowed for greater survival in uncharted territory. Furthermore, olfactory receptor 12D3 (OR12D3) is one of the Neanderthal genes that is essential for food digestion. Neanderthal DNA let humans quickly adapt to the wide range of novel foods they met during their migration to Europe. Our teeth's shape may potentially have been influenced by some genes! "So, if you are not African, your DNA contains a dash of Neanderthal genes" (Ottenburghs 5).

The majority of harmful alleles are exclusive to humans or Neanderthals prior to admixture, which means that when introgressed Neanderthal alleles are introduced at low frequencies, purifying selection will not find them. Despite having a significantly larger recessive burden than human haplotypes, Neanderthal haplotypes are protected against detrimental human variation because they rarely exhibit deleterious alleles at the same places as human haplotypes do. It is important to note that these simulation results presume that Neanderthals and archaic humans mated randomly; if consanguinity were common in either group, this may remove a significant amount of recessive harmful variation (Harris and Nielsen 881-891).

Genetic studies of ancient descendants of hominid populations revealed that Neanderthal DNA is present in the genomes of non-African/white-skinned populations, which includes the people of Mesopotamia and other regions in the ancient Near East. The degree of Neanderthal admixture can vary among different human populations, but it is generally accepted that Neanderthal genetic contributions are part of the broader genetic heritage of these Anglo-Saxon, European, Neanderthal, and troglodyte populations.

Although the precise amount of Neanderthal genetic admixture in any Anglo-Saxon community may change, it is evident that Neanderthals and anatomically modern [hu]mans (who are distinct from Neanderthals) are related. Evidence suggests that Black and heavily melanated humans from Africa and other regions of the world shared a common genetic past through interbreeding during their time of cohabitation in what is now Mesopotamia. This is modern-day Iraq, and

Iran is not very far from the African continent; Egyptian culture was the center of the globe. It is inconceivable for a group of people devoid of literacy to get to a high level of civilization; this is bigotry. Racism that is anti-Black In 2023, it is exceedingly difficult to receive accurate, true information due to white supremacist practices.

2

The Psychopathic Invasion of European/Asian into Egypt

"Kemetic Africa played a major creative role in the cultural patterns that are uniquely thought of as Greek civilization."
--Asa Hilliard, III

Why do white supremacists (those who practice their culture) and the so-called scholarship of archaeologists, anthropologists, historians, and Egyptologists frequently attempt to create a rivalry between Mesopotamia and Egypt by claiming that both cultures emerged at roughly the same time? Is it to further continue the status quo of white supremacy and anti-black hatred?

The ongoing debate over the age of the Sphinx pits mainstream Egyptologists against a newer faction of independent thinkers, revealing a substantial discrepancy spanning several thousand years. This latter group vehemently contends that the grand limestone statue predates the timeline proposed by mainstream archaeologists and Egyptologists. Amidst this dispute, suspicions arise concerning potential interference by racist white supremacists who may have distorted historical records

39

to conceal the truth, echoing the sentiments expressed by Dr. Diop. In his words, "Egyptologists were dumbfounded with admiration for the past grandeur and perfection discovered in Egypt; they gradually recognized it was the most ancient civilization that had engendered all others. But imperialism being what it is, it became increasingly inadmissible to continue to accept the theory, evident until then, of negro-Egypt. The birth of Egyptology thus marked by the need to destroy the memory of negro Egypt at any cost and in all minds, henceforth the common denominator of all" (Diop 45). This perspective sheds light on the potential motivations behind the conflicting narratives surrounding the Sphinx's age.

Mainstream archaeologists initially determined the construction of the Sphinx to have taken place between 2558 and 2532 BCE. However, in 1992, John Anthony West challenged this consensus by proposing that the Sphinx was carved 10,000 years earlier, during a time when Egypt wasn't yet a desert. West and others argued that the scientific community had overlooked a crucial detail—the distinctive markings of water erosion on the sculpture's body.

Robert Schoch, a geology professor at Boston University, supported this viewpoint by asserting that academia had overlooked signs of erosion caused by intense rainfall. The downpour that caused the erosion was not typical for the Egyptian plateau 5,000 years ago but was common 10,000 to 12,000 years ago. Schoch found this discovery fascinating, but it was met with ridicule and denial from mainstream science.

Despite extensive evidence underscoring the lasting influence of Egyptian civilization and culture, with traces dating back nearly 800,000 years, recent research by Manichev and Parkhomenko suggests that the Sphinx monument might have been partially submerged by "large bodies of water," leading to distinct "wave-cut hollows on its vertical walls." Notably, a specific erosion mark found within one of these pronounced hollows on the Sphinx appears to match the water level during the early Pleistocene Age. This geological evidence has led to the conclusion that the statue likely stood on the Giza Plateau during that ancient period (Shayne n.p.).

As discussed in the preceding chapter, one of the characteristics associated with psychopathic behavior is a pattern of habitual lying. In this chapter, we will thoroughly examine the lineage of certain groups, colloquially referred to as white supremacists, who have sought to distort historical facts for their own agendas.

"History is always written by the winners. When two cultures clash, the loser is obliterated, and the winner writes the history books-books which glorify their own cause and disparage the conquered foe. As Napoleon once said, 'What is history, but a fable agreed upon?"
— Dan Brown, The Da Vinci Code *(Brown, Dan. The Da Vinci Code, Doubleday, 2003.)*

This is a synopsis of the appearance and disappearance of what are known as evolved troglodyte encounters—people who invaded Egypt, an African country, without the use of written language or knowledge of astrology, medicine, agriculture, or spirituality. I aim to present evidence that highlights the similarities between the destruction that occurred during the period when the troglodytes left their caves, inter-bred with [hu]mans, and evolved into the modern Europeans we recognize today.

It is known that early Greek philosophers, as well as experts in as-tronomy, mathematics, and other fields, derived their knowledge from the ancient Egyptian schools of Mysteries. The teachings of the Egyp-tian Mysteries had already been disseminated to various regions before reaching Athens. Historical documentation suggests that Pythagoras, having received his education in Egypt, briefly established his order in his native Samos before eventually relocating to Croton in what is now known as southern Italy around 540 B.C. His order flourished there until he was eventually expelled. Similarly, Thales, who lived around 640 B.C. and also received education in Egypt, along with his colleagues

Anaximander and Anaximenes, originally hailed from Ionia in Asia Minor. This region served as the bastion of the Egyptian Mystery Schools, and these philosophers continued their teachings there.

According to some accounts, Pythagoras traveled to Egypt as a young man and studied mathematics and other subjects at the temple of the god Djehuty/Thoth in the city of Heliopolis for 20 years. It is believed that he may have learned about geometry, astronomy, and other subjects from the priests at the temple, who were known for their advanced knowledge of mathematics and science.

Pythagoras is also said to have studied with the Egyptian mathematician and philosopher Ankhmahor, who is known for his work on geometry and the division of the circle into 360 degrees. Ankhmahor was a contemporary of Pythagoras and lived in the 6th century BC, around the same time as Pythagoras.

The Pythagoreans were known to study the geometry of shapes (e.g., the Platonic solids), which was a subject of great interest in ancient Egypt. They were also interested in the concept of the "golden ratio," which was used extensively in ancient Egyptian architecture and art.

Some historians believe that Pythagoras's travels to Egypt and his exposure to the advanced knowledge and practices of the priests at the temple of Djehuty/Thoth had a significant influence on his own philosophical and mathematical ideas. It is possible that his studies in Egypt helped shape his belief in the spiritual and mystical significance of mathematics and his views on the nature of the universe and its underlying structure.

Greek physicians held the Egyptian physicians in the highest regard and believed their therapies to be exceedingly successful. Hippocrates studied in Alexandria and Egypt in 216 CE. Hippocrates, the so-called "father" of modern medicine, studied in 460–370 BCE and made the same claims about illness that Imhotep had made 2,000 years before. There were other doctors mentioned by name, both male and female.

Magnificent architect Imhotep is the only other fully deified Egyptian, apart from Amenhotep; his name translates to "He Who Comes in Peace." An Egyptian physician genius, Imhotep, an architect who lived between 2667 and 2600 BCE and is most known for creating the Step Pyramid of Djoser at Saqqara, was dubbed the "first physician" and was worshiped as a god of health and healing. He eventually rose to become the deity of knowledge and healing (or, in some accounts, the god of science, medicine, and building). Imhotep was an astronomer, mathematician, physician, poet, architect, and vizier to King Djoser (and possibly to the Third-Dynasty rulers who followed). He was a true polymath (Mark n.p.).

Despite Hippocrates acquiring medical knowledge from the writings of Imhotep, an Egyptian who predates him by thousands of years, the designation of Hippocrates as the "Father of Medicine" persists in European tradition. Western perspectives often assert that true civilized society originated in Greece, likely aimed at shaping the mindset of the uninformed. Still, Ptolemaic architecture and the blending of common sculptural styles show centuries of interaction between Egypt and Greece, the cradles of Greek civilization. Imhotep remains a mysterious figure, credited as the true father of medicine and an expert in architecture, achieving semi-deified status due to his remarkable reputation and contributions. His life was exemplary both during and after his time. It is plausible that additional artifacts detailing Imhotep's accomplishments and teachings remain undiscovered. The destruction of the Library of Alexandria, unfortunately, limits our access to such information.

Pythagoras and Fibonacci may get credit from the white supremacists of today's standards, but they are only "Hippocrates." The idea that a group of people who practiced a culture centered on ignorance, brutality, and cannibalism and who had just emerged from evolutionary development did not acquire higher levels of knowledge is ludicrous and hypocritical. The Egyptian people and their culture had a higher order of intelligence, after all.

"Nevertheless, it would long
continue to initiate the younger
Mediterranean peoples (Greeks

and Romans, among others)
into the enlightenment of civilization. Throughout antiquity,
it would remain the classic land
where the Mediterranean peoples went on pilgrimages to
drink at the fount of scientific, religious, moral, and social
knowledge, the most ancient
knowledge that mankind had
acquired." —Cheikh Anta Diop

There were secret schools that resembled lodges that existed outside of Egypt. These organizations aligned themselves with the Grand
Lodge of Egypt and followed the Osiriaca's beliefs. These schools were
established by initiates of the Egyptian mysteries and are sometimes
called private or philosophical mysteries. Notable instances include the
Ionian temple at Didyma, Euclid's lodge at Megara, Pythagoras's lodge
at Crotona, and the Orphic Temple at Delphi, along with the educational institutions linked to Plato and Aristotle.

It's crucial to dispel the notion that Greek philosophers independently crafted new doctrines. Rather, their philosophies were passed
down via the mysteries of the esteemed Egyptian hierophants. In
Plato's *Timaeus*, it is revealed that those in pursuit of mystical wisdom
journeyed to Egypt for initiation. The priests of Sais conveyed the profound understanding that, within the domain of the Secret Doctrine,
"you Greeks are but children." However, they were bestowed with the
knowledge to aid their spiritual advancement (James 27–29).

After Alexander the Great's conquest of Egypt, the Greeks, fasci-
nated by the mystical worship in the Nile land, began imitating the
complete Egyptian religion. This emulation spread throughout the
Roman Empire, reaching Brittany. The Greeks primarily adopted the
gods of the Osirian cycle and the Graeco-Egyptian Serapis, striving to
faithfully reproduce ancient Nile land traditions.

The grandeur of Egyptian architecture, the intricate hieroglyphs on temples, the presence of obelisks and sphinxes, the unique attire of priests, and the elaborate rituals left the Greeks in awe. They considered these customs steeped in profound mysteries, which hindered the ascent of Christianity. However, the Greeks, unable to fully emulate Egyptian conservatism, blended Egyptian deities with Greek and Asiatic names and mythologies. Consequently, Isis and Osiris retained little of their original Egyptian essence.

Egypt's Influence on Greek and Roman Religion:

The earliest theory of salvation is the Egyptian theory. The Egyptian Mystery System had as its most important object the deification of man and taught that the soul of man if liberated from its bodily fetters, could enable him to become godlike, see the Gods in this life, attain the Beatific Vision, and hold communion with the Immortals. Greek mythology and religious beliefs influenced Roman religion. Many Greek gods and goddesses were equated with their Roman counterparts. For example, Zeus became Jupiter, and Aphrodite became Venus. The Romans incorporated Greek myths and religious practices into their own pantheon (James 23).

Plotinus, a Greek philosopher, lived after Plato and Aristotle and also studied the Egyptian Mystery System He defines his experience as the liberation of the mind from finite consciousness and becoming one with the infinite. This liberation entails freedom from bodily impediments and the cycle of reincarnation. The Egyptian Mystery System, comparable to a modern university, served as the organized center of culture, emphasizing the salvation and immortality of the soul. According to Pietschmann, the system had three student grades: *mortals* (probationary students), *intelligence* (those with inner vision), and *Creators or Sons of Light* (those united with spiritual consciousness). These grades underwent rigorous intellectual and bodily disciplines, tests, and ordeals before actual initiation.

Egyptian education involved cultivating ten virtues for eternal happiness, mastering the seven liberal arts for soul liberation, and accessing greater mysteries for esoteric philosophy. Grammar, Rhetoric, and Logic purged irrational tendencies, while Geometry and Arithmetic delved into transcendental space and numeration. Astronomy explored latent forces in man and destinies. Music (harmony) was therapeutic, aligning human life with God. The Egyptian theory of salvation aimed at making Black people godlike on earth, promoting everlasting happiness through personal efforts, arts and sciences cultivation, and virtuous living—without the need for a mediator, in contrast to the Christian theory. (James 23-24)

The early Greek philosophers attempted to hijack Egyptian philosophy and faced indictment and prosecution for introducing new divinities into the Nile Valley. Anaxagoras, Socrates, and Aristotle were among those accused. The most notable case was against Socrates, who was charged with not believing in the city's gods and corrupting the youth. The accusations were rooted in Aristophanes' portrayal of Socrates as an evildoer investigating matters beneath the earth and in the sky, making the worst appear to be the better reason.

It is evident that Socrates and other philosophers faced persecution from the Athenian government because of their studies in astronomy and possibly geology. In order to become a member of the Egyptian Mystery System, which sought to free the spirit from physical restraints, one had to pursue science. Greek thinkers met this need and agreed with the goal of the system, whether they had direct contact with Egypt or through its educational system.

The teachings of the soul attributes required of a beginning aspirant in the Egyptian Mysteries include:

- Control of thought and action: Plato referred to this combination as justice, representing unswerving righteousness in both thought and action.

- Steadfastness of purpose is equivalent to fortitude.
- Identity with spiritual life or higher ideals is equivalent to temperance, attained by conquering the conscience of nature.
- Evidence of having a mission in life and a call to spiritual orders or the priesthood: Equivalent to prudence, reflecting deep insight and graveness befitting the faculty of seership.

Additional requirements in the ethical system of the Egyptian Mysteries included:

- Freedom from resentment: courage under persecution and wrong.
- Confidence in the power of the master (as teacher) and confidence in one's own ability to learn are both known as fidelity.
- Readiness or preparedness for initiation: guided by the principle, "When the pupil is ready, then the master will appear," indicating a condition of learning and efficiency at all times.

This suggests the influence of Egyptian Mysteries on Plato, his colleagues, and those who came after him had to know about the four Cardinal virtues from the Egyptian ten, emphasizing that Greek philosophy was bastardized imposters of ideas from the Egyptian Mystery System. Additionally, it mentions a Grand Lodge in Egypt with associated schools and lodges in the ancient world.

Concerning Plato's travels, it is documented that at the age of 28, Plato visited Euclid at Megara with other pupils of Socrates. Over the next ten years, he journeyed to Cyrene, Italy, and eventually Egypt, where he received instruction from Egyptian priests. Similar to previous invasions, such as the Persian invasion of Egypt and the Roman capture of Athens, Alexander the Great and his armies likely sought treasures in the form of gold, silver, sacred books, and manuscripts held in temples and libraries.

Contrary to the belief that Greeks independently established a renowned university in Alexandria, it is more accurate to understand that, given Egypt's rich tradition of temples and libraries, the Greeks, including Alexander the Great, Aristotle's school, and the Ptolemies, acquired knowledge by stripping Egyptian libraries of their books. Aristotle's school, along with its pupils, including Alexander, played a crucial role in turning the looted Royal Library of Alexandria into a research center. The students at this library received instructions from Egyptian priests and teachers until the tradition gradually faded. The linguistic challenges necessitated that the Greeks collaborate with Egyptian teachers. (James 34-40).

In the initial four centuries of the Christian era, the Egyptian religion endured. However, the landscape changed after the issuance of the Edict of Theodosius in the late 4th century A.D., mandating the closure of Egyptian temples. This marked a pivotal moment as Christianity gained traction, ushering in what some refer to as the era of "The Destruction of Whiteness." The ascendancy of Christianity contributed to the waning influence of both Egyptian science and Greek religions. Once the cornerstone of the Ancient World Religion, the Egyptian Mysteries traversed the Roman Empire, extending into Italy, Greece, Asia Minor, and various parts of Europe, including Brittany. Yet, with the dismantling of the Egyptian Mysteries, an opening emerged for the ascendance of Christianity. In its pursuit of absolute dominance, the Roman government aimed to eradicate the lingering influence of these mysteries on religious thought. This initiative laid the groundwork for the emergence of the "New World Religion," Christianity, which rapidly rose to prominence following Justinian's Edict of Toleration. (James 31-34)

The influx of Greeks to Egypt for educational purposes commenced following the Persian invasion in 525 B.C. and persisted until the Greeks gained control of Egypt, obtaining access to the Royal Library through Alexander the Great's conquest. Alexandria underwent transformation into a Greek city, emerging as a hub of research and the capital of the newly established Greek empire under the Ptolemies' rule. Despite this Greek influence, Egyptian culture thrived until the

4th century A.D., when Theodosius' edicts, and later Justinian's in the 6th century A.D., led to the closure of mystery temples and schools.

Cheikh Anta Diop famously made the following statement about how knowledge was sought after in Egypt: "Nevertheless, it would long continue to initiate the younger Mediterranean peoples (Greeks and Romans, among others) into the enlightenment of civilization. Throughout antiquity, it would remain the classic land where the Mediterranean peoples went on pilgrimages to drink at the fount of scientific, religious, moral, and social knowledge, the most ancient knowledge that mankind had acquired."

The abolition of the Egyptian Mysteries presented an opportunity for the rise of Christianity. The Roman government, aiming for complete conquest, sought to eliminate the mysteries that still influenced the religious mindset. This paved the way for the establishment of the "New World Religion," Christianity, which rapidly gained prominence following Justinian's Edict of Toleration. (James 31-34) Throughout Persian, Greek, and Roman invasions, Egyptians fled to desert and mountain regions, as well as adjacent lands in Africa, Arabia, and Asia Minor. There, they clandestinely preserved and developed teachings from their mystery system.

Accordingly, we are told that Ptolemy I Soter, in order to elicit the secrets of Egyptian wisdom or mystery systems, ordered Manetho, the High Priest of the temple of Isis 42 at Sebennytos in Lower Egypt, to write the philosophy and history of the religion of the Egyptians. Accordingly, Manetho published several volumes concerning these respective fields, and Ptolemy issued an order prohibiting the translation of these books, which had to be kept on reserve in the library, for the instruction of the Greeks by the Egyptian Priests.

Here it becomes quite clear that the first professors of the Alexandrine School were the Egyptian Priests, and that the scholars and pupils of Aristotle's transferred school received their training directly from the Egyptian Priests. It is also well to note that the chief text books of the Alexandrine School were Manetho's books. (James 44)

The Greeks owe their initial civilization to the Egyptians, as Greece was first influenced by colonies from Egypt, followed by those from Phoenicia and Thrace. Governed by wise leaders, these colonies not only tamed the unruliness of an uneducated populace through civil institutions but also established a robust foundation of religion and the fear of the gods. The profound dogmas regarding divine and human matters from their respective homelands were imparted to these nascent societies to instill virtuous discipline.

The practice of conveying religious doctrines through myths, a method originating in Egypt and later adopted by the Phoenicians and Thracians, eventually made its way to the Greeks. In a somewhat less honorable light, Greek philosophers engaged in plagiarism. Pythagoras, in particular, had teachings so comprehensive that his successors, influenced by his frequent visits to Egypt for education, embraced and disseminated portions of his doctrine.

This suggests two clear points: first, Greek philosophers did not introduce entirely novel concepts but rather practiced plagiarism, and second, the source of their teachings was the Egyptian Mystery System—either directly through contact with Egypt, indirectly through Pythagoras, or via tradition. These assertions find further support through an examination of the doctrines of Pythagoras and the identification of philosophers who echoed his teachings (James 60).

Destruction of Black Civilization

But according to Dr. Williams' book "Destruction of Black Civilization," African civilization was suppressed as a result of a plot involving white invaders as well as unrelenting natural forces that turned formerly fertile areas into vast, destructive battlefronts.

Due to the barbaric nature of the newly formed "mankind," which previously had no civilization and whose culture was savage at best. African people were forced into the harrowing of what Williams refers to as the "starving times" in Africa, marked by the struggle for survival, where children resorted to eating dirt and bark from trees and finding food for two or three meals a week was a significant occasion. Mothers, faced with the heartbreaking choice, would retreat into the bush with their emaciated children to die quietly in the shade. The Sahara Desert, metaphorically described as a blazing white monster on the move, serves as a poignant symbol of the challenges faced by African peoples, suffering horrific abuse and barely escaping with their lives due to "The Whiteness of Destruction."

Dr. Williams posits that the conspiracy against Black people involves two formidable adversaries: the unforgiving forces of nature and the actions of the white man. This dual oppression, symbolized by the "starving times," continues to impact Mother Africa, contributing to a lack of long-term planning for the future. The day-to-day survival struggles dictate a hand-to-mouth existence, hindering the ability to think beyond immediate needs.

Acknowledging that Black people were once the most progressive people on Earth, Dr. Williams outlines the preconditions for progress. These include becoming famine-free, settling in suitable territories, engaging in negotiations for nation-building, fostering a sense of national community, establishing a strong defense, and ensuring the rule of law and justice that apply equally to all members of society. Achieving these conditions can lead to internal peace, stability, and confidence, providing the opportunity for contemplation and forward-thinking. "Next, they tried in vain to find a white origin for Egyptian civilization. They finally came down in their own contradictions, sliding over the difficulties of the problem after performing intellectual acrobatics as learned as they were unwarranted. They then repeat the initial dogma, judging that they have demonstrated to all honorable folks the white origins of Egyptian civilization" (Diop 45).

Diop posits a theory suggesting a historical mingling of different populations in Egypt. He suggests that the Berber type, representing indigenous North African people, experienced extensive mixing in Egypt. The theory proposes the influence of African Berbers from the West, specifically the brown Libyans. Following this, there was an invasion by North African Libyans with European ancestry. The statement describes these invaders as having "white skin and blue eyes." The theory suggests that this group, through hybridization, may have modified the early Egyptians. The concluding idea is that the European blood introduced by these North African Libyans could connect certain elements of the Egyptian population to the broader European race, including the concept of the Aryan race.

It is essential to approach such theories with caution, recognizing that interpretations of ancient populations involve a combination of archaeological evidence, historical records, and genetic studies. "In Egypt, the Berber type is too mixed. According to this theory, the African Berbers from the West, the brown Libyans, but almost immediately, or shortly afterwards, and an invasion of Europeans hybridized the North African Libyans. This Libyan mix of blood "with white skin and blue eyes" may have modified the early Egyptians. By his European blood, this Egyptian could be related to the end of European race and the Aryan" (Diop 64). Additionally, terms like "Aryan" may reflect outdated and controversial racial classifications. Modern research tends to use more precise and scientifically grounded terminology.

Diop states, "Encompassing even the Prophet, the heritage of all Arabs is entwined with African lineage, and this awareness is ingrained among all educated Arabs." As Cheikh Anta Diop underscores, "As in Egypt, belief in the future was already prevalent. Dead ancestors were deified" (Diop 127). The groundwork for the flourishing of Islam was already laid, with all the essential elements in place over a millennium before the birth of Muhammad. Thus, the entire Arab people, including the Prophet, are a blend of diverse ethnic backgrounds, and this consciousness prevails among the educated Arab populace. Diop highlights this reality by referencing the famous hero of Arabia, Antar, who himself is acknowledged as a "mixed breed" (Diop 127).

The historical narrative of Nubia and the surrounding regions unfolds with a succession of dynasties and transitions. The initial Nubian dynasties, strongly influenced by Egyptian counterparts, persisted until the intrusion of European forces in the 5th century B.C. This marked the beginning of a new chapter in the region's history, as external influences began to shape the course of events.

Despite external influences, Nubia maintained its significance as a cultural and civilizational hub until the sixth century A.D. The enduring legacy of Nubian contributions to culture and civilization plays a pivotal role in the broader historical narrative of the region.

As the historical timeline progressed, the spotlight shifted to Ghana from the 6th Century onward. Ghana, during this period, emerged as a prominent center of cultural and economic activity. This era of Ghanaian prominence continued until 1240 when the capital faced a pivotal moment in its history with its destruction by Sundiata Keita.

The fall of Ghana's capital in 1240 marked a turning point, heralding the rise of the Mandingo Empire. Under the leadership of Sundiata Keita, the Mandingo Empire became a significant political and cultural force in the region. This transition represented a transformative phase in the historical and cultural trajectory of West Africa, with the Mandingo Empire leaving an indelible mark on the shaping of societies and civilizations in the centuries that followed.

"The first Nubian dynasties were prolonged by Egyptian dynasties until the occupation of Egypt by the-Europeans, starting in the 5th Century B.C. Nubia remained the sole source of culture and civilization until about the sixth Century A.D., and then Ghana saw the torch from the 6th Century until 1240, when its capital was destroyed by Sundiata Keita. This heralds the launching of the Mandingo Empire (Capital Mali)" (Diop 147).

The historical narrative of Nubia and the surrounding regions unfolds with a succession of dynasties and transitions. The initial Nubian dynasties, strongly influenced by Egyptian counterparts, persisted until the intrusion of European forces in the 5th Century B.C. This marked the beginning of a new chapter in the region's history, as external influences began to shape the course of events.

Despite external influences, Nubia maintained its significance as a cultural and civilizational hub until the sixth century A.D. The enduring legacy of Nubian contributions to culture and civilization plays a pivotal role in the broader historical narrative of the region.

As the historical timeline progressed, the spotlight shifted to Ghana from the 6th Century onward. Ghana, during this period, emerged as a prominent center of cultural and economic activity. This era of Ghanaian prominence continued until 1240, when the capital faced a pivotal moment in its history with its destruction by Sundiata Keita.

The civilizations traditionally attributed to Europeans invariably find their roots in the heart of the African continent, encompassing Egypt, Arabia, Phoenicia, Mesopotamia, Elam, and India. As Cheikh Anta Diop poignantly asserts, "In all those lands, there were already negro civilizations when the Europeans arrived as rough nomads during the second millennium" (Diop 152). The conventional narrative often entails illustrating that these perceived savage populations carried with them all the essential elements of civilization, wherever their journeys took them. This prompts a crucial question: why did numerous creative aptitudes only emerge when there was contact with black civilizations, rather than in the original cradle of the Eurasian steppes? Why did these populations not initiate the development of civilization and settlements before embarking on migrations? The contemplation of such inquiries gains significance in envisioning a scenario where the modern world disappears, allowing for the easy detection of traces of civilization in Europe, as alluded to by Diop.

The Moors, who originated in Mauritania in North Africa, entered Spain in the eighth century A.D. and brought with them the remnants of Egyptian culture. The transmission of ancient knowledge, especially the Wisdom Teaching or Mysteries of Egypt, which the Greeks called Sophia, was essential and continues to be so today (Blakemore, n.p.).

During this time, Cheikh Anta Diop emphasized the moral stance of "Negroes," stating, "Negroes are of all people those who most abhor injustice. The sultan pardons no one who is guilty of it" (Diop 132). Additionally, he highlighted the safety prevalent throughout the land, where travelers faced no reason to fear thieves or ravishers more than those who stayed at home. Moreover, Diop pointed out the ethical practices among blacks, noting, "The blacks do not confiscate the goods of whites, i.e.,. North Africans who die in their country, not even those consistent with big treasures. They deposit them, on the contrary, with a man of confidence among the whites until those who have the right to the goods present themselves and take possession" (Diop 162).

In the same historical context, between 700 and 1200 A.D., Makuria, encompassing today's northern Sudan and southern Egypt, exhibited characteristics more aligned with an empire than a kingdom. Structured into thirteen major states, each with its own sub-king, the region was united under the overarching authority of the "King of Kings." Despite the apparent power of individual kings, the ultimate authority rested with the traditional African Council. The ceremonial grandeur of the "King of Kings" was evident in the size hierarchy of parasols, where the monarch's parasol had to surpass those of divisional kings, and theirs, in turn, exceeded those of lesser officials.

In 745, during Cyriacus's reign as "King of Kings," Egypt's governor, Omar, intensified the persecution of Christians in what resembled a Muslim Holy War. This campaign involved the destruction or conversion of churches into mosques and the imprisonment of the Patriarch. As the head of all Christian churches in Africa, the Patriarch's confinement was perceived as both an affront and a violation of the nearly century-old peace treaty. Remarkably, lower Egypt witnessed the most severe destruction of churches by the Muslims. In response to Omar's dismissive stance, the African king marshaled an army of 100,000 men and advanced towards the Arab power center in Lower Egypt. Faced with resolute opposition, the governor promptly released the Patriarch and pledged to cease hostilities against Christians and their places of worship. Satisfied with these assurances, Cyriacus withdrew his army from Egypt. (William 148).

The Emergence of Colonization in Africa:

"Colonialism hardly ever exploits the whole of a country.
It contents itself with bringing to light the natural resources,

> *which it extracts and exports to meet the needs of the mother country's industries, thereby allowing certain sectors of the colony to become relatively rich. But the rest of the colony follows its path of underdevelopment and poverty, or at all events, sinks into it more deeply."* — (Franz Fanon, "The wretched of the Earth")

A wicked and catastrophic phenomenon known as "The Whiteness of Destruction" occurred in Africa during the 19th century as a result of many European powers' imperialist goals, which were motivated by a combination of economic prosperity and desires for military and political supremacy. Attempts to profit from the wealth of resources found on the African continent were made by countries such as Britain, France, Germany, Belgium, and Portugal during this period of imperialism. Both the impacted African territories and the European powers were significantly impacted by this upsurge in imperialist endeavors.

Motivated primarily by the desire for economic gain, European nations embarked on a quest to steal the wealth and resources of Africa and its people. This lust for economic gain and power was closely tied to the Industrial Revolution, as European powers sought raw materials for their industries and new markets for their goods. Additionally, the quest for political dominance played a crucial role as nations vied for strategic advantages, territorial control, and geopolitical influence.

In the historical context described, imperialism is portrayed as a policy pursued by European powers with the aim of conquering and dominating foreign territories and peoples for economic benefits. The strategy involved a combination of military force, political maneuvering, and economic control. The primary objective was not only the acquisition of valuable resources but also the establishment of political authority and control over African territories, impacting and subjugating local populations.

The impact of this wave of imperialism was profound and enduring. It led to the redrawing of political boundaries, the imposition of

European administrative systems, and the exploitation of African labor and resources for the benefit of the imperial powers. The consequences of this imperialistic era are still felt in contemporary geopolitics and have left a lasting imprint on the socio-economic and political landscapes of the African continent ("Imperialism: A Study," 2005).

Imperialism prompts contemplation on the lasting repercussions of imperialist endeavors, drawing inspiration from the proverb often attributed to Napoleon: "Great empires die of indigestion." It serves as a poignant reminder of the enduring significance of imperialist processes that persist well beyond the formal period of expansion. As a metaphorical expression, it suggests that large and powerful empires can fail due to their inability to effectively manage or deal with the vast amounts of resources they accumulate. Just as overeating can lead to physical indigestion, an empire taking on more than it can handle can lead to its downfall. The actions of major powers like Russia, Germany, France, and Great Britain have figuratively taken substantial "bite-sized pieces" of Africa and Asia. What stands out is that these acquisitions have not yet been fully digested, broken down, or assimilated. This metaphor implies that the aftermath of imperialist actions continues to pose challenges and complexities, akin to the troubles one might face after overindulging.

Furthermore, this underscores the ongoing nature of these challenges, suggesting that the repercussions of imperialist actions linger. Despite the formal cessation of expansionist efforts, some regions still resist assimilation, maintaining their independence despite potential threats.

In my reflection, I am reminded that the legacies of imperialist/ white supremacist actions cast a long, dark shadow on Western global affairs. The metaphorical indigestion highlights the potential pitfalls of expansive ambitions without a comprehensive plan for integration and governance. It serves as a cautionary tale, urging a just understanding of the enduring problems and challenges brought about by historical white supremacist imperialist processes ("Imperialism: A Study," 2005).

The Berlin Conference

The apex of these imperialistic endeavors manifested in the Berlin Conference of 1884–1885, where European powers assembled to formalize the partitioning of Africa among themselves, regardless of Africa's existing socio-cultural fabric. On February 5, 1885, Belgian King Leopold II established the Congo Free State by brutally seizing the African landmass as his personal possession. The colonized people were deprived of their independence, wealth, and territory. The king's stated goal was to bring civilization to the people of the Congo, an enormous region in Central Africa. The precise number of African lives lost due to Leopold's psychopathic barbarianism is unimaginable to ascertain. Nevertheless, it is widely acknowledged that millions of Congolese people perished due to forced labor, violence, starvation, and diseases like smallpox and sleeping sickness. Historians and scholars estimate the death toll in the Congo-free state under Leopold's savagery to range from several million to over 10 million. The absence of accurate records and the deliberate destruction of numerous documents by the colonial administration make it arduous to pinpoint an exact figure. The atrocities committed in the Congo during this era are frequently regarded as one of the most egregious instances of colonial exploitation and brutality in modern history ("Feb 5, 1885 CE: Belgian King Establishes Congo Free State").

Here are some examples of these barbaric, psychopathic forms of abuse:

Forced slavery and exploitation:

Leopold instituted a brutal system of forced labor, coercing Congolese Black people into grueling work on rubber and ivory extraction with extreme brutality. The imposed quotas were exorbitant, leading to severe physical and psychological abuse as the Congolese were compelled to meet unrealistic production targets.

Mutilations and Violence:

Failure to meet these imposed quotas often resulted in severe punishment, including mutilation. Hands were amputated, and Black people faced other brutal forms of violence. Local officials and overseers were incentivized to meet quotas through violent means, fostering a climate of fear and brutality.

Mass Killings and Starvation:

The ruthless exploitation and forced labor perpetrated by Leopold's regime led to widespread malnutrition and starvation among the Congolese population. The relentless demand for results pushed overseers to extreme measures, resulting in mass killings and deaths due to overwork, exhaustion, and disease.

Disease and Neglect:

The harsh working conditions and forced labor significantly contributed to the spread of diseases like smallpox and sleeping sickness, further decimating the population. With virtually nonexistent medical facilities, the Congolese were left without adequate care, exacerbating the impact of diseases on their already dire circumstances.

The Berlin Conference represented the culmination of the European scramble for African territory. This gathering established the framework for the subsequent colonization of the continent.

Countries Scramble for Africa's demise:

The late 19th century witnessed a profound transformation known as the Scramble for Africa, wherein European powers, notably Britain, engaged in a fervent race to establish colonies/domination across the African continent. Greed and a sense of superiority drove European nations to engage in a brutal race for dominance over African countries during the era of conflict among white conquerors, particularly with regard to Africa.Those psychopaths tortured and killed Africans out of a fetishistic and savage desire. the violent tactics used by colonial powers to establish their supremacy and take advantage of Africans and their resources for their own personal benefit.

These psychopaths saw African populations as nothing more than commodities to be used for financial advantage, and they were obsessed with enslaving and abusing them. The primary driving force behind this was the desire for financial gain via the exploitation of labor, agricultural products, and minerals—all at the expense of the lives, well-being, and welfare of African peoples. Not to mention that during this time, borders were arbitrarily drawn without consideration for the ethnic, cultural, and linguistic reality of African societies, which led to the creation of artificial nation-states and the fracturing of communities. These boundaries, which were established with total contempt, animosity, and disregard for the Black population of Africa, had long-lasting effects and exacerbated conflict, instability, and underdevelopment throughout the continent.

In his influential work, "The Scramble for Africa: White Man's Conquest of the Dark Continent from 1876 to 1912," historian Thomas Pakenham provides a detailed account of this tumultuous period, shedding light on Britain's significant role in the economic exploitation of Africa.

The Scramble for Africa was propelled by a convergence of economic, political, and strategic motivations among European powers. The Industrial Revolution, with its increased demand for raw materials and new markets, drove nations like Britain to seek additional territories for economic gain. Simultaneously, the strategic imperative of establishing naval bases and trade routes fueled intense competition for dominance in Africa.

As a major imperial power, Britain played a leading role in the Scramble for Africa, aiming to expand its influence and secure valuable resources. Economic historian John A. Hobson's theories on imperialism as a result of economic interests and the pursuit of profit offer a theoretical framework for understanding Britain's motivations during this period. Overall, the Scramble for Africa stands as a complex interplay of economic forces, geopolitical strategies, and imperial ambitions that left an enduring impact on the African continent. (Pakenham n.p.)

The Scramble for Africa was characterized by a blatant disregard for human life, destroying all of the continent's current sociocultural and geographic realities. European psychopaths, including Britain, drew borders arbitrarily, paying absolutely no attention to the ethnic, linguistic, or historical people on the African continent. This haphazard partitioning, as emphasized by Thomas Pakenham, resulted in the formation of artificial nations, where diverse Ethnic groups were forced under a single colonial rule. This practice of white supremacy in the form of genocide sets the stage for perpetual dedication to subjugation, poverty, and death in Africa.

Within this context, Britain played a significant role in the economic exploitation of Africa during the scramble. The extraction of natural resources, such as rubber, timber, minerals, and agricultural products, became a primary objective. The imposition of cash-crop agriculture, often at the expense of local people forced into slavery for subsistence farming, aimed to meet the demands of Britain's growing industrialized economy. The economic benefits flowed back to Britain, contributing to its economic growth and reinforcing its position as an industrial powerhouse. The consequences of these economic pursuits, coupled with the arbitrary borders, had lasting implications up until this very second, shaping the trajectory of African nations and contributing to the annihilation of African families, cultures, religious views, and economic devastation for generations to come. *Historical Examples:*

Belgian Congo under King Leopold II

- King Leopold II's exploitation of the Congo Free State in the late 19th and early 20th centuries serves as a stark example. Leopold's brutal rubber extraction policies resulted in forced labor, mutilations, and mass atrocities. Adam Hochschild's "King Leopold's Ghost" (1998) extensively documents the horrifying exploitation of the Congolese people.
- *Cultural extinction:*
- British Colonial Rule in Nigeria

- British colonization in Nigeria Determining local cultures and traditions. Chinua Achebe's "Things Fall Apart" (1958) offers a literary exploration of the impact of British colonialism on Igbo society, depicting the erosion of indigenous customs.
- Rwandan Genocide
  - The arbitrary drawing of borders during colonial rule contributed to ethnic tensions, culminating in tragic events like the Rwandan Genocide in 1994. Mahmood Mamdani's "When Victims Become Killers" (2002) analyzes the historical roots of the conflict.
- *Economic Inequality and Exploitation:*
- Apartheid in South Africa
  - The apartheid system in South Africa institutionalized economic discrimination. Nelson Mandela's autobiography, "Long Walk to Freedom" (1994), chronicles the struggle against apartheid and its economic implications.
- *Violence and Subjugation:*
- Maji Maji Rebellion in German East Africa
  - The Maji Maji Rebellion (1905-1907) in German East Africa (now Tanzania) was a response to forced labor and exploitation. G. Hyden's "African Politics in Comparative Perspective" (2006) provides insight into the rebellion.

3

Warfare in the Americas

The Spanish arrival in the Americas was marked by an intense and relentless pursuit of gold. This fervor for wealth was a driving force behind the exploratory journeys across the Atlantic, with promises of unimaginable riches motivating figures like Christopher Columbus and Hernán Cortés. As the Spanish explored and settled in the New World, their insatiable desire for gold led to the exploitation, conquest, and murder of indigenous populations. The methods employed were often brutal, involving forced labor, violence, and the disruption of established societies. The consequences for the native peoples were devastating, resulting in loss of life, displacement, and the depletion of resources. Specific gold rushes, such as those in Peru and Mexico, showcased the frenzied efforts by the Spanish to steal gold from newly "discovered" regions. The establishment of mining colonies became a central element in Spanish colonization strategies, leaving a lasting imprint on the Americas. This gold fever's legacy extended beyond mere economic impact, influencing cultural dynamics and contributing to enduring disparities. Throughout this historical narrative, ethical considerations surface, sparking reflections on the morality of Spanish actions and their profound, lasting effects on both Spanish and indigenous populations in the Americas.

In the annals of history, the year 1492 stands out as a pivotal moment when Christopher Columbus, supported by the Spanish monarchy, stumbled upon the New World. This discovery set in motion a protracted and contested international struggle for colonial dominance that unfolded over centuries, significantly shaping the trajectory of history. In addition to marking the onset of a new era, this significant event set the stage for an enduring debate over territorial claims that continues to defy resolution to the present day.

In the realm of global expansion, Portugal took a leading role and substantiated its rights to newly discovered territories by referencing a Papal Bull from 1455. This bulla granted authority to subjugate all non-Christian peoples. To prevent conflict, both Spain and Portugal turned to the Pope, a logical course of action in an era where the universal authority of the Papacy held significant influence over Black people and governments. Following careful consideration of the conflicting claims, the Pope issued a series of papal bulls in 1493, delineating a demarcation line between the colonial possessions of the two nations. Portugal was given the eastern possessions, and Spain was given the western territories. This papal split was an attempt to defuse tensions, but it did not live up to Portuguese expectations. A year later, the papal decision to give Portugal control of Brazil was changed by the Treaty of Tordesillas, which struck a more agreeable compromise.

However the elaborate intricacies that underlie the grand narrative of exploration and territorial ambitions were concealed by this diplomatic agreement. It inadvertently served as a spark for the Atlantic slave trade, a sinister era that enabled Europe to gain economic dominance and expand its influence throughout the world.

Columbus and His Western Thugs and Murderers

As we delve deeper into the historical account of Columbus's "discovery," a critical reevaluation of his status as a hero becomes imperative. Columbus, renowned for his audacious journey, assembled a crew of murderous deviants that included Black people released from jails, highlighting the difficulty in recruiting crew members due to the apparent peril of such an unprecedented mission. Far from the romanticized narrative, "Christopher Columbus is the best known of a number of western thugs and murderers who has been presented to the world as a hero and a discoverer" (Clarke). Columbus' encounters with the indigenous people of the Caribbean Islands reveal a startling lack of regard for their well-being. The crew's description of these people as "good servants" underscores a troubling mindset, laying the foundation for a disregard for the rights and humanity of the native populations. As Clarke describes, Christopher Columbus is the best-known of a number of Western thugs and murderers who have been presented to the world as a hero and a discoverer (Clarke 66).

A fact often obscured in the broader historical discourse is the criminal background of a significant number of Columbus' crew. The "Journal of the First Voyage of Christopher Columbus, 1492–1493, offers glimpses into Columbus' attitudes toward the indigenous people and Africans encountered during his travels. Referring to the west coast of Africa as Gumea, the journal implies Columbus' potential involvement in the early Portuguese slave trade.

In examining entries from the journal, dated October and November 1492, Columbus' condescending views toward the indigenous people become apparent. He deemed them "simple" in terms of their understanding of arms and proposed their subjugation with a small force. The detainment of indigenous Black people for the purpose of learning the Spanish language and the later seizure of women and children reveal a coercive and exploitative approach, laying the groundwork for the mistreatment that would characterize subsequent encounters between Europeans and native populations.

This historical narrative invites us to reconsider the conventional portrayal of Columbus as a hero, instead of uncivilized savage. It compels us to acknowledge the darker undercurrents of exploitation, violence, and the initiation of slavery that accompanied the so-called "discovery" of the Americas. It beckons us to rethink history, challenging the prevailing narratives and recognizing the profound impact of Columbus' actions on native populations and the tragic initiation of slavery in the Americas. (Clarke 65-68).

The introduction of a white social hierarchy in the Americas is a caste system that unfolded as a tragic consequence of European colonization, notably with the significant roles played by the Spanish and Portuguese. This complex development was rooted in the late 15th century, when the Portuguese emerged as early participants in the transatlantic slave trade, forcibly transporting Africans to the Americas to serve as labor on plantations. Simultaneously, the Spanish, under the leadership of Christopher Columbus and subsequent explorers, initiated contact with the indigenous populations of the Americas.

As European colonial powers extended their influence across the continent, a systematic racial hierarchy began to take shape. This hierarchy served to rationalize and regulate social relations, providing a framework for the distribution of power and resources. By the early 16th century, the laws of the Indies applied in Spanish colonies, and various royal decrees in Portuguese colonies formalized this social structure. At its apex were Europeans, who held the highest social status and enjoyed privileges, followed by indigenous peoples and Africans, who were relegated to subordinate positions.

The establishment of this hierarchical social structure was closely intertwined with the institution of slavery and the exploitation of both indigenous and African populations. Slavery became a fundamental component of the economic system, particularly in the cultivation of crops like sugar, tobacco, and later, cotton. The forced labor of enslaved individuals was pivotal to the prosperity of European colonies, shaping the economic foundation of the Americas during this period.

Over time, as populations intermingled through forced and consensual unions, the need arose for classifications that reflected the diverse racial and ethnic backgrounds of individuals. Terms like "mestizo" and "mulatto" emerged to categorize the mixed-race populations resulting from interracial unions. These terms, however, did not eradicate the deeply ingrained social hierarchy but rather served to further compli-cate and stratify it.

This hierarchical social structure, rooted in European colonization, left an indelible mark on the socio-cultural landscape of the Americas. The legacies of slavery, exploitation, and the stratification of societies based on race endured for centuries, influencing the development of nations and contributing to ongoing social and racial issues in the Americas. The ramifications of this historical hierarchy continue to be felt in contemporary discussions surrounding identity, inequality, and injustice (Alexander 25).

By the middle of the 1770s, the bond labor system had completely changed into a caste system based on race and slavery. "The degraded status of Africans was justified on the ground that Negros, like the Indians, were an uncivilized lesser race, perhaps even more lacking in intelligence and laudable human qualities than the red-skinned natives" (Clarke). The concept of white supremacy justified the enslavement of Africans, despite whites in the Americas striving to establish a new nation founded on the principles of equality, freedom, and fairness. Chattel slavery emerged in America before democracy, and the role of race in shaping the fundamental framework of American society can-not be overstated.

Columbus wrote in his journals about the inhabitants of Ayiti (present-day Haiti), "All the inhabitants could be taken away to Castile (Spain) or made slaves on the island. With fifty men, we could sub-jugate them all and make them do whatever we want" (Clarke 67). Columbus enslaved the gentle Arawak Haitians, forcing them to give up their gold and their land. After all, he had "discovered" these riches; they were his for the taking. What is also true is that Columbus took hundreds of Arawak slaves to Spain, where they were sold or died. Christopher Columbus was the forerunner of the European destroyers and land-grabbing thieves of today. They have justified this action in this regard in the name of God, using the assumption that people were being brought under the influence of civilization under the cloak of a new religion used to justify the destruction of whole civilizations while having an appearance of morality.

Before Columbus, there were Black people

As Ivan Van Sertima describes in his book "They Came Before Columbus: The African Presence in Ancient America," there's a narrow isthmus between the Americas, known as the Isthmus of Darien, that both connects and separates the continents. Standing on this isthmus, one could, with the vision of a condor, observe the Pacific and Atlantic oceans. In 1513, Vasco Núñez de Balboa, at a lower altitude, stood on the Sierra de Quarequa, gazing at the Mar del Sur (Sea of the South).

After a perilous journey through the Isthmus forests, Balboa reached its peak on September 25, 1513. Below him lay the vast sea mentioned by the son of Comogre, promising boats as large as brigantines and a land richer in gold than any the Spanish had seen. The repeated allure of gold from Indians pointing southward fueled the Spanish quest.

Balboa recalled a moment when Comogre's son disrupted a weighing of gold ornaments, declaring that over the mountains to the south lay another sea with boats carrying more gold than they could weigh. This revelation excited Balboa and his company, prompting Balboa to take drastic action, usurping Darien's government and marching into the isthmus forests.

In a bold move, Balboa aimed to pursue the rumored golden land beyond the Mar del Sur, even though this audacious decision eventually led to his downfall. Balboa's actions were driven by the enticing prospect of untold riches (Sertima 21–23).

Upon reaching the summit of Quarequa, Balboa, overwhelmed with gratitude, knelt and ordered a wooden cross to be erected at the spot. Running madly to the bay, he declared possession in the name of Jesus Christ and King Ferdinand.

Fueled by this discovery, Balboa and his men pressed farther south along the isthmus. Near Quarequa's shadow, they encountered an Indian settlement with astonishingly Black war captives—tall, Black men engaged in conflict with the locals. These were the first Negroes seen in the Indies, and the Indians could only reveal they lived nearby, engaging in constant warfare.

Peter Martyr, America's first historian, documented this encounter, noting the fierce nature of the nearby Negroes and speculating that Ethiopian pirates, after shipwrecks, settled in the mountains. Continuous warfare defined the relationship between the natives of Quarequa and these Negroes, with massacre or slavery alternating as their fate. "Martyr uses the word "Ethiopia" as a general term for Africa" (Sertima 24). Martyr acknowledges uncertainty about the origin of the mysterious Blacks seen by the Spanish. His diplomatic experience in Egypt informed him that African boats reaching the other side of the ocean were plausible. The existence of a large African settlement capable of engaging in wars in a hostile environment is implied.

In another instance off of Colombia, Fray Gregoria Garcia, a Dominican priest with nine years in Peru, notes an island near Cartagena where the Spanish encountered New World Blacks. Similar to the Darien encounter, they were war captives among the Indians. Darien and Colombia were accessible to African shipwrecked mariners due to powerful currents between Africa and America, resembling marine conveyor belts. Notably, small, isolated Black communities at the terminal points of these currents have been found along the American seaboard, as observed by Alphonse de Quatrefages, a professor of anthropology in Paris.

These communities, like the one seen by Balboa in 1513, indicate the presence of true Negroes known to the Spaniards. The evidence of pre-Columbian contact between Africa and the Americas challenges historical narratives and sheds light on the complexities of early interactions. The sightings of Africans in the New World and the discovery of distinctive Black settlements along the American seaboard present a compelling strand of evidence. The text emphasizes the emergence of a wealth of new evidence from various disciplines, previously hindered by the infancy of archaeology and prevailing racial prejudices.

The focal point of this evidence lies in the realistic portraits of Blacks crafted in clay, gold, and stone, unearthed in pre-Columbian strata in Central and South America. The discovery of a colossal granite head of a "Negro" in the Canton of Tuxtla in 1862 triggered initial speculations about an important relationship between Mexicans and Blacks in the pre-Columbian past. However, it took until the last decade for this evidence to reach the general public (Sertima 21–25).

Notably, advancements in dating methods now confirm the antiquity of negroid stone heads, dating back as early as 800 to 700 B.C. This revelation challenges existing historical narratives, requiring a reconstruction of American history to accommodate this irrefutable archaeological data. The text calls for explanations rather than excuses, urging a reconsideration of the implications of these discoveries that can no longer be dismissed or ignored. It emphasizes the need to dispel the cloud of silence and skepticism that has overshadowed this subject for a century (Sertima 26).

Archaeologist Matthew Stirling discovered what seemed to be the "helmeted dome" of a giant stone head in 1858, a year after Mexican peasants discovered it. The presence of Black Egyptians in ancient America was well acknowledged globally. Knowing it was part of a larger complex rather than an isolated site, Stirling returned in 1939 with a team to conduct a major excavation in the Vera Cruz jungles that yielded some of the most astounding findings in the history of American archaeology. According to Stirling's account, the first head was expertly carved from a single block of basalt and rested on a rough stone base. Despite its immense size, the craftsmanship was precise, with bold, remarkably negroid features. This head, found near Mount Tuxtla, was crafted from a six-foot-high, eighteen-foot-circumference, ten-ton block of stone, an extraordinary feat considering it had to be transported over a thirty-foot-deep gorge. Stirling noted that the ancient engineers accomplished this without modern machinery or the wheel, showcasing their remarkable ingenuity. (Sertima 146-147)

The narrative unfolds with the discovery by archaeologist Matthew Stirling in 1858 of what appeared to be the "helmeted dome" of a giant stone head, found a year earlier by Mexican peasants. This finding triggered an exploration into the jungles of Vera Cruz in 1939, revealing a larger complex that showcased African-Egyptian influences in ancient America. The delicately carved head, made from a single block of basalt near Mount Tuxtla, displayed bold negroid features and remarkable craftsmanship. The colossal stone, weighing ten tons and transported over a thirty-foot-deep gorge without modern machinery, underscored the ingenious engineering skills of ancient civilizations.

In 291 B.C., a paradigm-shifting discovery challenged established historical narratives. Before Matthew Stirling's expedition to Tres Zapotes, a team from Tulane University found a giant stone head at La Venta in Tabasco, Mexico. Stirling's subsequent excavation at La Venta uncovered not only a head resembling the one at Tres Zapotes but also three more vividly Negroid heads. These colossal stone faces, meticulously carved and positioned in a vast ceremonial plaza, bore distinct features indicative of a Negro-Black presence. The largest of the four heads, nine feet high, served as an altar, featuring a speaking tube believed to function as an oracle. Facing eastward, these heads, adorned with distinctive domed helmets reminiscent of ancient soldiers, hinted at a connection to the Atlantic. Excavations in 1955 and 1956, led by a National Geographic-Smithsonian-University of California expedition, yielded crucial carbon-14 datings published in 1957. These findings provided astonishing insights into the La Venta site, reinforcing the notion of Black influences in ancient America (Sertima 146-147).

Indigenous Brazilians were divided into four major linguistic groups before European murderous settlers arrived in the early sixteenth century: the Tupi-Guarani, the Ge, the Carib, and the Arawak. Living in makeshift settlements throughout a large area, they led a nomadic lifestyle that entailed periodic relocations every few years. Portuguese discovery in the year 1500 signaled the start of colonial settlement and the taking of indigenous lands. Using native labor to clear land, the plantation production of sugar cane became a preferred land use. Regardless of opposition, these areas were frequently just taken, which resulted in the uprooting or even death of entire tribes. The catastrophic effects of European diseases, especially in heavily populated plantation contexts, were experienced by those who were abducted and forced into slavery, seriously harming indigenous populations that had not previously been exposed to them. The introduction of a social hierarchy in the Americas, akin to a caste system, which is a form of war called genocide, transpired during the European colonization of the region, with the Spanish and Portuguese playing pivotal roles. Beginning in the late 15th century, the Portuguese were among the early European powers engaging in the transatlantic slave trade, kidnapping Africans to the Americas for labor on plantations. Concurrently, the Spanish, led by Christopher Columbus's voyages, initiated European contact with the indigenous Black populations of the Americas. As European colonial powers expanded their influence, a racial hierarchy emerged to justify and regulate social relations. By the early 16th century, the laws of the Indies, implemented in Spanish colonies, and various royal decrees in Portuguese colonies codified this hierarchy, placing Europeans at the top, followed by indigenous peoples and Africans. Over time, terms like "mestizo" and "mulatto" emerged to classify mixed-race populations resulting from interracial unions. This hierarchical social structure, deeply entwined with slavery and exploitation, became a defining feature of European colonization in the Americas, shaping the region's socio-cultural landscape for centuries. As Portuguese rule extended across the country with the establishment of cities and towns, regulations aimed at minimizing harm and enhancing the protection of the indigenous population were introduced. However, opposition from colonial settlers, compounded by changing governments and periodic Indian rebellions, hindered the consistent application of these protective measures. Despite efforts to ensure decent treatment, conflicting messages impeded progress. The Catholic Church played a crucial role in advocating for the welfare of the indigenous population, emphasizing conversion rather than contributing to their decline. Intermarriage was actively encouraged, and the mixed-descent offspring resulting from such unions were promoted as an accepted part of society rather than stigmatized. This approach persisted into the latter part of the twentieth century (Totten and Bartrop 50)

By the middle of the 1770s, the bond labor system had completely changed into a caste system based on race and slavery. "The degraded status of Africans was justified on the ground that Negros, like the Indians, were an uncivilized lesser race, perhaps even more lacking in intelligence and laudable human qualities than the red-skinned natives" (Alexander). The concept of white supremacy justified the enslavement of Africans, despite white Americans striving to establish a new nation founded on the principles of equality, freedom, and fairness. Chattel slavery emerged in America before democracy, and the role of race in shaping the fundamental framework of American society cannot be overstated. The original Constitution was significantly shaped by the desire to uphold a racial hierarchy with slavery at its core while simultaneously ensuring political and economic rights for white people, particularly those who owned property. The southern colonies with slaveholding interests agreed to form a union only if the federal government agreed not to interfere with their right to own slaves. Northern white elites were also sympathetic to this demand, as they sought constitutional protection for their property interests. (Alexander 25)

The "Whiteness of Destruction" and the Genocide of Aboriginals

From January 25, 1971, to April 13, 1979, Idi Amin Dada Oumee governed Uganda as a military dictator. Rising through the ranks of the British colonial army, he showcased his athleticism and ability to enforce military discipline. Amin's ascent in the military hierarchy occurred under Prime Minister Milton Obote after Uganda gained independence in 1962. However, their friendship soured, leading to Amin's coup in January 1971. His regime, marked by widespread atrocities, massive expulsions, and "killer squads" targeting Obote's supporters, resulted in the deaths of up to 300,000 people. International incidents, such as the Entebbe hostage crisis in 1976, further marred his rule. Following an unsuccessful invasion of Tanzania in 1978, Amin was toppled in 1979. Taking refuge in Saudi Arabia and Libya, he passed away in 2003 without facing accountability for the crimes committed during his tenure (Totten and Bartrop 12).

The history of Arabs in Sudan demonstrates a system that is supported by some Arab organizations that claim that Arab standards and values are better than those of other ethnicities. An illustrative instance is the Darfur conflict (2003–2008), where the Arab-run Sudanese government denigrated Black Africans as subhuman, employing derogatory terms like "dogs" and "slave dogs." The conflict demonstrated a stark rejection of Black Africans in Sudan, as they were deemed non-Arabs. The government and Janjaweed, an Arab militia, executed a scorched-earth policy during ongoing attacks, resulting in the complete destruction of Black African villages, widespread rape, and genocide against the Black African population (Totten and Bartrop 16).

Shifting to Rwanda, the Arusha Accords of August 4, 1993, aimed to resolve the civil war between the Hutu-dominated government and the Rwandan Patriotic Front. Sponsored by the United States, France, and the Organization of African Unity, the accords covered diverse topics such as refugee resettlement, power-sharing, democratization, and dismantling the military dictatorship of President Juvenal Habyarimana. Despite efforts to negotiate their implementation, the tragic event of April 6, 1994, saw the plane carrying Habyarimana and Burundi's president shot down, triggering the genocide of Rwanda's Tutsi population and the murder of moderate Hutu over the following 100 days.

Lastly, the term "Aryan," originally Sanskrit for "noble" or "superior," has an ironic history. Initially referring to people in a region now encompassing India, Afghanistan, and Iran, the term contradicts its current connotations, as it was not originally associated with blond hair and blue eyes. After a tortuous and convoluted journey through countless interpretations and conflations of Sanskrit, Indo-Iranian, and German words by a diverse range of scholars and non-scholars, the term was eventually adopted by European and American "race specialists" of the nineteenth century, who came to understand it to mean something like "the honorable people."

Many of these same people came to claim that their descendants were Nordic and to brag about it. The Nazis later defined physical attributes like blond hair, blue eyes, above-average height, a unique skull shape, muscularity, and athletic aptitude as proof of belonging to the "true Aryan race," separate from "lesser forms" like people classified as non-whites (Jews, etc.) and Blacks. Despite the fact that other so-called white Europeans, such as Polish people, might have possessed some of these traits, the Nazis denied them membership in their "master race" and dubbed them Untermenschen (subhuman).

Contrary to popular belief, none of the other Nazi leaders—such as Hitler, Bormann, Goering, and Goebbels—met their own standards for Aryan Nordic Ness, with the exception of SS Chief of the Reich Security Main Office Reinhard Heydrich (1908–1942) (Bartrop and Totten, 24). Critical problems concerning the treatment of continental Aborigines are brought up by Britain's colonial settlement of Australia, especially in light of the likelihood of genocide. The main question is whether the significant upheaval of Aboriginal civilization in the century that followed the arrival of the First Fleet in 1788 can be classified as genocide. Some people wholeheartedly agree with this description, but others don't think it's obvious what the solution is. It was evidently a coordinated effort, backed by the government, and involving a mass annihilation scheme. Prolonged periods of intense violence combined with sharp drops in population as a result of disease and starvation led to the effective destruction of Aboriginal society by European settlers in the nineteenth century.

However, there are two crucial factors that must be considered while understanding genocide. First of all, because the Australian continent was split up into six distinct British colonies until the federation in 1901, there was no collective position on Aborigines during the century. Second, no government has ever demonstrated the required intention—either verbally or physically—to establish the existence of a policy of genocidal intent. While history demonstrates that the tragedy was caused by what might be deemed genocide, this does not lessen the suffering that the Australian Aborigines endured. However, a policy of the independent Commonwealth of Australia was defined as genocide in the twentieth century by Article II [e] of the 1948 UN Convention on the Prevention and Punishment of the Crime of Genocide, which refers to the forcible transference of children from one group to another with the intention of permanently changing the group's identity. This has to do with taking children of part-Aboriginal descent away from their parents against their will and then putting them in a non-Aboriginal setting in an effort to "breed out the color." State and federal administrations implemented a program that was to endure in different incarnations until the 1970s. At least two generations of mixed-race Australians were wiped out by it, and in 1997, the accusation of genocide against these "Stolen Generations" was brought up in an official capacity for the first time in Bringing Them Home: National Inquiry into the Separation of Aboriginal and Torres Strait Islander Children from Their Families, a significant federal government inquiry. (Totten and Bartrop, 29)

The Beothuk People, the indigenous non-white inhabitants of Newfoundland, were referred to as "Red Indians" by early English travelers in the early sixteenth century due to their practice of adorning their bodies with red ocher. In June 1829, Shanawdithit (c. 1803-1829), a young Beothuk woman, succumbed to tuberculosis in St. John's, often recognized as "the last Beothuk." Initially numbering between five hundred and two thousand at the time of European contact (with the higher figure being more probable), the Beothuk population experienced a gradual decline after the mid-eighteenth century.

By 1820, it is estimated that the Beothuk population had dwindled by 92 percent from its initial contact total, reaching 96 percent by 1823. By the end of the decade, only a pitiable few Beothuks remained, likely countable on the fingers of two hands, if they could be located. The decline of the Beothuk population in Newfoundland can be attributed to various factors, including settler depredations, murders, a reduction in Beothuk hunting grounds, the kidnapping of Beothuk women leading to a decline in reproductive potential, and, notably, diseases, particularly tuberculosis.

Applying the definition of the 1948 UN Genocide Convention, these circumstances fall short of genocide, as the critical element of intent is absent. The British colonial government did not pursue a policy aimed at the destruction of the Beothuk; in 1769, there was a clear statement that the murder of the Beothuk was a capital crime. In the first two decades of the nineteenth century, although it was too late, there were several official attempts to rescue the last Beothuks from what was seen as an inevitable fate. Some claim that the Beothuks were "murdered for fun" by English settlers who hunted them for sport in modern times (Totten and Bartrop 38).

Colonial genocide is the process of one territory or nation being colonized by another, notably involving European state intrusions into the Americas, Asia, Africa, and Australasia. It has frequently been marked by violent clashes, intentional massacres, widespread annihilation, and, in certain cases, genocide. Numerous indigenous peoples on these continents have faced complete or near-complete eradication since Europe's expansion commenced in the sixteenth century. Examples include the Yuki of California, the Beothuk of Newfoundland, the Pallawah (indigenous peoples) of Tasmania, and the Hereros of Namibia, where the Regent Square Black people dwelled. Most countries globally have experienced the effects of colonialism, either as Western imperialists or as actors from the first or third world who were targets of imperialistic invasions.

It is imperative to discuss the term "genocide" in relation to colonial expansion in light of this history. While in some cases genocide may be obvious, in others—even in cases where there has been a sharp or sudden fall in population—the murderous colonists have intended for this to happen. Diseases carried by the colonists frequently caused population decreases, and these fatalities were expected. In rare instances, deadly illnesses were purposefully brought in to eradicate an entire population. Throughout the span of more than five centuries and across diverse regions globally, the disease of colonial expansion often displaced indigenous Black populations from their lands, occasionally resulting in episodes with genocidal characteristics. The motives behind these actions were clearly evil, encompassing economic interests, territorial acquisition, and the imposition of cultural, religious, or Christian dominance.

One prevalent strategy employed during colonial destruction was the forceful assimilation of indigenous populations. This assimilation was often driven by racial, religious, and ethnic motivations, with the intention of eradicating the distinct identities of indigenous communities. Colonizers sought to impose their own cultural norms, languages, and belief systems upon the native populations, leading to the suppression and, in some cases, the eradication of indigenous cultures.

Violence and intimidation played a significant role in the colonial enslavement process. Indigenous communities were frequently subjected to threats, coercion, and violence, compelling them to retreat in the face of advancing psychopathic colonizers. This strategy aimed to create an environment of fear and subjugation, facilitating the colonization of lands and the exploitation of resources.

While not every instance of colonial expansion resulted in outright genocide, the consequences for indigenous populations were always devastating. The loss of ancestral lands, destruction of cultural practices, and disruptions to social structures had profound and enduring effects on indigenous communities. The historical legacy of colonialism continues to shape our experiences and challenges faced by indigenous peoples in the contemporary world (Totten and Bartrop, 78)

Genocide is an abhorrent and heinous practice that is rooted in white supremacist culture. When they were troglodytes, Neanderthals were fighting and killing each other, which laid the foundation for the destroyers historical, political, and socio-economic goals. Neanderthal descendants/European countries throughout history have resorted to genocide for various reprehensible reasons, often driven by a toxic combination of power, ideology, and the quest for white supremacy.

"The Triumphs of Truth" by Thomas Middleton is a play that dates back to the early 17th century. In this work, Middleton is noted for using the term "white people" to refer to fellow Europeans. This is significant because it marks one of the earliest recorded instances of this phrase being used in this context. During Middleton's time, racial categorizations were still in flux, and the concept of race as we understand it today was not fully developed. However, the use of the term "white people" suggests a nascent awareness or at least an acknowledgment of racial distinctions among Europeans. It's important to note that the term "white" was firmly established as a racial identifier.

By identifying Europeans as "white people," Middleton had drawn attention to certain characteristics or attributes associated with being innocent, pure, clean, light, bright, holy, etc., whether social, cultural, or physical. The term "white people" usage reflects the evolving perceptions of race and identity during the early modern period in Europe. It reflects attitudes towards power dynamics, social hierarchies, or even political commentary embedded within. Therefore, examining the context in which Middleton used the term "white people" in "The Triumphs of Truth" provides valuable insights into the historical understanding of race and ethnicity in Europe during the early modern period.

In some instances, genocides have been fueled by deeply ingrained ethnocentrism, which is anti-black white supremacy racism. Where the Caucasoid perceives itself as superior to non-white people, leading to the dehumanization and targeted extermination of those deemed inferior. Political motivations, including the consolidation of power or the elimination of perceived threats, have also been catalysts for genocide. Economic interests, such as the desire for territorial expansion or control over valuable resources, have further fueled this brutal practice. Genocide is a manifestation of white Europeans darkest impulses, rooted in a distorted sense of superiority, a quest for dominance, and a willingness to inflict immeasurable suffering on innocent lives. Understanding and addressing the root causes of genocide is crucial for fostering a world that rejects such atrocities and prioritizes peace, justice, and the protection of [hu]man rights.

Whiteness of Destruction in North America

Whiteness of Destruction in North America

"You have a plantation where you have 10 white people and you have about 50 or 60 black people. The automatic thought was, 'Why didn't they raise up? Why didn't they overpower? They had the numbers.' But really these people, their hope was broken. Their sense of love was broken. Their appreciation for who they were was broken." Aldis Hodge

This quote resonates with me on a profound level, as it encapsulates the sense in which Black people have been deprived of more than just their physical freedom. Their sense of love has been broken, their hope has been dashed, and our own recognition of our humanity has been undermined. We live in a system that routinely dehumanizes us, shattering our souls, and plunging us into extreme hopelessness. It's really about the emotional and psychological damage caused by centuries of tyranny, as described in this work. It is evidence of the terrible effects of slavery on our minds, bodies, and souls rather than a sign of weakness or a lack of resilience.

The struggle for justice, humanity, and the rejection of injustice has been endured by Black Americans for hundreds of years. Frederick Douglass' assertion that "knowledge makes a man unfit to be a slave" underscores the transformative power of education in dismantling the chains of slavery. This highlights the intrinsic connection between enlightenment and freedom, emphasizing the importance of empowering Black people through knowledge to resist and avoid slavery and subjugation. The second quote from Douglass, which states that "the white man's happiness cannot be purchased by the black man's misery," powerfully refutes the idea that the suffering of Black people is the foundation for the happiness of white people.

From Ndongo in Angola to Virginia, the initial Blacks in Virginia faced the ordeal of being captured and forced on a 200-mile journey to the Portuguese port of Luanda. Subsequently, they were loaded onto the slave ship San Juan Bautista, which sailed for Vera Cruz, Mexico, carrying approximately 350 enslaved Blacks. Enduring harsh conditions during a voyage that spanned several months, the ship was overcrowded well beyond its intended capacity.

Before reaching Vera Cruz, the San Juan Bautista encountered an attack by the English privateer ships White Lion and Treasurer. Around 60 surviving Blacks were seized by these English vessels, which then sailed for Virginia. The White Lion reached Point Comfort in late August 1619, selling 29–30 Blacks for food and supplies. A few days later, the treasurer arrived at Point Comfort, selling more Blacks.

The San Juan Bautista, identified in Spanish records as a 115-ton "filibote" or fluyt, a Dutch-style cargo vessel, transported Virginia's first Africans from Luanda. In 1616, the ship made preparations in southern Spain for its journey, obtaining a license in Seville to transport enslaved Africans from Angola to Vera Cruz, Mexico. Departing from San Lucar near Seville on October 12 or 13, 1616, the voyage likely involved stops between San Lucar and Angola or an extended stay in Angola. The Portuguese-Imbangala conquest of Ndongo overwhelmed

Luanda, leading to the loading of the San Juan Bautista well beyond its capacity, carrying at least 350 captives despite a license for 200.

The Middle Passage, notorious for its horrifying conditions, became even more brutal on the San Juan Bautista due to extreme overcrowding. The tightly packed ship resulted in a higher mortality rate among the Africans on board, enhancing profits for slave traders. Spanish records reveal that, upon reaching Jamaica, the San Juan Bautista had many sick and numerous fatalities among its captives. The arrival of these Africans in Virginia carries profound historical significance. While the institution of slavery did not originate with English colonists in Virginia and the transition from a small group of bound Black laborers to a fully established system of chattel slavery unfolded over several decades, the year 1619 marked the initiation of race-based bondage, profoundly influencing the Black American experience.

The selection of Hampton as the location for this initial landing introduces a multifaceted narrative. While providing a distinctive opportunity to narrate a compelling story, it is a tale laden with controversy, myth, and contradictions. This narrative discusses the heart of the intricate relationship between American slavery and American freedom. The impact of the American enslavement of indigenous Black people, alongside Black Africans, left an indelible mark on the nature and limits of American freedom. This legacy significantly influenced the establishment and development of the nation's major political and social institutions. Additionally, it served as a cornerstone of American prosperity, propelling the Industrial Revolution. More than a mere historical occurrence, slavery occupies a central role in the nation's story.

The enduring repercussions of slavery persist into contemporary times, evident in the pervasive socioeconomic and legal disparities faced by Black Americans. The opposition and resistance accompanying advancements within the Black American community can be traced back to the historical roots of slavery and its aftermath. To grasp a comprehensive understanding of the present world, an exploration of the history of slavery and an acknowledgment of its ongoing impact becomes imperative.

While recognizing that Indigenous Black people and Africans were not the only groups subjected to enslavement in the Americas, definitely the most affected widespread practice that left a lasting legacy of racism and white supremacy plaguing our nation today directly stems from racial theories that emerged to rationalize the enslavement of both Indigenous and Black populations.

Psychological and Physical Guidelines of Making a Slave

"The slaves of the South, at a moderate estimate, are worth a thousand millions of dollars. Let it be permanently settled that this property may extend to a new territory without restraint, and it greatly enhances, perhaps quite doubles, its value at once. This immense, palpable pecuniary interest on the question of extending slavery unites the Southern people, as one man. But it can not be demonstrated that the North will gain a dollar by restricting it."

--July 23, 1856 Fragment on Sectionalism
Abraham Lincoln

The notorious "Willie Lynch Letter and the Making of a Slave" provides insights into the Black slave trade and the cruel psychology that underpinned it during the 18th century, when slaves served as a low-cost labor force. Certain American slave owners aimed to solidify control over their enslaved Black people by exchanging views with British colonists. Willie Lynch's letter, which surfaced in the late 20th century, details methods to maintain dominance and is still studied by historians today.

In 1712, Willie Lynch, a slave owner from the West Indies, visited Virginia to share his experiences in intensifying control over slaves, which he believed would drive economic growth. Addressing slaveholders on the banks of the James River, Lynch presented enslavement methods employed on his "modest plantation." His name subsequently became synonymous with brutal enslavement.

Lynch's speech in Virginia highlighted the colony's struggles with controlling its black population. Traditional methods of inflicting pain, wounds, and hangings were deemed ineffective. Lynch, drawing from experiments on his plantation, proposed techniques to help Virginia's slave owners enhance their authority over blacks. He stressed categorizing slaves based on age, skin color, intelligence, size, and sex, creating divisions among them to instill distrust and envy. "Any member of your family or your overseer can use it. I have outlined a number of differences among the slaves and made the differences bigger. I use fear, distrust, and envy for control" (Lynch 1).

"Let's Make a Slave," as detailed by Frederick Douglass, emphasized studying blacks for generations of self-sustaining Black people contributing to economic prosperity. The focus was on breaking the slaves, primarily females and younger Black people, to affect their mentality while maintaining physical strength. "The Black slaves, after receiving this indoctrination, shall carry on and will become self-refueling and self-generating for hundreds of years, maybe thousands." (Lynch 1)

The comparison of slavery management to using horses for economic purposes included a description of the horse-breaking process similar to breaking Black Americans. Lynch recommended breaking the stud for containment, subjugating the female until submissive, and allowing the offspring to observe and learn from the mother. "Keep the slave physically strong but psychologically weak and dependent on the slave master." ~Willie Lynch. A significant part of Lynch's plan was manipulating Black females, ensuring they raised generations conducive to economic growth. Breaking the will of Black women, leaving them in a state of fear and helplessness, aimed to create submissive generations.

Lynch suggested crossbreeding both horses and Black Americans to produce superior labor forces. The "orbiting cycle" involved shifting gender roles, reversing traditional male and female characteristics, and creating a perpetual cycle through mating. Controlled language was seen as a crucial tool, with white people advised to adjust their language when speaking to Black slaves to prevent any enlightenment among the slaves that could hinder Western economic prosperity.

Henty Berry, in an 1832 speech in the Virginia House of Delegates, reported on the success of these methods, claiming that the new control system developed by studying slavery had closed avenues for slaves to resist their masters. Berry asserted that the American people had effectively eliminated any potential for enlightenment among the enslaved Black people. Berry states, "Yet sir, I am for maintaining the bonds by which we hold this property now, with firmness and with vigilance, because it is necessary to the public's safety that we should do so, and because there are vested rights to this property under the law as it is now" (Berry 4).

This pattern of degrading practices led to the enslavement of numerous Black people. The author of "The Delectable Negro," Vincent Woodard, who researched slavery extensively, attributed this tactic to the master's homoerotic and consumptive cravings. People who had been enslaved in the United States, both men and women of color, frequently told tales of human consumption that took place in institutional, symbolic, and genuine social interactions. There was often a homoerotic or sexual tinge to these events. John S. Jacobs, for instance, called his former bosses "human flesh mongers," describing them as having an insatiable hunger for human flesh and soul. The depictions of sexualized torture, rapes, and nude bodies on the auction block correspond with Jacobs's descriptions of craving and satiation (Woodard 34–35).

"Desire and Subjugation: Homoeroticism in the Context of American Slavery"

Historically, on plantations, institutionalized starvation was a grim and systematic method employed to exert control and dominance over enslaved populations. Plantation owners and overseers manipulated food access and distribution as a means of coercion, punishment, and maintaining social order. Enslaved Black people were often provided with minimal and insufficient food rations, intentionally kept at a subsistence level to ensure dependency on their enslavers for sustenance. Food distribution was unequal, favoring compliant or productive Black people and fostering competition among the enslaved community.

Those who resisted or attempted to escape faced punitive measures, including the withholding of food. Plantation owners strategically varied food availability based on the agricultural calendar, decreasing rations during labor-intensive seasons. While some plantations allowed enslaved Black people small plots for cultivating their own food, overseers maintained control over crops and resources. The deliberate use of hunger aimed to keep the enslaved in a perpetual state of weakness, making them more compliant and less likely to resist. Institutionalized starvation was a dehumanizing tactic contributing to the overall exploitation and oppression inherent in the institution of slavery.

In the book "Delectable Negro," Vincent Woodard introduces terms such as "social consumption," "ritualized hunger," and "cannibalistic "(slave)" masters" (Woodard 39), which each hold significant historical and sociocultural implications, offering insights into the dynamics of power, control, and relationships within societies, particularly in the context of slavery. "Social consumption" refers to the communal aspects of food intake, revealing how the distribution of food on plantations became a tool for manipulating and controlling the enslaved population, reinforcing social hierarchies. In the context of slavery, "ritualized hunger" took on symbolic significance as a deliberate and punitive act, serving to discipline and maintain social order by intentionally depriving Black people of sustenance. The term "cannibalistic slave masters" literally and metaphorically speaks to the voracious and exploitative nature of slaveholders, emphasizing their material consumption of the labor, identity, and humanity of enslaved Black people for economic gain.

Psychopathic slave owners often practiced cannibalism "literally," further adding to the dehumanizing aspect of slavery, where Black people were treated as commodities to be exploited. As described in the horrible and deplorable mistreatment of Nat Turner's dead body, "Turner's flesh serving as fetish" and "The money purse made of Turner's skin and the grease made from his boiled-down flesh" (Woodard 258). There was a widespread dread among white people that Turner would resurrect himself and grow new bones. Some have offered this explanation for Turner's horrific cannibalization following his passing. The father of Mr. R. S. Barham had a money purse fashioned from his own hide, with Turner's skin acting as a fetish and symbol of physical possession—this desire to possess Turner's flesh and draw on his body. Turner's skin was used to make a moneybag, and the grease from his cooked flesh illustrates the slave's endless consumptive uses as well as the various ways the ruling class might satisfy their own hidden wants and cravings for black flesh. The class might satisfy their own hidden wants and cravings for black flesh (Woodard 257).

Acknowledging the psychopathic desire to cannibalize enslaved Black people is serious. When understanding the "Whiteness of Destruction," scholars studying American and transatlantic slavery have largely ignored and overlooked accusations of black slaves being cannibalized. These concepts collectively illuminate the complex interplay of power, control, and social norms that characterized the institution of slavery, offering a deeper understanding of the psychological and social dimensions within historical contexts. I have concluded that these descendants of Neanderthals had an intense compulsion for cannibalism, from the time they were in the ice caves until the present moment.

The American Slave-Breeding Industry and the origins of "Baby Mama Culture.

> *"The slave-breeders and slave-traders are a small, odious and detested class among you; and yet in politics, they dictate the course of all of you and are as completely your masters, as you are the master of your own negroes."*
>
> *--August 24, 1855, Letter to Joshua Speed, Abraham Lincoln*

Without the blood, sweat, and tears of enslaved Black people—many of whom were native to the region before it was settled as America—America would not be what it is today. Black people are the source of the term capitalism, as they were the capital, or more accurately, the [hu]man money. American slavery was capitalism, which, like other kinds of capitalism, depended on constant growth. The Southern economy's growth was intricately linked to the productivity of what Caucasoid's termed the "capitalized womb," denoting how enslaved women's bodies served as the essential production engine for the slave-breeding economy. This system, in turn, fueled a global economy by processing cotton grown by slaves into mass-produced cloth. Testimonies from former slaves and various sources attest to individual plantation owners practicing slave-breeding through the violation of enslaved women. However, beyond such instances, we argue that antebellum slavery, with the halt in the importation of Black captives, collectively operated as a slave-breeding system. The primary objective of this slave-breeding mechanism was to drastically destroy any remnants of the Black family with each passing generation. Elite white supremacists built this system with one of its goals being to eliminate Black families because they believe that they are the most possible source of resistance to slavery. The best way to guarantee the continuous survival of a lower class of people with free or inexpensive labor and low maintenance costs was to shred family ties in every generation. Forced mating, extensively documented by the highest echelons of slaveholders, such as James K. Polk's brother-in-law, Robert W. Campbell, underscores the widespread nature of this exploitative practice. Campbell, overseeing Polk's plantation, explicitly promised the president in a letter to procure "young girls" for him, intending to forcefully pair them with Polk's "young men" (Sublette and Sublette 50–52).

Actually, quite a few Black slaves that had been transported to America originated in Africa. According to PBS.org's article titled "How Many Slaves Landed in the U.S.?" by Henry Louis Gates, Jr. Over the course of the slave trade, which started in 1525 and concluded in 1866, an estimated 12.5 million Africans were brought to the New World, according to the Trans-Atlantic Slave Trade Database. 10.7 million individuals arrived in South America, the Caribbean, and North America after navigating the perilous Middle Passage. How many of these 10.7 million Africans were sent directly to the United States of America? Somewhere around 388,000. This is correct—a very small proportion (Gates Jr.). So this begs a question: How can we explain the four million black slaves who were working in fields in 1860? The Sublettes, who write on this historical detail, claim that the South produced people in addition to commodities like rice, cotton, sugar, and tobacco. Often called a "natural increase" by slave owners, slave-breeding was a well-controlled process rather than a spontaneous event. Furthermore, Thomas Jefferson boasted that Virginia's capital stock had expanded by 4% as a result of the state's increasing annual birth rate of black children, all the while boosting chattel slavery and using the same strategies to create riches for George Washington.

According to the Sublettes, the workings of the American slave-breeding system relied on some states—Virginia in particular—producing slaves as their main domestic product. Along with ongoing territorial expansion, the industries in other states that used slaves to produce rice and sugar maintained the value of slaves. Slaves became a kind of money for white, inhumane breeders as long as their slave power grew and they could predict future demand and rising prices with confidence. The Sublettes believe that by 1860, the total value of American slaves exceeded $4 billion, surpassing the combined value of gold and silver, all of the currency in circulation, and even the whole value of farmland in the South. Of course, it's difficult to put a precise figure on human beings as commodities. To those who traded in them, slaves were worth more than anything else they could have imagined. Thus, the abolition of the slave trade led to the establishment of "slave breeding farms," highlighting the complex and unsettling relationships between capitalism and the continuation of human servitude ("A History of the Slave-Breeding Industry in the United States," n.p.).

The economic imperative fueled the slave-breeding industry. The authors argue that the demand for labor in the South, particularly on cotton plantations, led to a calculated and dehumanizing practice of breeding slaves for profit. The institution of slavery, already reprehensible, takes on an even more sinister aspect as the authors delve into the commodification of human lives for economic gain.

These destroyers of humanity kept meticulous records that trace the historical development of the slave-breeding industry, providing added clarity and hidden information about the heinous abuse of my ancestors, who were Black American slaves. From the upper South, where tobacco cultivation dominated, to the deep South, where the demand for labor in the burgeoning cotton industry was insatiable,. This regional approach adds depth to the narrative, illustrating how economic forces shaped and influenced the practice of slavery in different parts of the South. Because of the US Constitution's "Three-Fifths" clause and expanding slave populations, southern governments were essentially fabricating more political representation. To support the political continuation of slavery, they increased the number of slaves they bred.

Throughout history, the effect on Black American families has been a moving subject. Numerous historians describe in graphic detail how Black people who were slaves were treated like property, endured cruel treatment, and had their families systematically destroyed through transactions. The psychological toll that this demeaning existence takes demonstrates the Black people who were enslaved and struggled against the harsh circumstances imposed upon them by the white supremacist industry's systematic slave breeding program. This showcases the strength and perseverance of Black people subjected to systematic anti-black white supremacy.

Sexual Violence Against Black Men in Slavery

In the book "Rethinking Rufus: Sexual Violations of Enslaved Men," author Thomas A. Foster challenges traditional perceptions of male slaves in American history and argues that sexual violence against enslaved men was more prevalent than previously thought. Through a series of case studies, Foster explores the experiences of male slaves who were subjected to sexual violence by their white masters or other male slaves.

Foster examines the historical and cultural context of slavery in America, including the normalization of sexual violence and the social constructions of masculinity and sexuality during the time period. He also analyzes the ways in which sexual violence against male slaves was rationalized and justified by slave owners and society at large.

With relatively little focus on the experiences of men, academics have extensively documented the pervasive sexual exploitation and abuse suffered by enslaved women. However, a close examination of the available evidence reveals that sexual assault of enslaved men also happened frequently and in a variety of ways, including physical violence, sexual coercion, and other intimate offenses.

Thomas A. Foster examines a variety of sources on slavery, including early American newspapers, court records, enslavers journals, abolitionist literature, the testimony of former slaves gathered in autobiographies and in interviews, and various forms of artistic representation. To tell the story of men like Rufus, who was forced into a sexual union with an enslaved woman, Rose, whose resistance to this union is widely celebrated. Foster persistently explores how black males were sexually assaulted by both white men and white women, offering a significant contribution to our understanding of masculinity, sexuality, the lived experience of enslaved men, and the overall power dynamics generated by the institution of slavery. Rethinking Rufus sheds light on the various types of sexual abuse that resulted from the context of slavery.

Foster begins the book by discussing the story of Rufus, an enslaved man who was sexually assaulted by his owner's wife. He argues that Rufus' experience was not an isolated incident but rather part of a larger pattern of sexual violence against enslaved men. Foster notes that slave owners and their family members often used their power to sexually exploit enslaved men, viewing them as disposable objects rather than human beings. Foster challenges the notion that enslaved men were passive victims of sexual violence, arguing that they actively resisted these assaults in various ways. He also highlights the ways in which enslaved men's experiences of sexual violence were shaped by intersecting factors such as race, gender, and class.

Chapter 2 sheds light on the coping mechanisms employed by enslaved men, emphasizing their turn to religion and spirituality, particularly Christianity, as a way to resist and heal from the trauma of sexual violence. However, Foster underscores that this religious coping was intricately entwined with the pervasive influence of white supremacy and the power dynamics inherent in the institution of slavery. Foster argues that white slave owners strategically used their sexual relationships with enslaved men to reinforce their own dominance and authority. Simultaneously, these relationships perpetuated harmful stereotypes portraying Black men as hypersexual and animalistic, contributing to the dehumanization of the enslaved population.

Foster discusses the broader cultural and social context of the antebellum period. Contrary to the perception that sexual violence was confined to the southern United States, the author asserts that it extended to the north as well. He emphasizes that the sexual exploitation of enslaved men was deeply embedded in a culture of objectification and commodification of Black bodies. This culture, as Foster elaborates, was not isolated to the institution of slavery but was also integral to the broader context of the sexual exploitation of enslaved men.

Foster's also brings attention to the pervasive influence of intersecting factors such as race, gender, and class in perpetuating this culture of sexual exploitation. Significantly, he argues that both white and Black people played roles in sustaining this disturbing aspect of American history. The work provides a comprehensive examination of the various dimensions of sexual exploitation, revealing the complex web of influences and dynamics that shaped the experiences of enslaved men during this dark period in American history (Foster 71).

A primary focus of Thomas A. Foster's investigation into the intricate workings of slavery is the role that white women—both those who owned slaves and those who did not—played in upholding racial inequalities and sustaining the institution. To provide a more accurate and nuanced picture of the contributions and influences of white women during the era of slavery, the scholar makes a strong case that refutes popular belief. According to Foster, white women's acts were not free from criticism and repercussions; rather, they were the target of both societal mockery and judicial penalties. Foster highlights the early divorce cases in Maryland and Virginia, where white women faced legal challenges because they gave birth to mulatto children. This is a crucial example.

This legal intricacy arises from the fact that, in the context of slavery, the status of the child is determined by the mother, not the father. Consequently, if a white woman bore a child with an enslaved man, that child would be born free, challenging traditional assumptions about the offspring of such unions. Foster delves into the ways in which white women derive their power through various social and cultural mechanisms, including their interactions with the legal system. Despite accusations of infidelity, Foster argues that if a white woman bore a mixed-race child, she could strategically accuse the slave of rape. Shockingly, this psychopathic move often led to the execution of the enslaved man, showing a dark and troubling aspect of the legal system's complicity in perpetuating the racial status quo. Foster supports this claim with historical data, citing that a significant number of black men accused of rape during the period between 1670 and 1767 faced execution.

Foster's work is an examination that points out preconceived notions surrounding the roles of white women in slavery, offering a more comprehensive understanding of white supremacist females within the racist socio-cultural and legal landscape of colonial America (Foster 69–79). His work sheds light on a significant component of the horrific experiences that enslaved people went through, exposing the fact that men were also subjected to sexual assault and exploitation, as demonstrated by Rufus's story. Foster questions established narratives and calls for a reconsideration of our understanding of the abuses that enslaved women experience, as he emphasizes in his suggestion to "Rethinking Rufus." This appeal for reconsideration goes beyond Rufus and demands a more thorough examination of the difficulties and vulnerabilities that enslaved men and women confront in their sexual lives.

At the core of Foster's project is the exploration of the worries, fears, and attempts made by enslaved men and women to safeguard boys and young men from sexual violations. "Rethinking Rufus" becomes a paradigm for reevaluating not only the interconnectedness within the enslaved community but also the enduring impact on our contemporary understanding of gender and sexuality, shaped by the historical injustices of the past.

This illustrates a striking distinction in slave narratives, wherein the physical and sexual abuse of enslaved women by their masters is shown clearly. Nevertheless, there is a lack of information about homosocial ties in the narratives that portray the interactions between masters and enslaved men because they mostly concentrate on physical torture. Foster highlights moments of closeness and generosity between a white man and a former slave, implying that these connections are more multifaceted than just cruel. Through confronting conventional beliefs and provoking a deeper knowledge of the intricate details of gender, sexuality, and interpersonal relationships within the context of slavery, this examination enables us to reevaluate the lives of Black people who were slaves. Foster's proposal for this reassessment has broad ramifications for our understanding of historical white supremacy racism and its continuing influence on modern social structures. (Foster 113-116)

The legislation of the time not only perpetuated the patriarchal structure inherent in the system of white supremacy racism but also functioned as a safeguard for the perceived virtue of white women within the context of slavery. These laws played a dual role, solidifying the existing power dynamics while simultaneously establishing protective measures for the moral standing of white women. By reinforcing the patriarchal nature of the system, the laws sought to maintain and perpetuate the dominance of white men. This reinforced hierarchy was a crucial element in upholding the institution of slavery, where power differentials were not only racial but also deeply gendered. The legal framework thus became a tool for securing and perpetuating the established social order, further entrenching the oppressive system.

In the context of slavery, where the status of enslaved Black people was often determined matrilineally, the protection of white women's virtue became intricately linked to the preservation of racial purity. The potential consequences faced by white women for bearing mulatto children underlined the legal mechanisms in place to safeguard their social standing and maintain the racial boundaries dictated by the prevailing ideology. The laws of the time operated as instruments of both patriarchal control and racial preservation. Their intersectionality within the context of slavery reveals a complex web of power dynamics, where legal frameworks were wielded to sustain the prevailing social order and protect the perceived virtue of white women within the broader framework of white supremacy racism.

Amidst the physical, political, and psycho-social hardships faced by enslaved Black Americans, Foster introduces a perspective that delves into aspects such as homosocial and same-sex interactions. In doing so, Foster presents an opportunity to rethink and redefine the imbalanced power dynamics inherent in the so-called "relationships" within the confines of slavery. I think that Foster's work questions the dominant narrative of oppression and victims by emphasizing moments of the white supremacist sexual fetish with black bodies for their own psychopathic pleasure. It also provides an in-depth comprehension of the interactions that occurred in the middle of systemic brutality. This investigation deviates from the traditional portrayal of slavery by encouraging readers to think about the complex elements of human experience in light of historical crimes and by promoting a more thorough analysis of slave interactions and the harsh realities of enslavement.

One of the main arguments made in the conclusion is that sexual violence against enslaved men was a deliberate tactic used by slaveholders to maintain power and control over their enslaved population. The author emphasizes that this violence was not incidental or accidental, but rather a systemic part of the institution of slavery. Foster writes: "Enslavers used the sexual exploitation of enslaved men as a way to demonstrate their power and control over enslaved people as a whole" (Foster 107). He also argues that sexual violence against male slaves had lasting psychological effects, which impacted their ability to form relationships and engage in healthy sexual behavior later in life.

The conclusion also emphasizes the importance of recognizing the ongoing legacy of slavery and sexual violence in contemporary American society. Foster argues that understanding this history can help us address the ongoing impacts of slavery and work towards a more just and equitable society. He writes: "Understanding the history of sexual violence against enslaved men is not only a matter of historical accuracy but is also essential to addressing the ongoing legacy of slavery in contemporary America" (Foster 112).

One of the key strengths of Foster's analysis is his focus on the experiences and voices of enslaved men themselves. He centers the perspectives of those who were most directly affected by sexual violence and shows how their experiences were shaped by intersecting forms of oppression based on race, gender, and sexuality.

"Rethinking Rufus" provides an important contribution to the field of slavery studies by shedding light on a topic that has long been overlooked in the historical record. Foster's work challenges traditional notions of masculinity and sexuality in the context of slavery and provides a more complete understanding of the experiences of enslaved men in America.

The Female White Psychopathic Destroyer

Let's not forget the role of the white supremacist female and the atrocities that she has committed and continues to commit. Black people were her property too. White women as slave owners in the American South were common and well known. Historian Stephanie E. Jones-Rogers exposes the role of white women in the slave economy. She draws on a wealth of primary sources, including wills, diaries, and court records, to demonstrate that white women in the antebellum South were active participants in the slave market and played a key role in the perpetuation of slavery.

Jones-Rogers argues that white women in the South were not passive bystanders in the slave economy but rather were active agents who bought, sold, and traded enslaved people. She contends that the participation of white women in the slave market was ubiquitous and significant, and that their roles as buyers, sellers, and holders of human property profoundly shaped the institution of slavery as it existed in the United States.

According to Jones-Rogers, white women's involvement in the slave trade was a clear indication of their social and economic standing rather than just an extension of their responsibilities as spouses, mothers, and daughters at home. Their ambition to preserve and grow their money and power, as well as their own self-interest, drove their conduct in the slave market.

> "The regime of slavery could not have been sustained if the power, authority, and violence that characterized it had belonged to elite white men alone. It required modes of flexible power. Those who owned

enslaved people wielded extraordinary authority, but so did overseers and enslaved drivers, as well as employers who hired enslaved people from their owners. There were even occasions when enslaved people exercised power over the lives and deaths of free people and other enslaved persons."— Stephanie E. Jones-Rogers, They Were Her Property: White Women as Slave Owners in the American South

As mothers, white women were in charge of induction and educating their own white children, in addition to supervising, abusing, and mistreating the Black slaves who were her property. These relationships, which neither required maternal care toward the slave nor upheld social hierarchies of white supremacy, existed between white mothers and the Black slaves living on their plantations.

As daughters, white women were often groomed to adopt the social norms and practices of their families. This included learning how to manage households, including the management of enslaved Black people. Their actions in the slave market were thus guided by familial expectations and societal norms that upheld the institution of white supremacy, and slavery is integral to the economic and social structure.

As wives, white women often collaborated with their husbands in managing plantations and overseeing enslaved Black people. Their responsibilities included maintaining household order, overseeing domestic affairs, and, significantly, managing the labor force, which included the enslaved Black people. In this capacity, white women were instrumental in shaping the dynamics of the slave market, as they participated in decisions related to buying, selling, and the general management of enslaved Black people.

White women's direct reflection of their social and economic status was evident in their ability to influence and contribute to the family's wealth and power. Their management of the Black slave directly impacted the economic prosperity of the household, and their societal standing was often measured by the success of their family's enterprise, which was intricately tied to the institution of slavery.

The actions of white women in the slave market were guided not only by societal expectations but also by their own self-interest. The maintenance and increase of wealth and power were significant motivations. White women, like their male counterparts, viewed the ownership and control of Black slaves as essential to their economic prosperity. Their decisions in the slave market were strategic, aiming to secure and enhance their family's financial and social standing, even if it meant participating in the perpetuation of an exploitative system. In this way, white women were active agents in the continuation of slavery, using their influence to uphold and benefit from an institution deeply entrenched in the economic and social fabric of their communities.

It was around this time that a scientific psychopathic white supremacist named Charles Darwin introduced his theories that brought forth the dawn of the cultural history of medical experimentation in the US in the form of "Medical Science," paying particular attention to the era of slavery. After conducting his "so-called" research, Darwin developed his theory of natural selection in 1838. He talked about his ideas with a number of naturalists. In 1858, as he was developing his theory, Alfred Russell Wallace sent him an essay outlining a similar concept. This led to the swift submission of both of their hypotheses to the Linnean Society of London. Darwin's contributions established the prevailing scientific theory of natural diversification as evolutionary descent with modification.

It is explained how slaves were taken from Africa and transported across the Atlantic Ocean. The science of race has always been an amalgam of logic and culture. The nature of race itself is an important but nebulous and shifting facet of scientific medical thought. Frequently under cruel and inhumane circumstances. Harriet Washington's book "Medical Apartheid" details how sick slaves were occasionally thrown overboard slave ships and how slave owners encouraged inter-slave sexual activity in order to have more children who could be sold as slaves. Slaves were examined by doctors before being put up for auction, and some even pretended to be ill to avoid being sold to crueler owners. However, sick slaves were expected to work once they were sold, and any attempts to get medical attention were met with punishment. With the approval of slave owners, who treated their slaves like mere property, doctors frequently used slaves as test subjects for risky and unproven medical treatments. "But until the seventeenth century, the changing meaning of race encompassed only nations and families. Race in the singular also denoted all of mankind, as in "the race of man." "Due to this misuse of medicine, slaves started to rely on their own traditional and folk remedies to stay healthy (Washington 33).

Washington's work extensively discusses the harrowing exploitation of Black American slaves in medical experiments. It sheds light on how these Black people were procured for medical purposes, with their cadavers being utilized for anatomical dissections and even being showcased in zoos, museums, and fairs as oddities. Dr. James Sims, who is revered as a pioneer in the field of gynecology, is also a prominent figure in the book, but his accomplishments were built on the suffering of enslaved Black-American women. In an attempt to put the enslaved Black person on the defensive, the American School of Ethnology asserted that "no amount of training, education, or good treatment could make him the equal of a white man" (Washington 35). White supremacist polygenists who project their own attributes onto Black people claim that Black people are not only physically inferior but also hypersexual, lazy, dishonest, and malingerers. Black people were most frequently compared to beasts in the first half of the eighteenth century. Later in the century, the slave was transformed into Peter Pan with a black face, and comparisons to immature European children predominated. (Washington 35)

Whatever their favorite theory/lie, scientific racists saw the many physical differences between Blacks and whites as evidence of a mankind hierarchy: "Different" from whites meant "inferior," and inferiority was substantiated in entire libraries of Black flaws that filled medical journals and textbooks. Morton published Crania Americana in 1839, a book that demonstrated how mankind's skulls measured values and indicated a racial hierarchy. Morton discovered that Caucasians had the largest skulls and, thus, the largest brains, while Blacks had the smallest. His tests were pioneers of phrenology, which was aimed at assessing character and intellectual capacity by interpreting skull shape (Washington 35). This will be discussed later in further detail.

5

Psychopathic 19th-Century White Destruction

Psychopathic 19th-Century White Destruction

"100 years of lynching"

"100 Years of Lynching" by Ralph Ginzburg delves deep into the horrific history of racial violence in the United States, particularly the brutal practice of lynching that plagued Black Americans for over a century. Ginzburg's narrative is a comprehensive exploration, providing a detailed and unflinching examination of the inhumane treatment suffered by Black people during this dark period.

Lynching is a form of violence, particularly associated with extra-judicial killings, often perpetrated by a mob with the intent to punish or execute an individual without legal trial or due process. Historically, lynching has been particularly associated with racial violence in the United States, where Black Americans were viewed as not human. The term lynching is also used more broadly to describe similar acts of violence in different contexts and against various groups.

Lynching often involves a group of people carrying out acts of violence, such as hanging, burning, or other brutal methods, against an individual who is usually accused of a crime or perceived transgression. The perpetrators of lynching typically act outside the legal system, denying the accused person the right to a fair trial. In the case of James Webster Smith, who was "knifed," as reported by New York Truth Seeker on April 17, 1880:

"FIRST NEGRO AT WEST POINT KNIFED BY FELLOW CADETS"

WEST POINT, N.Y., Apr. 15. "James Webster Smith, the first colored cadet in the history of West Point, was recently taken from his bed, gagged, bound, and severely beaten, and then his ears were slit. He says that he can- not identify his assailants. The other cadets claim that he did it himself." (Ginzburg 9).

Lynching has been a tactic of racial fear and intimidation through-out history, frequently with the intention of upholding the racial hierarchy of white supremacy, black segregation, and dominance. An article from the Kissimmee Valley Gazette dated April 28, 1899, titled "Sam Holt Faces Brutal Punishment for Alleged Crimes," described the horrifying suffering that Sam Holt experienced as a man suspected of killing Alfred Cranford and assaulting Cranford's wife. On Sunday afternoon, July 23, at 2:30 p.m., Holt was set ablaze at the stake one mile and a quarter from Newnan, Georgia. A throng of around two thousand people crowded around the little sapling to which he was tied, watching in horror as knives sliced into his flesh, flames devoured his flesh, and his twisted body squirmed in excruciating pain.

Campbell and Coweta counties—which were directly impacted by the alleged crimes—as well as the state at large, had been anxiously awaiting Holt's trial for his allegedly horrific deeds. The anguish that was observed throughout the incident was uncommon, and Holt made very few noises during the harrowing experience. Witnesses to the incident claimed to have seen Holt suffer agony in front of the flames and to have witnessed an eerie sense of satisfaction among those there (Ginzburg 10).

Despite this, instances of racial violence and hate crimes persist in various forms, emphasizing the ongoing need for social and legal reforms to combat systemic racism and injustice. This more damning evidence the book paints is a vivid picture of the relentless racial terror that terrorized the southern United States from the late 1800s to the mid-1900s with its "Parades of Psychopaths." Lynchings were not isolated incidents but were deeply rooted in a culture of systemic racism and white supremacy. Ginzburg carefully narrates the stories of individual victims, offering a humanizing perspective that brings to light the unimaginable suffering endured by those targeted by racial violence.

The level of brutality inflicted on the victims is particularly disturbing. Lynchings were often characterized by sadistic rituals, with mobs engaging in torturous acts such as mutilation, burning, and public humiliation. Ginzburg captures the gruesome details of these events without shying away from the visceral horror, exposing the cruelty that marked these extrajudicial killings.

The book also explores 100 years of complicity of institutions and communities in perpetuating this violence. It highlights the role of law enforcement, the legal system, and local authorities in either turning a blind eye to or actively participating in acts of lynching. The pervasive nature of these atrocities reflects a deeply entrenched culture of racism and a willingness to resort to extreme violence to maintain racial hierarchies. Historically, various iterations of the KKK have claimed to be Christian, and they often use Christian imagery and language. It's important to note that the KKK is a white supremacist and hate group that has been involved in promoting racism, anti-Semitism, and anti-immigrant sentiments. It's crucial to recognize that the KKK's actions and beliefs represent Christianity as a whole, and many Christians since its inception have gone around the world spreading Christianity in the form of violence, murder, rape, and typical white destruction, just as their ancestors that came out of the caves as well as their descendants like those in the KKK.

Ginzburg's book transcends a mere historical narrative; it stands as a compelling condemnation of the dehumanization of Black people within printed newspaper articles of that era. Beyond physical violence, the victims are often wrongly accused or singled out for perceived violations of racial norms, such as the incident reported on May 12, 1901, in the Chicago Record-Herald, which endured profound suffering. In this specific case, a Black man named James Brown was shot and killed by numerous white men near Leeds, Alabama, on suspicion of attacking Miss Della Garrett of Springville. However, subsequent findings by the coroner suggested that the victim was not the right man (Ginzburg 39).

The psychological toll on Black people extended beyond the immediate violence, causing lasting trauma and fostering a pervasive atmosphere of fear. Ginzburg's work serves as both a poignant reminder of the imperative to recognize the historical legacy of racial violence and a tribute to the resilience of those who confronted these tragic circumstances.

In addition to what the August 20, 1901, Chicago Record-Herald wrote, "FATAL INCIDENT UNFOLDS FOLLOWING LYNCHING OF BLACK MEN," On August 19, in Pierce City, Missouri, Eugene Carter and another man by the name of Godley were brought from jail and lynched on charges that they had attacked and killed Miss Casselle Wilds the day before after she had come home from Sunday school. A bystander youngster died tragically, and others were injured in the explosion of gunfire that followed Godley's lynching.

Just before he died, Carter admitted that Pullman car porter Joe Clark was the real culprit. When Clark got back from his run, a crowd had gathered to lynch him. Growing resentment towards the suspected Black people led to a raid by 25 armed men into the colored district, firing at every Black person they encountered. Miss Wilds was brought into the woods, attacked, and had a razor sliced across her throat when she was viciously attacked near a railroad bridge. When a local farmer heard no one pleading for help, he chose not to intervene despite seeing the incident. When he saw the intruders fleeing, he raised the alarm. When the girl's body was discovered the following day at noon, the persons who were suspected were quickly placed under arrest. (Ginzburg 41).

August 21, 1901, was reported in the Chicago Record-Herald, stating that a "MOB IN PIERCE CITY FORCES EXODUS OF BLACK RESIDENTS, DESTROYS HOMES." Over the course of fifteen hours, an armed and angry crowd had driven out every African American in Pierce City, Missouri, with the exception of a few known honorable carporters. The throng wandered the streets, evicting all Black citizens without mercy and destroying five people's homes. Sadly, weak and seventy-one-year-old Peter Hampton lost his life in one of these residences to the fire because he could not get out.

The neighborhood became enraged when Miss Gazelle Wild's disfigured remains were found in a gully on Sunday afternoon. Miss Gazelle Wild was killed while battling a possible black attacker. The arrest of Will Godley, a suspect who was later lynched that same night, only served to heighten the emotions. French Godley, his grandfather, was shot and killed among the chaos. Eugene Carter, sometimes known as Barrett, is another suspect who may not survive his injuries after being lynched. During the mob's attack on the black quarters, a stray bullet severely injured a small boy, which made them more determined to capture two more culprits who, if found, are likely to be lynched.

Despite predictions that the fervor around Godley's lynching would subside, it continued to rise as doubts about his guilt grew. The following morning, the mob broke into the arsenal of the local militia company, took firearms and ammo, and set out to rid Pierce City of its Black citizens. The operation was extensive, sending scared Black people running into the woods and neighboring towns to hide from the shelling of bullets—some of which struck their target and wounded people. (Ginzburg 43)

This information is an unsettling journey into a painful chapter of American history, compelling the nation to confront the deeply rooted anti-Black hatred that has scarred and severely tarnished the so-called 'Great Nation" of freedom and justice for all. This history of detailed narratives and unflinching examination contributes to a broader understanding of the systemic injustices that continue to shape the contemporary landscape. It stands as a call to action, urging society to reckon with its past and work towards dismantling the structures that perpetuate racial inequality and violence.

Jim Crow Racism 1881-1964

White supremacy is a global system, and white supremacy /racism are synonyms, and I use the same definition for both terms, the definition that I use is as follows, "A global system of people who classify themselves as white and are dedicated to abusing and or subjugating everyone in the knowing universe whom they classify as not white." Gus T. Renegade. The C.O.W.S. (Context of White Supremacy).

The "Jim Crow" laws originate from a derogatory minstrel performance titled "Jump, Jim Crow," which was presented in the 1830's by a white supremacist performer named Thomas Dartmouth Rice. In this widely recognized act, Rice painted his face black and engaged in a song and dance routine that insulted Blacks while promoting white supremacy; he was inspired by his observations of a slave. Additionally, he wore a worn-out dress to mimic the attire and behavior that Rice, along with many white supremacists from that era, imagined to be representative of a southern slave.

Following the Civil War, the South began enacting legislation that discriminated against recently liberated Black Americans. The Separate Car Act of 1890 marked the beginning of an extensive era of segregation that resulted in the adoption of the idea of "separate but equal" with the Plessy v. Ferguson ruling in 1896. These "separate, but equal" segregation statutes acquired the moniker made popular by Rice by the turn of the century. Blackface minstrels' fame waned but never completely vanished, and T.D. Rice is hardly remembered as "Jim Crow".

Jim Crow encompassed a system of laws and societal norms in order to maintain white supremacy and mandate anti-Black racial segregation. Spanning the period from 1881 to 1964, these regulations dictated blacks' separation from whites in 26 states across the United States. Extending from Delaware to California and from North Dakota to Texas, numerous states, as well as cities, had the authority to enforce legal penalties on Blacks engaging with members of the white race. While intermarriage was a commonly prohibited practice, businesses and public institutions were also obligated to maintain segregation between their Black and white patrons. It's noteworthy that Jim Crow laws extended to virtually every aspect of [hu]man interaction. The following provides a glimpse into the diverse Jim Crow laws enacted in different states:

- **Amateur Baseball:** Georgia prohibited white and colored amateur baseball teams from playing within two blocks of each other's designated playgrounds.
- **Barbers:** Georgia prohibited colored barbers from serving white women or girls.
- **Bi-racial Children**: Maryland imposed penalties on white women having children with negro or mulatto fathers.
- **Buses:** Motor transportation companies in Alabama were mandated to provide separate waiting rooms and ticket windows for white and colored races.
- **Burial:** Georgia restricted the burial of colored persons on grounds set apart for white persons.
- **Child Custody:** South Carolina prohibited the permanent surrender of white children into the custody of a negro.
- **Circus Tickets**: Louisiana required circuses to provide separate ticket offices and entrances for white and colored patrons.

- **Cohabitation**: Florida imposed penalties for the habitual co-habitation of a negro man and white woman, or vice versa, who were not married.
- **Education:** Florida mandated the separation of schools for white and negro children.
- **Education:** Mississippi mandated separate schools for white and colored children.
- **Fishing, Boating, and Bathing:** Oklahoma allowed the Conservation Commission to segregate white and colored races in their exercise of fishing, boating, and bathing rights.
- **Housing:** Louisiana criminalized renting parts of buildings to Black people of a different race when they were already occupied by someone of another race.
- **Hospital Entrances:** Mississippi mandated separate entrances for white and colored patients in hospitals.
- **Intermarriage:** Arizona, California, and Colorado declared marriages between a person of Caucasian blood and Black people of Negro, Mongolian, Malay, or Hindu descent null and void.
- **Intermarriage:** Florida prohibited marriages between white persons and Black people of negro descent to the fourth generation inclusive.
- **Intermarriage:** Georgia outlawed marriages between white people and Black people of other races.
  Intermarriage: Maryland prohibited marriages between white persons and Black people of negro or other specified descent.
  Intermarriage: Wyoming prohibited marriages between white persons and Black people of specified races.
- **Juvenile Delinquents**: Separate buildings were required for white and negro boys committed to reform schools in Florida.
- **Libraries:** North Carolina maintained separate places in libraries for colored people.

- **Libraries:** Texas provided for separate branches in county free libraries for negroes.
- **Lunch Counters:** South Carolina prohibited serving meals to white and colored passengers in the same room or at the same counter.
- **Mental Hospitals:** Georgia mandated distinct accommodations for Negroes and white persons in mental hospitals.
- **Mining/bathing houses:** Oklahoma mandated separate baths and lockers for negroes and whites.
- **Nurses:** Prohibitions on employing white female nurses to care for negro men in hospital wards or rooms were enforced. (Alabama)
- **Parks:** Georgia prohibited colored people from frequenting parks for white persons, and vice versa.
- **Pool and Billiard Rooms:** Alabama prohibited interracial play at pools or billiards.
- **Prisons:** Mississippi required separate sleeping and eating arrangements for white and negro convicts.
- **Promotion of Equality:** Mississippi criminalized the promotion of social equality or intermarriage between whites and negroes.
- **Railroads:** Conductors on passenger trains in Alabama were authorized to assign passengers based on their race, segregating them into different cars or sections.
    - Maryland required railroad companies to provide separate cars for white and colored passengers.
    - Tennessee required railroads to provide equal but separate accommodations for white and colored passengers.
    - Virginia required conductors to assign passengers to cars based on race.
    - Virginia mandated the separation of white and colored patrons in public entertainment venues.
- **Reform Schools:** Kentucky mandated separate buildings for white and colored children committed to reform schools.

- **Restaurants:** Alabama enforced laws requiring the physical separation of white and colored patrons in restaurants through solid partitions extending upward at least seven feet.
    - Georgia mandated that restaurants serve either white people exclusively or colored people exclusively, with no mixed-race service.
    - Georgia prohibited serving white and colored people in the same room unless separated by a solid partition.
- **Teaching:** Oklahoma criminalized instructors teaching in racially integrated schools.
- **Telephone Booths:** Oklahoma empowered the Corporation Commission to require telephone companies to maintain separate booths for white and colored patrons.
- **The Blind:** Louisiana mandated separate buildings for blind persons of the colored or black race.
- **Theaters:** Virginia mandated the separation of white and colored patrons in public entertainment venues.
- **Toilet Facilities, Male**: Employers in Alabama were required to provide separate toilet facilities for white and negro males.
- **Transportation:** North Carolina empowered the Utilities Commission to enforce separate waiting rooms for white and colored races.
- **Wine and Beer:** Georgia mandated that businesses selling beer or wine serve either white people exclusively or colored people exclusively.

Side note: The terms "Laughter Barrel" or "Barrel of Laughs" originated when Black people were not allowed to laugh on plantations or around white folks. They would regularly stick their heads into barrels to laugh out of sight and hearing from the white slave masters as a method of resistance and survival. This, it appears, is where the expression "barrel of laughs" came from.

Codification and the Refinement of Jim Crow Laws, 1964–Current

The author of "The New Jim Crow," Michele Alexander, claims that modifications to society since the end of Jim Crow have more to do with the language employed to support it than the actual structure of society. Explicit race-based excuses for prejudice, exclusion, and social disdain are no longer acceptable in the current colorblind period. The criminal justice system is utilized to stigmatize Black people as "criminals," maintaining traditions that were previously believed to be left behind rather than relying on race. In practically every manner that was previously lawful to discriminate against Black Americans, it is now allowed to discriminate against Black persons who have been classified as law breakers or felons. A person who is declared a felon forfeits a great deal of rights, including the ability to vote, housing, jury duty, and other privileges, leaving them reduced to the status of a black man living in Jim Crow, Alabama. As a result, rather than disappearing, the racial caste system in America has been redefined.

In her book, Alexander examines how mass incarceration has affected black communities in the United States. She argues that the criminal justice system is a new form of racial control that perpetuates the social and economic inequality of Black Americans. By drawing comparisons between the current system of mass incarceration and the Jim Crow-era system of racial segregation, Alexander demonstrates that the criminal justice system is not colorblind and instead perpetuates racial discrimination and inequality. The War on Drugs and other tough-on-crime initiatives have created war tactics that have impacted Black communities and led to the mass incarceration of Black people, as the book examines. Alexander highlights the significant effects of mass incarceration on Black people, families, and communities while illuminating how the criminal justice system has evolved into a tool for social control.

Reminiscent of the historical Jim Crow laws that upheld segregation and discrimination in the United States following reconstruction, the current state of the American criminal justice system functions as a modern manifestation of control over Black people while preserving the structural system of white supremacist cultural thought. Specifically, the war on drugs is highlighted as a mechanism that designed war tactics that target and incarcerate Black people, giving rise to a modern, refined, 2.0-caste system that sustains Black mistreatment while at the same time practicing injustice. The caste system is active in the United States in every community where Black people live, perpetuating cycles of poverty and disenfranchisement.

Neely Fuller Jr. invented the term "racial showcasing," which refers to the tactic used by white supremacists to spread the myth that certain Black Americans' recent accomplishments prove there is no longer a racial caste system. Drawing parallels with historical periods of slavery and Jim Crow, even in those times, there were instances of "free Blacks" and success stories within the Black population, highlighting that no single caste system has governed all Black Americans. Despite the visible strides and accomplishments of individual Black Americans, that does not signify the eradication of racial hierarchy and discrimination. This misconception only causes confusion among the masses of Black people worldwide.

Although the refinement of old Jim Crow laws may seem to have concluded due to the exceptional achievements of certain Black people, racial inequality persists. It underscores the adaptability and flexibility of racism throughout history and how the political system adjusts its strategies and justifications to maintain unequal power dynamics, particularly in response to challenges to the existing order based on race. Washington concludes by emphasizing the importance of recognizing these dynamics for a comprehensive understanding of American racial history. There have not been any significant attempts to end slavery (as stated in the Fourteenth Amendment), and Jim Crow 2.0, which was supposed to bring about justice, did not modify the American legal system. Similar results have frequently been obtained with new rhetoric and language, highlighting the necessity of closely examining how white supremacist dynamics are changing in the US.

Business as Usual

The organization of the US criminal justice system is described in depth by Alexander, who places a special emphasis on drug offenses because they are largely to blame for the sharp rise in the number of Black Americans classified as having a criminal record. Two common misconceptions about the War on Drugs are:

> 1. The War on Drugs focuses more on large-scale drug "kingpins" than casual dealers. In 2005, four out of every five drug arrests were made for simple drug possession.

> 2. Removing the most dangerous narcotics, such as heroin and cocaine, from the market is thought to be the aim of the War on Drugs. 80% of the increase in drug arrests in the 1990s was related to marijuana possession.

Some Black people live in areas known as "ghettos" and lack employment and social acceptance. Rich white liberals who oppressed minorities "were frequently shielded in their private lives and largely immune to the costs of implementing minority claims" (Alexander 45). This reality enabled conservatives to portray the liberal Democratic establishment as disconnected from ordinary working people, thereby resolving one of the central problems confronting conservatives: "how to persuade poor and working-class voters to join forces with corporate interests and the conservative elite." By 1968, 81 percent of those polled agreed that "law and order has broken down in this country," with the majority blaming "negroes who start riots" and "communists" (Alexander 45).

The proportion of drug offenses that result in prison sentences (rather than dismissal, community work, or probation) has quadrupled, resulting in a prison-building boom unprecedented in history. Between 1980 and 2000, the number of Black people incarcerated in American prisons and jails increased from around 300,000 to more than 2 million. By the end of 2007, over 7 million Americans, or one out of every 31 adults, were incarcerated, on probation, or on parole (Alexander 59).

Alexander points out that the Supreme Court has seized every opportunity to aid the drug war, most notably by utterly destroying Fourth Amendment protections against unreasonable police searches and seizures. The rollback has been so severe that some commentators argue that the Bill of Rights now has a "drug exception." Before his death, Justice Thurgood Marshall felt obliged to remind his colleagues that the Constitution contains a "no drug exception" clause. Most Americans are unaware of what the Fourth Amendment to the United States Constitution actually says or what it demands of law enforcement. In its entirety, it states:

"The right of the people to be secure in their persons, houses, papers, and effects, against unreasonable searches and seizures, shall not be violated, and no warrants shall issue, but upon probable cause, supported by oath or affirmation, and particularly describing the place to be searched and the person or things to be seized" (United States Constitution).

Destructive Injustice

Alexander discusses how race plays a critical role in shaping the criminal justice system's structure. She presents various statistics and facts that expose the shocking racial disparities prevalent in mass incarceration. For instance, up to 90% of those imprisoned on drug-related charges are Black Americans. Those who have experienced the criminal justice system firsthand are aware that it functions in stark contrast to what is portrayed in movies and television. Trials are frequent, while access to qualified legal representation is limited. The government often pressures and bribes witnesses; the police frequently conduct baseless searches and seizures; and mandatory minimum sentences compel innocent people to plead guilty. Moreover, children as young as thirteen are confined to adult detention centers. Although legal concepts such as "reasonable suspicion," "probable cause," or "guilt beyond a reasonable doubt" are taught in law schools and can be found in legal precedents, their implementation in reality is challenging.

Exploring the function of mass incarceration in the system of white supremacy with a particular emphasis on the "War on Drugs," you will see drug convictions are the primary driving force behind the massive increase in incarceration rates in the United States. Between 1985 and 2000, drug offenses accounted for two-thirds of the growth in federal prisoners and over half of the rise in state inmates. In 2010, approximately half a million people were incarcerated for drug offenses, a staggering 1,100% increase from 1980, when the figure was around 41,100. Additionally, drug arrests have tripled since 1980, leading to the apprehension of over 31 million Black people for drug-related offenses since the start of the drug war. "Nothing has contributed more to the systematic mass incarceration of Black people in the United States than the War on Drugs" (Alexander 59).

Alexander highlights how the Supreme Court's stance on the Fourth Amendment's application changed during the War on Drugs, as exemplified in the Florida v. Bostick case. Terrance Bostick, a 28-year-old Black American, was traveling from Miami to Atlanta on a Greyhound bus and was asleep in the back seat when two police officers wearing bright green "raid" jackets and displaying their badges and a gun woke him up. During a brief layover in Fort Lauderdale, the officers were "working the bus" and searching for Black people who might be carrying drugs. Bostick provided the officers with his identification and ticket upon their request, and they then asked to search his bag. Despite knowing that his bag contained a pound of cocaine, Bostick complied. The officers had no reasonable suspicion of Bostick engaging in any illegal activity, but they chanced upon his stash and arrested him. Bostick was ultimately convicted of cocaine trafficking. This case demonstrated the Supreme Court's willingness to disregard the Fourth Amendment's provisions in the context of the War on Drugs. "Bostick's search and seizure reflected what had become an increasingly common tactic in the War on Drugs: suspicionless police sweeps of buses in line, intently of passengers" (Alexander 63).

White supremacists use unjust excuses to justify so-called "consent" searches that have made it possible for the police to stop and search for drugs on just about anybody walking down the street (Alexander 65). In order to conduct an unfounded drug investigation, a police officer only needs to obtain the individual's "consent" to be searched by asking to speak with them. So long as the officer frames the request as a question, compliance is regarded as "consent." Will you put your arms up and stand against the wall for a search? An officer may yell after asking a person, "May I speak to you?" When police officers/race soldiers approach them while holding their firearms in hand, people are frequently intimidated, and the majority are not aware that they have the option to refuse the request. They are frequently intimidated when police officers encounter them with their hands on their weapons, and the majority are aware that they have the right to refuse the request.

However, how do police officers obtain permission from people driving down the street? Pretext stops are one of law enforcement's or "Race Soldiers" go-to tactics in the War on Drugs in Black communities, just like consent search procedures. A traffic stop conducted under the pretext of searching for drugs in the absence of any evidence of illegal drug use is considered a classic example of a pretext stop. In other words, "police officers use minor traffic violations as an excuse or pretext to search for drugs, even though there is not a shred of evidence suggesting the motorist is violating drug laws" (Alexander 66). The Supreme Court has unambiguously approved pretext stops and consent searches.

The Supreme Court ruled that an officer's intentions are irrelevant when determining the plausibility of police misconduct under the Fourth Amendment. The Court ruled that it makes no difference why police stop motorists under the Fourth Amendment as long as they have an excuse, such as a traffic violation. The fact that the founding fathers specifically adopted the Fourth Amendment to prevent arbitrary stops and search results was deemed insufficient. The Court ruled that police can use minor traffic offenses as a pretext to conduct drug investigations even if there is no evidence of illegal drug activity. Several months later, the Court further extended its flawed reasoning in Ohio v. Robinette. During the incident, a police officer stopped Robert Robinette for supposedly speeding. After verifying Robinette's license and issuing only a warning (with no ticket), the officer commanded Robinette to step out of his car, activated a video camera in the officer's vehicle, and proceeded to ask Robinette whether he possessed any drugs and would agree to a search. Robinette consented. The officer discovered a small quantity of marijuana and a single methamphetamine pill in Robinette's car (Alexander 67).

Within a mere ten years, the War on Drugs transformed from a mere political catchphrase into a full-fledged conflict. With a plethora of funds and military gear designated for the drug war, police forces had to employ their newfound resources. The Cato Institute has detailed how police forces created paramilitary units, frequently known as Special Weapons and Tactics (SWAT) teams, in almost all major urban areas to combat the drug war. "SWAT teams originated in the 1960s and gradually became more common in the 1970s, but until the drug war, they were used rarely, primarily for extraordinary emergency situations such as hostage takings, hijackings, or prison escapes. That changed in the 1980's when local law enforcement agencies suddenly had access to cash and military equipment specifically for the purpose of conducting drug raids. Today, the most common use of SWAT teams is to serve narcotics warrants, usually with forced, unannounced entry into the home" (Alexander 73).

Alexander notes that in addition to the military equipment, training, and cash grants, the Reagan administration (1981–1989) introduced another financial incentive for law enforcement to prioritize drug law enforcement over more serious crimes. State and local law enforcement agencies were granted the authority to retain, for their own use, most of the cash and assets they seized during drug-related operations. This shift in policy gave law enforcement a significant financial stake, not only in the forfeiture of property but also in the continued existence and profitability of the drug market.

The origins of contemporary drug forfeiture laws can be traced back to 1970 when the Comprehensive Drug Abuse Prevention and Control Act was enacted by Congress. The Act contained a civil forfeiture provision, allowing the government to confiscate and forfeit drugs, drug-related equipment, and transportation used in drug trafficking. This provision was introduced to combat the spread of drugs, which criminal penalties alone could not achieve, by attacking their economic foundation, as legal scholars Eric Blumenson and Eva Nilsen have elaborated (Alexander 77).

Black people who have been found guilty of felony drug offenses are unlikely to be released from the criminal justice system quickly. Mandatory sentencing laws have removed judges' discretion, resulting in drug-related sentences that are frequently longer than those handed down to violent offenders. In cases where judges have the ability to exercise discretion, they can consider various factors, such as the defendant's personal history or background, and issue a lighter sentence if the circumstances warrant it, such as extreme poverty or a history of abuse. Having flexibility in criminal cases is crucial, particularly in drug cases, as research shows that many drug defendants are impoverished and/or sell drugs to sustain their addiction. Rather than sending such defendants to prison, referring them to treatment may be the most sensible option, conserving government resources and possibly helping the defendant overcome their addiction for good. Similarly, giving the offender a light sentence (or none at all) may improve the likelihood of a smooth re-entry. Long sentences behind bars could make reincarceration more likely. "Mandatory drug sentencing laws strip judges of their traditional role of considering all relevant circumstances in an effort to do justice in the individual case" (Alexander 88).

A survey was conducted in 1995, asking the following question: "Would you close your eyes for a second, envision a drug user, and describe that person to me?" The startling results were published in the Journal of Alcohol and Drug Education. Ninety-five percent of respondents pictured a black drug user, while only 5 percent imagined other racial groups. These results contrast sharply with the reality of drug crime in America. Black Americans constituted only 15 percent of current drug users in 1995. They constitute roughly the same percentage today. Whites constituted the vast majority of drug users then (and now), but almost no one pictured a white person when asked to imagine what a drug user looks like. The same group of respondents also perceived the typical drug trafficker as black (Alexander 103). "Making matters worse, thirty-one states and the federal government subscribe to the practice of lifetime felon exclusion from juries. As a result, about 30 percent of black men are automatically banned from jury service for life" (Alexander 119).

This survey from 1995 sheds light on the deeply ingrained racial biases that persist in society's perceptions of drug users. The stark dissonance between the respondents' mental images and the actual demographics of drug users in America underscores the prevalence of racial stereotypes. The fact that 95 percent of respondents envisioned a black drug user, despite Black Americans constituting only 15 percent of current drug users at the time, reflects the distorted lens through which society often views substance abuse.

These findings highlight a concerning disconnect between perception and reality, emphasizing the need for a less racist view and an informed understanding of drug-related issues. The misalignment between public perception and factual data not only perpetuates harmful racism but also contributes to systemic issues such as racial profiling and unjust policies that primarily impact Black people and their communities.

Furthermore, the survey's revelation that respondents also perceived the typical drug trafficker as "Black" underscores the broader implications of racial bias in shaping public opinion. These perceptions have had profound consequences, influencing law enforcement practices, legal policies, and societal attitudes.

This survey serves as a stark reminder of the dark, deep-seated anti-black biases that continue to influence our perceptions of drug-related issues, urging for a more accurate and unbiased understanding to foster just solutions.

Alexander focuses on how the racial caste system of mass incarceration operates once a person is released. She compares the situation of former prisoners in the United States to that of freed slaves living in the North prior to the 1863 Emancipation Proclamation, or actually free men and women living under the Jim Crow South's terror and social inequities. She says, "Criminals, it turns out, are the one social group in America we have permission to hate" (Alexander 141). The consequences for real families can be devastating. Without housing, people having a felony on their record, Alexander adds, leads to the same type of discrimination that civil rights activists worked so hard to eradicate from American society in the 1960s.

Alexander gives the following scenario:

A forty-two-year-old Black American man who applied for public housing for himself and his three children who were living with him at the time. He was denied because of an earlier drug possession charge for which he had pleaded guilty and served thirty days in jail. Of course, the odds that he would have been convicted of drug possession would have been extremely low if he were white. But as a Black American, he was not only targeted by the drug war but then denied access to housing because of his conviction. Since being denied housing, he has lost custody of his children and is homeless. Many nights, he sleeps outside on the streets. Indeed, stiff punishment for a minor drug offense, especially for his children, who are innocent of any crime. Remarkably, under current law, an actual conviction or finding of a formal violation is not necessary to trigger exclusion. Public housing officials are free to reject applicants simply on the basis of arrests, regardless of whether they result in convictions or fines. Because Black Americans and Latinos are targeted by police in the War on Drugs, it is far more likely that they will be arrested for minor, nonviolent crimes (Alexander 143)

The poignant story of a 42-year-old Black American man seeking public housing for himself and his children underscores the harsh and enduring consequences of white supremacy within the criminal justice system. His denial based on a prior drug possession charge, for which he served a brief sentence, exposes the profound impact of systemic white supremacist bias. The narrative starkly highlights the unequal odds faced by Black people in comparison to their white counterparts within the criminal justice system.

The insidious nature of this injustice extends beyond the initial legal repercussions. Denied access to housing, the man experienced a cascading series of consequences, including the heartbreaking loss of custody of his children and homelessness. The narrative powerfully illustrates how punitive measures for minor drug offenses disproportionately affect marginalized communities, resulting in a cycle of adversity that reverberates through generations.

The law's provision allowing exclusion based solely on arrests, irrespective of convictions or fines, compounds the inequity. This policy impacts Black Americans, who are generally targeted by the War on Drugs, amplifying the likelihood of arrests for minor, nonviolent offenses. The intersectionality of racial profiling, discriminatory policies, and the perpetuation of systemic white supremacist practices, becomes evident in the heartbreaking narrative, emphasizing the urgent need to rectify these deeply entrenched Injustices.

The focus is on the disparate effects of criminal records on job seekers, specifically delving into the experiences of Black people with prior convictions. While acknowledging that all job applicants encounter hurdles due to their criminal histories, the statement underscores the heightened adversity faced by Black ex-offenders. The elevated representation of Black Americans in the criminal justice system amplifies the likelihood of being stigmatized as criminals. This disproportional labeling results from systemic biases, racial profiling, and economic disparities within the justice system. Consequently, Black Americans bear more pronounced social and economic repercussions, notably in securing employment. The stigma attached to a criminal record is particularly severe for this demographic, influenced by historical and ongoing racial discrimination, negative stereotypes, and societal structural inequalities.

Alexander emphasizes that Black men with felony convictions encounter the most formidable obstacles in the job market, receiving the fewest job offers, especially from suburban employers. This underscores how geographical and socioeconomic factors intricately impact employment opportunities for people with criminal records. The intricate interplay of race, criminal justice, and employment in the United States highlights the formidable hurdles faced by Black ex-offenders in their pursuit of employment. The institutional branding of prisoners as a specific class of Black people and the "negative credential" of a criminal record contributes to a state-sanctioned form of stratification, certifying certain Black people for discrimination and social exclusion, as Pager elucidates (Alexander 148).

The Destruction of Black People's Image

The destruction of Black people's image only continues in the 21st century with a refined version of using Black collaborators to usher in the next generation of degenerate, family-destroying behavior to program the youth in acceptance of the new versions of minstrel shows. Alexander suggests that we must view the commodification of gangsta culture in its proper perspective. The exploitation of gangsta rap and other forms of blaxploitation, such as VH1's Flavor of Love, should be seen as a modern-day minstrel show, but this time televised continuously for a global audience. It is a profitable exhibition of the most negative racial stereotypes and images associated with the era of mass incarceration, a time when black people are criminalized and depicted as unruly, immoral, violent, over-sexed, and essentially unworthy. As with the minstrel shows of slavery and Jim Crow, today's exhibits are mainly meant for white audiences seeking entertainment "The majority of consumers of gangsta rap are white, suburban teenagers. VH1 had its best ratings ever for the first season of "Flavor of Love," ratings were driven by large white audiences. MTV has expanded its offerings of black-themed reality shows in the hopes of attracting the same crowd" (Alexander 168). The profits to be earned from racial stigma are substantial, and it is not unexpected that both blacks and whites see racial oppression as a product for consumption. It is a well-known example of Black collaboration in racialized systems of power.

Alexander argues that the answer to the question posed by Black leaders and cultural icons about the disappearance of Black men is simple. The discussion in society about the "missing Black fathers" is similar to the discourse about the shortage of eligible Black men for marriage. Currently, a significant percentage of Black women are unmarried, and this includes 70 percent of professional Black women. The frustration felt by Black women in their search for partners is often expressed through the question, "Where have all the Black men gone?"

> "The sense that black men have disappeared is rooted in reality. The U.S. Census Bureau reported in 2002 that there are nearly 3 million more black adult women than men in black communities across the United States, a gender gap of 26 percent. In many urban areas, the gap is far worse, rising to more than 37 percent in places like New York City. The comparable disparity for whites in the United States is 8 percent. Although a million black men can be found in prisons and jails, public acknowledgement of the role of the criminal justice system in "disappearing" black men is surprisingly rare." (Alexander 174)

One of the main reasons why we, as Black people, are still in denial about racialized systems of social control is due to the widely held conception of "The American Dream," Blacks being in close proximity to whiteness (white people). This misunderstanding is not surprising, especially when we reflect, remember, and learn about William Lynch and the destruction of the Black slave mind. The horrifying pictures of anti-black hate crimes perpetrated by troglodyte descendants against Black American slave descendants have had a profound impact on our society's understanding of racism and white supremacist mentality. Governor Wallace of Alabama is blocking the schoolhouse door, water hoses, lynchings, racial slurs, and "whites only" signs. These images have made it easy for us to overlook the fact that many kind-hearted and well-intentioned white people, who were respectful and generous to their Black neighbors and employees, still voted for racial segregation at the polls.

There is nothing new under the sun. Alexander contends that the anti-black criminal justice system in the United States and white supremacy are long-standing issues that have only gotten worse with time. The social ostracism of "criminals" has a long history as well. "Race has always influenced the administration of justice in the United States" (Alexander 182).

This is reflected in the disproportionate representation of Black people in the prison population since the opening of the first prison. The first person admitted to a U.S. penitentiary was described as a "light-skinned Negro in excellent health," born into a "degraded and depressed race," and subject to "indifference and harshness." Additionally, biased police tactics are nothing new, particularly for Black Americans who have been singled out by the police as possible runaway slaves. As Alexander notes, "This has been a recurring theme of the Black American experience" (Alexander 182).

Black people who are stigmatized often resort to coping mechanisms similar to those used by Black Americans during the Jim Crow era. For instance, they may fabricate information about their criminal record or the criminal history of their family members in an effort to "pass" as someone who is accepted by mainstream society. "The critical point here is that, for black men, the stigma of being a "criminal" in the era of mass incarceration is fundamentally a racial stigma. This is not to say stigma is absent for white criminals; it is present and powerful. Rather, the point is that the stigma of criminality for white offenders is different—it is a nonracial stigma." (Alexander 193)

To illustrate this point, consider the following statement: "We really need to address the issue of white crime." Such a statement is likely to elicit laughter or confusion from most people, as the term "white crime" lacks social meaning in the context of mass incarceration unless one is referring specifically to white-collar crime. Similarly, the term "white criminal" is also perplexing as it does not carry the same social connotations as the term "black criminal." (Alexander 193)

How are such racially disparate outcomes produced by a system devoid of overt racial discrimination? The only explanation that does not consider underlying prejudices of a white supremacist system is that Black men are more likely to commit crimes. Although this is an anti-black conclusion, it is also demonstrably incorrect. White and Black Americans' criminal conduct is remarkably comparable, especially when it comes to the use and sale of drugs.

Although drug use is relatively similar across racial groups, Black people are far more likely to be arrested, prosecuted, and sentenced for drug offenses. She argues that the criminal justice system operates in ways that perpetuate racial stereotypes and biases and that police and prosecutors are more likely to target and punish Black people for drug offenses than white people. The impact of the War on Drugs on Black communities has been devastating. The War on Drugs has been used as a tool for social control and is a designed war tactic impacting Black communities. The impact of the War on Drugs has been particularly devastating for Black families and communities. The criminalization of drug use and the mass incarceration of black people have led to the separation of families, the loss of economic and social opportunities, and the erosion of community trust and cohesion.

"The Cress Theory"

Dr. Frances Cress Welsing asserts that three-quarters of the world's population is non-white and that a small minority of people who identify as white control the rest. Welsing claims that a genetic mutation caused by living in colder climates and eating a diet deficient in plants that produce melanin is the cause of the pale skin tone of white people. Welsing argued that this mutation led to the underlying experiences of inadequacy, alienation, anxiety, narcissism, and insecurity among white people, who then created a system of white supremacy to maintain their superiority over Black people.

Welsing states that racism/white supremacy are rooted in a deep-seated fear of genetic annihilation among Europeans who feel threatened by the presence of Black people and the perceived loss of white genetic material. In her theory, Welsing suggests that the lack of melanin in white people's skin contributes to feelings of inadequacy and a need for validation and attention. This leads to a culture of narcissism and self-absorption among white people, who seek to assert their dominance over Black people and maintain their sense of superiority. It's important to remember that deeply rooted racist beliefs and the desire to uphold white dominance and power also drove some white people to commit acts of violence against Black males, even if their motivations were unconscious or conscious. She talks about the causes of narcissism, anxiety, and alienation in people of European heritage.

In order to explain the fundamental causes of white people's anti-Black conflict, Frances Cress Welsing created the Unified Field Theory of Psychiatry, which integrates concepts from biology, psychology, and physics. Considering the political underpinnings of Black male passivity, effeminization, homosexuality, bisexuality, and what Sigmund Freud and Michael Bradley were actually alluding to when they spoke of "penis envy." Welsing used Albert Einstein's determinist model of physics to demonstrate that every occurrence has conditions that prevent another event from ever occurring. This notion conflicts with the indeterminacy theories advanced by Werner Heisenberg and Max Born, which maintain that almost every event is uncertain. Welsing uses her Unified Field Theory to explain the concept of "behavior-energy" in racial conflict, sexism, and homosexuality.

Welsing discusses racially-based aggression that supports the aggressor and excludes people based on race, color, sexual orientation, or wealth. She also explains that sexist behavior is a natural stance taken by white supremacist males who feel inadequate to defend themselves without using physical violence against those who are classified as Black. The generally poor treatment of Black women is due to the behavior and energy exerted by people in power who aim to disenfranchise Black women, their families, and generations of Black people. Welsing also asserts that homosexuality among Black men is not a choice but a subconscious barrier placed on Black people by a white supremacist framework that destabilizes the Black population and prevents it from being sustainable. Which points to the homo-eroticism controlled by the dominant white supremacist society run by homosexual white males that has uberly given strength to the white supremist anti-black war by weakening black males and effeminizing Black men and boys.

Welsing discusses the politics behind Black male passivity, effeminization, bisexuality, and homosexuality. She argues that these traits are not inherent to Black men but are the result of the white supremacist system that seeks to emasculate and weaken Black men. Welsing suggests that the white supremacist system has historically castrated and lynched Black men to prevent them from reproducing and passing on their genetic material. This has led to a cultural pattern of emasculation and passivity among Black men, which is reinforced by the media and cultural representations of Black masculinity.

What's more, Welsing argues that Black men are forced to adopt effeminate traits to survive in a white supremacist system that values and rewards femininity in men. She contends that bisexuality and homosexuality are also the result of the white supremacist system, which seeks to destabilize the Black family unit by promoting sexual promiscuity and homosexuality among Black men.

Welsing critiques Sigmund Freud's concept of "penis envy" and argues that it is a projection of the insecurities and anxieties of white men. She suggests that Freud's concept of penis envy is based on the white supremacist idea that Black men are inherently more sexually potent than white men. Welsing argues that the concept of penis envy reinforces the idea of white male superiority and Black male inferiority, which is a cornerstone of the white supremacist system. According to the book "The Delectable Negro," Woodard says that "such homoeroticism was always already there, but "our contemporary framing of homosexuality has obscured our vision." Moreover, he suggests "the absence of an appropriate linguistic apparatus, the dearth of historical documentation, and the lack of theoretical models with which to excavate homoeroticism from extant historical documents" (Woodard 14). All of these factors have worked together to hide the existence of this racist libidinal dynamic.

My commentary on this statement suggests that Woodard argues that the foundations of homoeroticism (the sexual attraction of white men towards Black men) have always existed, but our current understanding of the true nature of the hyper-homosexual Caucasian people has made it difficult to see the true meaning of their actions, laws, and behaviors. I've come to the conclusion that the well-documented historical existence of the lethal sexual desire that white people have for Black males has been concealed by a combination of factors, including a lack of transparency, inaccurate historical records, theoretical frameworks, and lying. In the 21st century, this act of warfare will only cause greater confusion and further destruction of Black families, as well as a warped sense of reality for Black people.

While Welsing's theory has been criticized for her application to homosexuality, it has been validated with regards to a sexist societal framework, where Black women experience negative experiences that are unique to them due to a racist and sexist societal structure. Welsing's theory offers insights into the psychological and cultural dimensions of racism, sexism, and homosexuality.

Symbols of the White Supremacist

Dr. Ani and Frances Cress Welsing argued that symbols are important for understanding the collective consciousness of a society and how it shapes our individual behavior. Dr. Ani asserts that symbols are a form of language that can be used to transmit unconscious, implanted ideas, emotions, and beliefs across time and space. She contends that symbols can be powerful tools for shaping the perceptions and behaviors of Black people and groups. While Welsing suggests that symbols can be used to perpetuate systems of power and oppression. For example, she argues that the white supremacist system is supported by symbols that reinforce the idea of white superiority and Black inferiority. These symbols include the constant use of white as a symbol of purity and Black as a symbol of evil or negativity.

Both Welsing and Ani emphasize the importance of decoding symbols in understanding the cultural and psychological factors that contribute to racism and white supremacy. They suggest that symbols are a reflection of the collective consciousness of a society and can reveal hidden meanings and cultural assumptions that are not immediately apparent. Decoding symbols, therefore, is an important tool for understanding the ways in which cultural beliefs and values shape individual behavior.

Also, note that symbols can be used to perpetuate systems of power and oppression. In her essay, she discusses the symbolism of Christ, the cross, the crucifix, the communion, Christian holidays, guns, ball games, smoking objects, and rape. Decoding these symbols can help reveal the underlying cultural assumptions and values that support the system of white supremacy. Welsing argues that the systematic inferiorization of Black children within a white supremacist system is a serious problem. Also, she contends that Black children are deliberately taught to perceive themselves as inferior to white people, leading to adverse effects on their self-esteem and psychological development.

Welsing extends her exploration of racism's impact on Black youth, emphasizing how the white supremacist system perpetuates their inferiorization through the education system, media, and cultural portrayals of Black people. The part played by Black parents in the erasure of Black culture while arguing that Black parents have internalized the white supremacist system and are complicit in perpetuating the inferiorization and destruction of their own people. She suggests that Black parents must recognize their role in the system of white supremacy and work to counteract it.

Examination of the crises in Black male/female relationships. Welsing scrutinizes the role of media and cultural depictions in contributing to the challenges faced by Black couples. She contends that the portrayals of Black masculinity and femininity in media often perpetuate stereotypes and negative narratives, which, in turn, impact the dynamics within Black relationships. Welsing questions whether these perceived crises are, in fact, genuine issues or if they are exacerbated by external influences.

According to Welsing, challenging these representations becomes imperative for the Black community to foster healthier relationships. By actively confronting and dismantling stereotypical portrayals, she suggests that Black people can contribute to the creation of a more equitable and loving society. This involves a collective effort to reshape cultural narratives and redefine societal perceptions of Black masculinity and femininity, ultimately fostering an environment where Black relationships can thrive without the burden of harmful stereotypes. She also examines how Black women are adjusting to the 21st century. She contends that Black women ought to take ownership of their place in the struggle against white supremacy and strive for a society that is more just and equal. She contends that Black women must utilize their voices and influence to confront the white supremacist system in order to bring about change.

Frances Cress Welsing explores the concept of the "color of God" and its impact on Black mental health. She argues that the Eurocentric concept of a white God perpetuates the idea of white superiority and Black inferiority, which has a negative impact on the mental health of Black people. Welsing suggests that the Eurocentric concept of God as white reinforces the idea that white people are the chosen people of God and that Black people are cursed. This idea is particularly damaging to the mental health of Black people because it promotes feelings of inferiority, low self-esteem, and self-hatred. Welsing argues that the Eurocentric concept of God as white contributes to the development of internalized racism among Black people. She suggests that Black people who internalize the idea of white superiority may experience depression, anxiety, and other mental health issues as a result. Welsing proposes that the concept of the color of God should be reimagined to reflect the diversity and beauty of all people. She suggests that a more inclusive concept of God could promote self-love and cultural pride among Black people, which could contribute to improved mental health.

The importance of having a god or deity that reflects one's personal image is very important because having a god or deity that reflects their personal image can strengthen their cultural identity and sense of connection to their heritage. It may provide a source of familiarity, comfort, and resonance with their cultural and ethnic background. A deity that reflects the personal image of worshippers can enhance relatability. This can impact the worship experience, making it more meaningful and relatable to the individual or community. Feeling a personal connection to the divine figure can deepen spiritual engagement. Understanding the historical and social context is crucial. In situations where dominant cultural or religious narratives have been used to reinforce power dynamics or perpetuate inequality, reimagining the divine in a way that reflects the diversity of humanity can be a step toward challenging oppressive structures.

Conversations are "critical to have comprehensive analysis and definition of the opposing force," according to Dr. Frances Cress Welsing. She defines "racism-white supremacy" as:

> The local and global power system is structured and maintained by persons who classify themselves as white, whether consciously or subconsciously determined; this system consists of patterns of perception, logic, symbol formation, thought, speech, action, and emotional response, as conducted simultaneously

in all areas of people's activity (economics, education, entertainment, labor, law, politics, religion, sex, and war). The ultimate purpose of this system is to prevent white genetic annihilation on Earth, a planet in which the overwhelming majority of people are classified as non-white (black, brown, red, and yellow) by white-skinned people, period. All of the non-white people are genetically dominant (in terms of skin coloration) compared to the genetically recessive white skinned people (Welsing ii).

She goes on to explain that all Black crises (such as female-headed households, Black on Black crime, Black underachievement, poverty, Black male incarceration, etc.), "individual and group-destructive pathological forms of behavior are the *direct* and *indirect* byproducts of a behavioral power system fundamentally structured for white genetic survival, locally and globally. She states that "White supremacy, domination, and oppression of all non white people are essential for global white genetic survival. The prevention of white genetic annihilation is pursued through all means" (Welsing, iv).

The Black male continues to be central to the issue of white supremacy Either consciously or subconsciously, they "represent the greatest threat to white genetic survival, because only males (of any color) can impose sexual intercourse, and black males have the greatest genetic potential (of all non-white males) to cause white genetic annihilation. Thus, Black males must be attacked and destroyed in the power system designed to ensure white genetic survival.

According to Welsing, the strategy for white genetic survival that is being used today is more nuanced and systemic. In order to enable the Black male victims to be made to take part in and then be held accountable for their own mass deaths, Black men are currently being destroyed in an indirect manner. But the path to widespread Black male mortality can be identified with careful inspection and comprehension of white supremacy's ultimate goal—the genetic survival of the white race as a whole.

Benign Neglect of the Black Males

Benign neglect: an attitude or policy of ignoring an often delicate or undesirable situation that one is held to be responsible for dealing with

("Benign neglect." Merriam-Webster)

Benign neglect policies is a new refinement word used by white supremacists to ignore Black people's problems and issues, which are always caused by the white supremacist, directly or indirectly. We can see this, especially when we study Black males in America, Black males are always shown in a negative light– only promoting degenerate behaviors, and never properly being represented for the positive contributions that we provide for our wives, children, neighborhood, community, city, state, the entire country, or the world.

Dr. Curry describes the Psychological trauma that all Black people experience in America in his book, "The Man Not". The introduction starts with, "I see dead black bodies, black men and boys, in the streets. Dead niggers became YouTube sensations. I see their executions on the internet: the courts of Trayvon Martin, Michael Brown, and little Tamir Rice for eternity." And continues, "Black men are thought to be latent rapists-the Black macho of old-violent patriarchs, a privileged Black male, craving the moment he is allowed to achieve the masculinity of whites. These mythologies, decades long gone, remain the morality of discipline and the political foundation from which racist caregivers become revered concepts." (Curry 1)

The book explores why society tends to see Black men as overly masculine and violent stereotypes. He argues that unlike mainstream studies on masculinity, there hasn't been much effort to understand non-traditional Black masculinities separately. Instead of challenging criticisms of traditional white masculinity, hyper-masculinity is suggested as the biological marker of Black maleness. This leads to the perception that Black men embody the pathological excess of white masculinity. Curry also discusses how Black males are perceived as threats because they are excluded from theories based on their own experiences, which leads to the perception that they are flawed. Perspectives on Black masculinity and how Black men and boys are viewed by the community. It makes the case that comprehending the distinct experiences of Black males is essential to understanding how race, class, and gender intersect in America. Curry examines how Black males are oppressed and disenfranchised while also showcasing their resilience through a study of popular culture, history, and social science. The book offers a thorough analysis of the experiences of black men, illuminating the detrimental effects that gender, class, and race have on their communities and way of life.

In a society of white supremacy, we see Black men as hyper-masculine and violent stereotypes of "Big Black Boogie Man," fiendishly in pursuit of white women. The argument should be that there hasn't been enough effort to understand different types of Black masculinity. The stereotypes of Black men should be contested by Black people, who contend that knowledge of their experiences is essential to understanding the interplay of gender, race, and class. Additionally, black men encounter significant resistance and oppression in a number of facets of daily life.

The white supremacist traditional view suggests that Black and African cultures, considered "barbaric," lacked gender divisions and therefore couldn't appreciate concepts like truth, God, and poetry that stem from the distinctions between masculine and feminine. William Lynch taught this: "You must use the female vs. the male. And the male vs. the female" (Lynch 1). The idea was that the patriarchal race, organized similarly to patriarchal homes, aimed to civilize and advance what were perceived as savage races, primarily Black people. Ethnological thought classified all Black people as belonging to feminine-savage races, clearly dividing the Black and white races. This argument stated that Black men and women were not permitted to have different "genders" from the dominant white male race. Fallacies regarding gender and race surfaced in the nineteenth century. because it was believed that each racial group had produced a unique evolutionary species.

The dehumanization of Black men in a white supremacist system gives explicit permission for others, including other Black individuals and minorities, to abuse or exploit us without any fear or consequences. Curry emphasizes that society's perception of Black men as "nonhuman" allows perpetrators of violence against us to escape guilt, contributing to our inhuman subjugation. "Since Black males can never be victims, other Black people—even other Blacks and minorities have the power to abuse, exploit, or rape them without fear of sanction. In other words, the dehumanization of Black men and boys generally by society gives Black people explicit permission to dehumanize them as well. In this sense, perpetrators of violence against Black males are not guilty of any crimes at all. They are simply participating in the subjugation of nonhuman things that have no moral status or empathy in the larger society, especially in the case of personal or intimate partner violence." (Curry 117)

"The Man Not" challenges the notion of intersectionality, stating that even though Black maleness may encompass centuries of violence and set aside inhuman hardships, a heterosexual Black male is still considered a single subordinate group within intersectionality due to the analytical definition of maleness as a privilege. The concept of "intersectional invisibility" is introduced, highlighting how people with intersecting disadvantaged identities experience different forms of oppression compared to singularly subordinated groups. Intersectional invisibility proposes that the oppression experienced by people with intersecting identities is distinct from that experienced by groups that are subjugated separately, as opposed to comparing the drawbacks of different subjugated groups.

In a troubling reflection of societal attitudes, the dehumanization of Black males perpetuates a distorted narrative where they are denied victimhood. This pervasive belief suggests that Black individuals, including those within the same racial and ethnic communities, possess the authority to subject Black men and boys to abuse, exploitation, or assault with impunity. The overarching dehumanization of Black men by society at large becomes a disheartening permission structure, granting explicit approval for further dehumanization within their communities. In this context, those perpetrating violence against Black males are not held accountable for any criminal wrongdoing; instead, their actions are framed as participation in the ongoing subjugation of entities devoid of moral standing or empathy within the broader societal landscape. This alarming perspective particularly manifests in cases of personal or intimate partner violence, underscoring the urgent need to challenge and rectify the deeply ingrained patterns of dehumanization that perpetuate harm against Black males.

It is imperative to critically examine various dimensions of a Black person's identity, particularly when navigating a system inherently predisposed to harbor animosity towards this particular identity. When we explore the intersectionality of these aspects, certain categorizations may reveal inaccuracies. Take, for instance, the experience of being a Black man, which encompasses challenges ranging from the specter of violence and rape to elevated rates of mortality and incarceration. However, the application of the concept of "intersectionality" reveals a nuanced perspective, illustrating that a straight Black man is often perceived as part of a singular. However, the application of the concept of "intersectionality" reveals a nuanced perspective, illustrating that a straight Black man is often perceived as part of a singular group. Unfortunately, this grouping tends to downplay the unique challenges he may encounter, as societal perceptions tend to prioritize the presumed advantage associated with being male rather than recognizing the distinct issues he may face within the broader spectrum of discrimination. Also the idea of "intersectional invisibility," which means that when we try to fit a person with intersecting identities into existing categories, we might miss out on understanding their unique experiences. Instead of looking at how different groups face disadvantages, intersectional invisibility suggests that the types of challenges people with intersecting identities go through are different from those faced by people who belong to just one group (Curry 174).

Curry stresses the essentialist assertion that subordinate males in patriarchal societies are defined as "not male," or "Man-Not," is founded on a somatological epistemology that aims to articulate a specific history and perspective of a social structure while attempting to characterize one that needs not genuinely exist. However, a relationship is established between males of the dominant group and males of the subordinate group based on their sexual categorization, rather than their actual position in a given community or historical setting. The status of inferior males in patriarchal civilizations is substantially different from that of dominating guys. "Such conceptual schemas do not tell us about the disadvantage groups have in relation to one another; instead, these theories tell us that we should predetermine that the defect of maleness is its cost to our perception of femaleness. This theory insists: No matter how great the violence against subordinate males actually is, these males are privileged because they are targeted for the maleness they share with the dominant racial group" (Curry 175).

Dr. Curry also discusses the ways in which black men have been excluded from mainstream discussions around gender and sexuality. He argues that the dominant discourse on gender and sexuality has historically excluded black men and other men of color, leaving them without a voice or representation in these discussions. Curry calls for a recognition of the diversity of male experiences and a move towards more inclusive and intersectional discussions around gender and sexuality.

1. Recognition of the complexity of Black male experiences: Curry's work highlights the multifaceted nature of the experiences of Black men, including the ways in which they are shaped by factors such as class, gender, and historical legacies of racism.

2. Emphasis on the agency of Black men: The book challenges the perception of Black men as passive victims of societal forces and instead emphasizes their agency and ability to resist and challenge oppressive systems.

3. Critique of dominant narratives: The book offers a critique of dominant narratives about Black men, including those that perpetuate stereotypes about their supposed hypermasculinity and criminality.

4. Intersectional analysis: The book offers an intersectional analysis of the experiences of Black men, highlighting the ways in which their experiences are shaped by multiple factors, including race, gender, and class.

5. Focus on healing and empowerment: The book offers a framework for healing and empowerment for Black men, including the importance of building community and challenging systems of oppression.

6

Medical Experimentation on Black Lab Rats

"The ends justify the means mindset has been the impetus behind many a cruel medical or social experiment."— James Morcan, The Orphan Conspiracies

The history of medical experimentation on Black Americans in the United States is thoroughly and provocatively examined in Harriet Washington's book "Medical Apartheid." Washington examines the history of this practice, which dates to the middle of the 19th century, and makes the case that racism and discrimination have been major factors in how white doctors treat black patients. Washington's view is broken up into four sections, each of which focuses on a different era of American history. Washington illuminates the various manifestations of racial discrimination and segregation that have affected the relationship between black patients and the medical profession through vivid and compelling narratives.

"Three times as many Black Americans were diagnosed with diabetes in 1993 as in 1963. This rate is nearly twice that of white Americans and is sorely underestimated: The real Black diabetes rate is probably double that of whites" (Washington). She uses a variety of sources, such as historical documents, firsthand accounts, and scientific research, to back up her claims with convincing evidence of mortality. "Cancer, the nation's second greatest killer, is diagnosed later in blacks and carries off proportionately more Black Americans than whites. Black Americans suffer the nation's highest rate of cancer and cancer deaths" (Washington 3). Washington exposes the extent of medical experimentation conducted on Black Americans, revealing horrific acts such as involuntary sterilization, intentional infection of patients with diseases, and administration of experimental drugs without informed consent. Furthermore, the book delves into the impact of racism and discrimination on the evolution of medical practices and knowledge, leading to the emergence of racial disparities in healthcare outcomes. The book also highlights the inevitable disruptions caused by the domination of one group over another in society.

What exactly qualifies as a medical experiment? The Latin words "ex," which mean "from" or "out of," and periculum, "a dangerous trial," respectively, are the origin of the word experiment. The stakes are extremely high when human health and lives are on the line, making conducting an experiment a risky endeavor. The defining characteristic of scientific experimentation, however, Washington quotes renowned French researcher Claude Bernard, "An experiment is an observation induced with the object of control." As a result, a researcher conducting an experiment goes beyond merely observing a medical phenomenon. Instead, the researcher makes a change while carefully monitoring the situation, records the outcomes, and then applies logic to analyze them. To conduct an experiment is to risk success or failure, and when human health and lives hang in the balance, the stakes are high indeed" (Washington 55).

Therapeutic experiments are those in medicine that test potential therapeutic interventions for the experimental subject. Other research involves nontherapeutic tests that are not intended to benefit the research subject. The experimental standards that govern research today are very different from the ones that physicians used to follow before the 20th century. Informed consent is a necessary prerequisite for the majority of experiments involving humans today, and human subjects are protected by a variety of laws, at least in theory. The process by which a researcher fully discloses to a subject what he or she proposes to do, why it is being proposed, and what potential consequences the experiment carries is known as informed consent and does not involve a subject signing a piece of paper. Rather, informed consent is a fluid, ongoing process. The subject's written consent, which must be obtained, is only then requested by the researcher. The process has not ended despite the consent form being signed. The subject is free to leave the experiment at any time, but the researcher is required to keep him informed of any developments that might have an impact on him.

James Mccune Smith, M.D. is cited by Washington in chapter 3, "CIRCUS AFRICANUS," "The Popular Display of Black Bodies."

> "The Negro "with us" is not an actual physical being of flesh and bones and blood, but a hideous monster of the mind, ugly beyond all physical portraying, so utterly and ineffably monstrous as to frighten reason from its throne, and justice from its balance, and mercy from its hallowed temple, and to blot out shame and probity, and the eternal sympathies of nature, so far as these things have presence in the breasts or being of American republicans! No sir! It is a constructive Negro, John Roe and Richard Doe Negro, that haunts with grim presence the precincts of this republic, shaking his gory locks over legislative halls and family prayers."
> (Cooper, and McMorris)

In 1904, Samuel Phillips Verner, an adventurous missionary explorer, had gathered a diverse collection of exotic animals after embarking on three expeditions to the heart of Africa. However, on his last expedition in 1903, he was commissioned by around 1885, Ota Benga was born in the Congo, a country in central Africa.

After being taken prisoner from his native country, he was displayed at the 1904 Louisiana Purchase Exhibition at the St. Louis World's Fair. Upon returning to America, Verner was hailed as a modern-day Dr. David Livingstone, whom he regarded as his posthumous mentor. In addition to being an ordained minister in the Presbyterian Church, Verner was also highly regarded in church circles for his attempts to impart morality to the Congolese natives, whom he relentlessly admonished for their indecent clothing and sexual conduct at the Southern Presbyterian Missionary House in Luebo.

Little did his American admirers know that Verner had fathered a daughter and son on an African orphan between 1895 and 1899 (Washington 75). He wished to return home to the Congo, and when he realized he could never save enough for passage, his depression became profound. In 1916, Benga committed suicide with that ubiquitous icon of Western technological achievement, a handgun. Hornaday had the last word in his obituary of Benga, which appeared in the zoological bulletin, took a semi comic tone, and was filled with uncomplimentary untruths that fit his racist agenda.

Benga's tragedy illustrates how American scientists found black bodies useful even when they were not trying new medications or surgeries. This chapter focuses on the popular public display and imaging of Black bodies, but the boundary separating popular display from medical display was a porous one, a permeable membrane with copious migration in both directions. Some medicalized freak body types were exclusive to Blacks, who had a patent on "white Negroes" and, in the United States, a near monopoly on "primitive peoples." Even the Black idiot savant, a perennial attraction, was considered more freakish than the white variety because his intellectual gifts offered a greater contrast to Blacks' ostensibly low intelligence (Washington 79).

Henry Moss exhibited himself around 1790, realizing that his physique had begun a mysterious journey towards whiteness. Moss was his own barker, unlike sideshow freaks after him who had to stay silent while barkers trumpeted the contrived exotica that passed for their life stories. Moss unrolled his own tale while he sat proudly on a museum chair or ambled across a bar stage, peeling the linen off his multicolored body in a seductive medical striptease. From his modest yet free birth in Goochland County, Virginia, in 1754, to his heroics as a soldier in South Carolina and Virginia during the Revolutionary War, to the strangely slow spreading of his fame, Moss spoke for himself in front of rapt audiences in Philadelphia's taverns and museums, charging exorbitant fees for his 1796 address to the American Philosophical Society, which cost twenty-five cents per person.

Henry Moss became a household name in Europe, where his bald head adorned chocolates and German almanacs. When Moss did appear at Mr. Leech's local pub, the symbol of the Black Horse, in Philadelphia in 1796, President George Washington was among the crowd. So were prominent racial theorists of the time, such as Reverend Samuel Stanhope Smith and an enthralled Benjamin Rush, M.D., who is now known as the father of American psychiatry and who believed at the time that "Black skin was the manifestation of a type of leprosy that he called "Negritude." Calling Blacks lepers sounds like the pronouncement of a racist, and Rush is sometimes regarded." Rush thought that although Black people had a disease, it was curable. Rush believed that Blacks were diseased but that they could be cured. He welcomed albinos, leucoethiopes (elevated white blood cell count in the bloodstream), and vitiligo-stricken "white-Negroes" as "hopeful monsters," living proof that Blacks could become healthy white. Rush believed that a cure was desirable because removing black skin would eliminate the main social and religious reasoning for enslavement and because Blacks themselves preferred white skin (Washington 80).

Crowds of paying onlookers, including museum curators, medical students, experts, and university lecturers, flocked to medical exhibitions that involved gaping, drawings, paintings, photography, and provocative taunts. This spectacle inevitably led to physical violations. The showcased individuals of African descent were exploited to reinforce the perceived lower status of Black people along an evolutionary continuum, placing them between monkeys and whites. The observers not only posed derogatory questions about the subjects' personal habits and sexual abilities but also engaged in palpating, measuring, and making lewd comments about the labia and penile lengths. The culmination of this degrading display occurred during the presentation of the prisoner Saartje (Sarah) Baartman, also known as "Hottentot Venuses."

It's important to know historical instances in order to comprehend how someone like Ota Benga could be forced into a zoo in twentieth-century New York City. Saartjie Baartman, who was born in 1789 amid the French Revolution and the Declaration of the Rights of Man, was involved in one of the most notorious cases. Baartman, like Benga, was a hunter-gatherer from the Khoisan tribe who lived at the southeast tip of the continent in what is now South Africa. Saartje (Sarah) Baartman, a Khoikhoi woman, was horrifyingly shown as a freak show attraction throughout Europe in the 19th century, earning her the unfair nickname "Hottentot Venus." Unfortunately, this derogatory moniker was eventually applied to at least one other woman who met a similar fate (Washington 82).

The derogatory word "Hottentot" refers to a designation of the native Khoikhoi people of southwest Africa that dates back to colonial times and is now officially acknowledged as insulting. There are deeper ramifications to Baartman's portrayal as the "Hottentot Venus" than just commercial gain. It represents the height of racist colonial activities and draws attention to the dehumanization and monetization of Black people. The story of Sarah Baartman highlights the ways in which racism, misogyny, and colonialism are intertwined, revealing the significant injustices that were upheld during this time. Her terrible tale is a powerful reminder of the pressing need to address historical injustices and work toward a more just and inclusive society in the future.

Black bodies served various purposes in circuses, clinics, and hospitals. After the mid-nineteenth century, it became crucial for hospitals to ensure a steady supply of Black bodies to establish themselves as the central hub for American medical education and care. These Black bodies were strategically utilized as tools for medical instruction, training, and research. In specific southern locations, they became the exclusive choice, filling medical school rosters and clinical settings.

In the 1830s, Dr. T. Stillman advertised in the Charleston Mercury, primarily focusing on treating skin diseases. In an intriguing addition on October 12, 1838, he stated, "Wanted: 50 negroes. Any person with sick negroes, deemed incurable by their respective physicians and wishing to dispose of them [emphasis added]... the highest cash prize will be paid upon completion.

The majority of hospital "clinical material" was provided by slaves who had become too old or sick to work. With no legal rights, they couldn't contest their confinement or treatment in court. Stillman expressed his desire for Blacks with conditions other than apoplexy, kidney disease, stomach, intestinal, bladder, liver, and spleen disorders, as well as scrofula and hypochondria. He aimed to test new techniques and medications on debilitated and chronically ill Blacks in the same facility where he treated paying whites. The medications and techniques were then marketed by him. Slave owners were pleased to be relieved of old, sick, and unproductive slaves (Washington 103).

For minor infractions of the various rules that controlled how Black Americans behaved while free, black people also ran the risk of being imprisoned in jails or almshouses. The "hospital movement," which started in Europe and eventually spread to America, This movement resulted in the closure of one-year medical schools that prioritized scientific research and anatomical knowledge over the dispensing of a small number of treatments. Horrendous ineffective practices like cupping, bleeding, and purging, which led to a decline in their use, and it was mandated that medical students complete several years of clinical training in hospitals. Washington states:

"Diseases such as yellow fever, smallpox, malaria, and tuberculosis still flared into epidemics with regularity, and the dominant class of property-owning whites still relied upon private physicians to care for them and their families. However, they increasingly expected those physicians to have the professional benefit of hands-on clinical experience" (Washington 104).

Dissection and Exhibition of Dead Black Bodies

"In Baltimore, the bodies of colored people exclusively are taken for dissection, because the whites do not like it and the colored people cannot resist."

(Martineau, Harriet. Retrospect of Western Travel, vol. 1. Saunders and Otley, 1838.)

"No place in the United States offers as great opportunities for the acquisition of anatomical knowledge. Subjects being obtained from among the colored population in sufficient numbers for every purpose, and proper dissection carried on without offending any Black people in our community!" (*ADVERTISEMENT FOR THE SOUTH CAROLINA MEDICAL COLLEGE,C. 1831*) (Washington 115).

The Journal "Use of Blacks for Medical Experimentation and Demonstration in the Old South" by Todd L. Savitt writes about "AN ABUNDANCE OF MATERIALS IN THE SOUTHERN MEDICAL." According to J. Walter Fisher's 1968 paper detailing some of the medical uses of slaves in the old south, "journals reveal that slaves had a fairly significant role in medical education and in experimental and radical medical and surgical practice of the antebellum south" (Savitt). Additional research on this topic shows that white medical educators and researchers in the South heavily depended on the availability of

Black patients for a variety of reasons. Black remains were frequently discovered in operating rooms, dissection tables, classrooms, bedside demonstrations, and experimental facilities (Savitt n.p.).

Madame Delphine LaLaurie, a prominent socialite in 19th-century New Orleans, is infamous for her cruel mistreatment of slaves. Historical accounts describe horrifying instances of abuse and torture inflicted upon those enslaved on her property. Some of the reported mistreatment includes severe beatings, mutilations, and cruel punishments. Bullwhips with metal or burned tips inflicted more pain on her slaves (Love and Shannon 15). One notorious incident occurred in 1834 when a fire broke out at the LaLaurie residence. As firefighters arrived to extinguish the flames, they discovered a shocking scene in the attic. Slaves were found in various states of mutilation, and it is said that she was the first person to perform a sex change operation on two of her slaves. There was overwhelming evidence of extreme cruelty and inhumane practices. Some had been subjected to brutal experiments, while others were confined in small, cramped spaces. By 1825 surgical developments in England and France were rapidly finding their way to Louisiana (Love and Shannon 46).

Delphine Lalaurie was one of the sparkling queens of Creole high society. Dr. Louis Lalaurie was eclipsed by his stunning wife, who was disregarded and thought to be reserved by many (Love and Shannon 47). Note that Lalaurie would mercilessly beat her slaves, and that Devince, her slave, was the subject of Delphine Lalaurie's formal court petition on the day of his final beating. More evidence supporting the roles white women had in owning slaves, as discussed in the book "They Were Her Property."

The public was outraged by Madame LaLaurie's abuse of her slaves, which received extensive media coverage. Authorities intervened, but she managed to escape punishment by fleeing the city before facing any legal consequences. The details of her actions have become a symbol of the cruelty and brutality inflicted upon enslaved individuals during that dark period in history. Madame LaLaurie's legacy is often remembered as a stark example of the dehumanizing treatment that many slaves endured.

The disturbing history of medical research and abuse of Black Americans is a dark chapter that exposes the unethical exploitation of Black bodies for scientific advancement. Throughout history, Black Americans have been subjected to heinous experiments, serving as involuntary subjects in the development of surgery and medical science. This egregious exploitation underscores the deeply rooted racism and disregard for [hu]man rights that characterized these practices.

One chilling and particularly horrifying case illustrates the extent of this abuse. A Black man grappling with jaw bone cancer made a conscious decision to refuse surgery, exercising his autonomy over his own body. Shockingly, he became a victim of medical cruelty when he was forcibly operated on without his consent. This egregious violation of his bodily autonomy speaks to the systematic dehumanization and disregard for the agency of Black individuals within the medical field.

This historical context sheds light on the broader pattern of racism within medical research, where Black Americans were disproportionately targeted for experiments and subjected to procedures against their will. The legacy of such abuses continues to cast a long shadow over the relationship between the Black American community and the medical establishment, emphasizing the urgent need for ethical practices, accountability, and reparative efforts to address the historical injustices inflicted upon Black bodies in the name of medical progress.

Washington describes in detail the horrifying history of Black Americans being the focus of medical research and torture, as well as how Black bodies were utilized as test subjects for advancements in surgery and medical technology. Regrettably, this instance of medical ethics being broken came to light, but sadly, it wasn't unique. Surgeons, like the one who operated on the man, frequently operated on African slaves without getting their permission.

A pervasive stereotype at the time held that Black slaves did not experience pain like white people, which influenced how doctors treated them. This cruel practice of using Black-Americans for medical experiments continued through the late 20th century, as seen in the case of Casper Yeagin on September 11, 1977. Although his family sued the hospital where he was experimented on, the case was dismissed. In recent years, more evidence of such experiments has come to light, including the theft of tens of thousands of stolen bones from a Georgian medical college and the theft of numerous Black-American bodies from mortuaries for medical dissection.

In the chapter "Watching the Bones," Washington describes the postmortem display of Black American bodies as, for many, the culmination of medical racism. Stuffed, mummified, or skeletal Black bodies have been exposed without their permission in medical offices, anatomy labs, museums, traveling sideshows, and even private establishments. Books bound in the skins of Black Americans, which were typically purchased as souvenirs from grave robbers, can still be found in some libraries and medical offices. Black Americans were bought and sold even after they died. In 2001, retired Brooklyn teacher Frances Oglesby protested, "They put my mother on display like a monkey in the zoo" (Washington), announcing her complaint against the Medical College of Georgia for $800,000 in pain and suffering damages as well as the restoration of her mother's remains. Bessie Wilborn, Oglesby's mother, is a skeleton that has been on exhibit at the pathology lab for fifty years. Recent medical abuse and research involving Black-Americans includes incidents such as prisoner radiation exposure, drug testing, and blood transfusion (Washington 134). Black children were selected for studies to examine the link between genetics and violence. There are various examples of the government being complicit in medical experiments that were conducted on Black American people.

In examining historical census data, Washington brings to light unexpected revelations from the United States census of 1840. This comprehensive survey encompassed a total of 17 million Americans, of which three million were Black. A noteworthy and surprising revelation was the stark difference in health outcomes between free Blacks and enslaved Blacks. Contrary to conventional expectations, free Blacks exhibited significantly worse health, particularly in terms of mental well-being, compared to their enslaved counterparts, who demonstrated lower rates of illness and mental disorders. In 1841, the U.S. Department of State published a document that seemingly aligned with pro-slavery arguments. This publication presented statistical evidence asserting that slavery was essential for preserving the health of Black people. Despite its bias, the document maintained an appearance of impartiality, offering well-organized data collected by census takers without overt prejudice.

A consistent pattern emerged in the census data, revealing higher death rates and younger mortality among free Blacks, attributable to various diseases such as tuberculosis, malaria, pellagra, and syphilis. Additionally, the census brought to light elevated rates of pregnancy loss and infant mortality among free Blacks, often unjustly linked to perceived higher rates of sexual immorality and sexually transmitted illnesses. Perhaps one of the most disturbing indicators highlighted by the census data was the prevalence of madness among free Blacks, serving as a dramatic illustration of their perceived helplessness. The rates of mentally defective Blacks were eleven times higher among free Blacks in the North compared to slaves in the South. This stark contrast in mental health statistics fueled pro-slavery arguments, grounding their assertions in ostensibly unbiased research conducted by the U.S. federal government. Washington's examination sheds light on the complexities of historical data interpretation and the potential for such information to be manipulated to serve specific agendas, even at the expense of truth and justice (Washington 146).

Washington's research indicates Blacks' doom was not simply attributed to lower intelligence because their profoundly flawed bodies were prey to a slew of diseases that never struck whites: Cachexia Africana ("dirt eating," or pica), hebetude, pellagra, and dysthesia aethiopica, to name a few examples, were still being discovered, and new "Black" diseases were being discovered. Black fertility has also decreased, allegedly as a result of deadbeat fathers and murderously conflicted moms. Black children had an even lower likelihood of surviving than their parents without white participation. It was also thought that slavery was required to safeguard white people from diseased Black people who were thought to be free-roaming carriers of infectious diseases. Prior to 1950, the majority of medical professionals believed that sickle cell anemia, the predominant Mendelian disease, was exclusively experienced by Black Americans. According to Washington, social anxieties about interracial relationships had an impact on these beliefs (Washington 147).

Destruction of the Black Unborn

"We don't want the word to go out that we want to exterminate the Negro population."Letter to Dr. Clarence J. Gamble, December 10, 1939

During the 20th century, the medical doctrine of eugenics emerged, which was derived from the Greek term Eugenes, meaning "well-born." The term was coined by Francis Galton, a relative of Charles Darwin. Between 1900 and 1910, geneticists identified human characteristics that followed a Mendelian pattern of inheritance, where the breeding of two parents carrying certain traits resulted in a predictable combination of well-born, sick, and carrier offspring, including various metabolic disorders.

White supremacists and eugenicists are interchangeable terms that are a more sophisticated way of expressing the idea of "white supremacy." A group of ideas and methods known as eugenics attempt to improve the genetic makeup of the mankind's population by encouraging selective breeding and managed reproduction. Eugenics' main goal is to subtly destroy Black families because its supporters—many of whom are mentally ill white supremacists—see Black features as undesirable. Their motivation stems from the desire to eradicate Black infants due to these traits. Eugenicists suggest that this can be accomplished by passing laws that promote reproduction among white people who are thought to have favorable features while discouraging or outlawing the reproduction of those who are thought to have negative traits.

Essentially, eugenics becomes a tool used by white supremacists who believe that some racial characteristics are better than others in order to influence mankind genetics.

Eugenics, who also practice "The Whiteness of Destruction" had a particularly detrimental impact on Black people, as it was often used as a justification for anti-Black practices and policies. Here are some ways in which eugenics affected Black communities:

- *Forced Sterilization*: In the United States, eugenic ideas contributed to the implementation of forced sterilization programs, particularly during the early-to-mid 20th century. Black people, along with other minority groups, were exclusively targeted for sterilization without their informed consent. This practice aimed to reduce the reproduction of individuals considered socially and economically undesirable.

- *Racial Purity Ideology:* Eugenicists/white supremacists promoted ideas of racial purity, asserting that the pure white races were genetically superior to others. This ideology was used to justify segregation and discriminatory laws against Black people. The childish notion of a white racial hierarchy, which contributed to systemic racism, is dedicated to denying Black communities [hu]man rights.

- *Segregation and Discrimination:* Eugenics played a critical role in reinforcing racial segregation and discriminatory policies, particularly in the southern United States. The belief in the supposed genetic inferiority of Black people was used to legitimize unequal treatment in areas such as education, healthcare, housing, and employment.

- *Medical Exploitation:* Black people were often subjected to medical experiments and unethical practices under the guise of eugenic research. The Tuskegee Syphilis Study, conducted between 1932 and 1972, is a notorious example where Black men were deliberately infected and left untreated with syphilis without their knowledge, even after penicillin became a known cure.

- ***Biased Immigration Policies:*** Eugenic ideas influenced immigration policies that discriminated against individuals from certain racial and ethnic backgrounds. This had implications for Black immigrants seeking to enter countries where eugenic principles were influential.

By the 1930s, this objective had gained broad acceptance among scientists and the general public, not just in the United States but around the world, and eugenic standards were used to lower populations of Black people. The Eugenicists suggested that society utilize medical information regarding the inheritance of diseases and traits to combat societal issues by encouraging the birth of children with desirable, healthy, and attractive traits, which was known as positive eugenics. As Margaret Sanger says:

> *"I think the greatest sin in the world is bringing children into the world, that have disease from their parents, that have no chance in the world to be a human being practically... Delinquents, prisoners, all sorts of things just marked when they're born. That to me is the greatest sin that people can commit."* ~Interview with journalist Mike Wallace, 1957.

Eugenicists promulgated the weeding out of undesirable societal elements aka Black people by discouraging or preventing the birth of Black children. The ultimate goal is to eliminate healthy and beautiful Black genes and traits. This was positive for the eugenicists. This thought process caught the attention of many anti-Black hate groups, like the Ku Klux Klan:

"Today I received an invitation to talk to the women's branch of the Ku Klux Klan... I was escorted to the platform, was introduced, and began to speak...In the end, through simple illustrations, I believed I had accomplished my purpose. A dozen invitations to speak to similar groups were proffered" ~Margaret Sanger.

The intricate link between medicine and racism is evident through historical instances that extend beyond well-known cases like the "Tuskegee Syphilis Study," where Black Americans purposely infected with syphilis were left untreated for research purposes by the US Public Health Service. While this study is infamous, there are other medical experiments that have remained obscured from the public eye. This exploration delves into the chapters that particularly spotlight eugenics, a philosophy that gained traction in the 19th century and intensified the exploitation of Black people in America.

Eugenics, as a philosophy, proposed that medical knowledge about various diseases could be wielded to address social problems by permitting only Black people with perceived desirable traits to procreate. This disturbing approach sought to manipulate the genetic composition of the population based on discriminatory and often unfounded criteria. The implementation of eugenic principles led to unethical practices such as forced sterilizations, the propagation of racial hierarchies, and discriminatory medical experiments.

In essence, the fusion of eugenics with medical practices reinforced systemic racism, perpetuating harmful stereotypes and contributing to the marginalization and exploitation of Black communities. Understanding the historical context of these events is crucial for addressing the enduring impact of medical racism and working towards a more equitable and just healthcare system.

The First Birth Control

"Eugenics without birth control seems to us a house builded [sic] upon the sands. It is at the mercy of the rising stream of the unfit." — The Birth Control Review, Birth Control and Racial Betterment (1919).

The introduction of the first birth control, Norplant, was not only targeted at poor black women but also selectively marketed to thousands of young Black girls. In 1991–1992, approximately fifty thousand Norplant kits were implanted, including some in the overwhelmingly Black population of public high schools in Baltimore. This targeting was justified by referencing teenage pregnancy rates. However, this approach to addressing the issue of teenage pregnancy was rooted in racist myths rather than factual evidence. It's important to note that Baltimore, with its predominantly Black population and a teenage pregnancy rate three times the national average, is atypical. About 10 percent of girls aged fifteen to seventeen in the city are already mothers, making it a unique setting for a national experiment with racial implications. The Laurence G. Paquin Middle School clinic was the first site for Norplant implantation, with 345 of its 350 girls being Black. Policy makers concentrated on the fertility of Black girls, and Norplant was introduced through school-based health clinics, with the initial one hundred clinics opening at predominantly Black schools (Washington 207).

In 1992, statistics revealed that 75 percent of fifteen-year-old girls and 50 percent of seventeen-year-old girls were virgins, and more pregnancies occurred among white teenage girls than their Black counterparts. Unrecognized at the time by epidemiologists, the overall American teenage pregnancy rate was already declining, with the sharpest decrease observed among Black girls.

It's important to recognize the historical impact of eugenics on Black communities and to understand how these unjust practices contributed to the perpetuation of "The Whiteness of Destructions" in the form of racial inequality. These practices continue to shape discussions on white ethics, non-human rights, and social injustice. When attempting to create a society that is uniform, it often leads to the development of racist ideologies that view certain groups as either superior or inferior based on their genetics. This type of thinking is often utilized by the dominant group to mistreat, segregate, and discriminate against minority groups. During a time when many white Americans considered

Black Americans to be of lower status, they were seen as expendable and easy to exploit. Instead of prioritizing the belief that all [hu]mans possess inherent rights, racial stereotypes were adopted, which not only allowed for medical experimentation on Black patients but also made it seem acceptable. Washington supports this assertion by citing numerous sources, such as journals, legal documents, medical reports, and interviews with Black-American victims of medical experiments.

Radiation Experiments on Black Americans

The first recorded Black victims of radiation experiments lived around the turn of the century, long before the dropping of the atomic bomb. Near the end of 1895, German physicist Wilhelm Conrad Roentgen discovered a magical light. He found that passing electricity through special gases at low pressure generated electromagnetic radiation with strange and powerful properties. The rays imparted fluorescence and enabled him to make images that rendered solid objects transparent. Alive to the rays' potential for seeing inside previously opaque objects but confused by their mysterious nature, Roentgen resorted to calling them "X-rays." Doctors found with delight that the X-rays could reveal all manner of skin blemishes, cancers, and even previously hidden internal problems. During the same period, physicians successfully experimented with radium for the purpose of healing. Radiation enjoyed a beneficent medical image, and scientists sought to seduce Black Americans as well as whites with its power to heal and also purify. Any doctor who wished to embrace the newest fad in medicine could advertise his radium or X-ray treatments, and most of the doctors who did so treated patients in private clinics, rather recklessly by our standards. They were initially unaware of and later insufficiently concerned by the dangers of repeatedly bombarding patients with high radiation doses.

Black patients even received glass tubes containing small quantities of radium so they could cure their own superficial tumors or defects in their skin. Doctors immediately started investigating opulent cosmetic applications in addition to medical treatment, and as early as 1900, they promoted radiation therapy to Black patients as a means of becoming white. "BURNING OUT BIRTH-MARKS, BLEMISHES OF THE SKIN AND EVEN TURNING A NEGRO WHITE WITH THE MAGIC RAYS OF RADIUM, THE NEW MYSTERY OF SCIENCE"! This was the headline that appeared in the January 10, 1904, New York American. "All Coons to Look White: College Professors Have Scheme to Solve Race Problem," the New York Telegraph prophesied, while the Boston Globe pondered, "Can the Ethiopian Change His Skin or the Leopard His Spots': All claimed that the "scientific light" would be the leading edge technology that would erase the dark handicap of racial differences, and by all accounts, the Black subjects of the experiments were willing and eager. But the press reports were hazy and full of mistakes, and it doesn't appear that any of the tales were published in academic publications or that any additional research was done to monitor damage (Washington 225-226).

Doctors utilized varying levels of emitted radiation to determine the energy needed for specific degrees of burns. They induced radiation burns on the arms of forty-four whites across different hospitals for "investigational purposes." Using this data, they calculated the potential casualties from a nuclear bomb, like the one over Hiroshima. Analysis showed that Blacks experienced more severe burns than whites after the same exposure, leading to the conclusion that Blacks would suffer greater harm from radiation burns in a nuclear event. At the Medical College of Virginia, 460 Black and 770 white patients were injected with radioactive substances, including phosphorus, without their consent. Blacks comprised 37 percent of the experimental subjects, nearly four times their representation in the population.

The AEC sponsored fifteen radiation studies on three hundred Black patients at New Orleans Charity Hospital, conducted by Tulane University physicians. One study involved administering radioactive mercury to twenty-two Black patients to gauge symptoms and excretion time. In another experiment, doctors discreetly placed radioactive mercury in open sores after removing blisters from a dozen Black and three white patients, seeking insights into the metal's effects on healing times, yielding no clinically meaningful data (Washington 237).

In 1911, influential white scientist Cesare Lombroso, a Halan physician, made distinctions between Blacks and criminals. Lombroso asserted, "There exists a group of criminals, born for evil, against whom all social cures break as though against a rock, a fact which compels us to eliminate them completely, even if by death" (Washington 247). According to his theories, these individuals were inherently and immutably evil due to their deranged physiology, and he believed they were more likely to be Black than white.

When illustrating his concept of "criminal man," Lombroso chose the Dinka of the Upper Nile, an Black society, as the perfect example of born savage criminals. Despite the fact that the Dinka were not more bellicose than many other societies, Lombroso used their dark skin as a qualifying factor for this distinction. Lombroso considered dark skin and the associated inability to blush as physical stigmata that conclusively signaled their criminal nature, asserting that "inability to blush has always been considered the accompaniment of crime and shamelessness" and adding that "blushing is very rare among idiots and savages" (Washington 247).

Circumstantial Voluntary Jailhouse Experiments

In Philadelphia, Pennsylvania, the Holmesburg Prison experiments, spanning from 1951 to 1974, were led by Dr. Albert Kligman. Inmates at Holmesburg Prison were subjected to experiments testing various substances on their skin without informed consent. These incidents, while not directly involving the American Medical Association (AMA), prompted the medical community, including the AMA, to reevaluate ethical standards in medical research.

The role of the American Medical Association is significant in shaping ethical standards for medical research. The AMA's code of medical ethics provides guidelines for the ethical conduct of physicians and researchers, with a focus on protecting the rights and well-being of [hu]man subjects. The establishment of Institutional Review Boards (IRBs), mandated by the National Research Act of 1974, further ensures the ethical review of research involving human subjects. The AMA has advocated for informed consent, ethical treatment of research participants, and protection of vulnerable populations. During this period, inmates at Holmesburg Prison were recruited to participate in various medical experiments in exchange for a small financial compensation. In the book "Acres of Skin: Human Experiments at Holmesburg Prison," one inmate named Ponton recounted his involvement in "at least 25 biopsy tests," resulting in "about 6 different spots and 24 different marks" on his back that persist even after 25 years. Ponton endured weekly injections in the shoulder, followed by biopsies, earning $5 for each test site and $30 in total.

Ponton's resilience in enduring the pain and suffering from a range of tests is noteworthy, considering his initial reaction to the first experiment, which he described as nearly unbearable. The 10-day test involved a patch on his back covering a large area, and he was prohibited from taking a shower during that period, for which he received $10 or $15. The Holmesburg Prison experiments, conducted in collaboration with the University of Pennsylvania and prison officials, utilized hundreds of prisoners as subjects to test a variety of products, including facial creams, skin moisturizers, perfumes, detergents, and anti-rash treatments (Hornblum 9).

Holmesburg, now closed, was a significant county jail in Philadelphia where unsentenced prisoners awaiting trial were commonly held. Dr. Kligman, an expert in fungal skin disease, was initially invited to the prison around 1951 to manage an outbreak of athlete's foot. However, he quickly identified the prisoners as potential research subjects, leading to the establishment of Holmesburg as a laboratory testing ground. This extensive use of prisoners for experimentation raised ethical concerns, challenging the principles of the Hippocratic Oath and the Nuremberg Code within the American medical establishment (Hornblum 421).

Other experiments used the inmates as test subjects for far more hazardous, even potentially lethal, substances, such as radioactive isotopes, dioxin, and chemical warfare agents. Based on in-depth interviews with dozens of prisoners as well as the doctors and prison officials who, respectively, performed and permitted these experimental tests, this is an account of extreme abuse, moral indifference, and greed. Central to this account are the millions of dollars many of America's leading drug and consumer-goods companies made available for the doctors motivated by the desire for fame and money based on these medical experiments. According to the author, many of these doctors established their careers on the basis of their experiments on these inmate subjects, who were isolated, cheap, and locked away from the public eye.

The commitment to research involving [hu]man beings is further demonstrated by the creation of Institutional Review Boards (IRBs), which were required by the National Research Act of 1974. As part of their duty to examine and approve research methods, institutional review boards (IRBs) strive to respect moral standards such as the "Hippocratic Oath," which is covered in Chapter 2. Hippocrates, the Greek physician, is credited with adopting the Hippocratic oath, an ethical code that he received from Imhotep. It is still spoken during medical school graduation ceremonies today and has been used by medical practitioners as a code of conduct throughout history. The AMA and other organizations support it as well. Possibly the worst abuse done under the pretext of scientific research. This chapter will discuss a handful of the many trials that targeted predominantly or solely Black children for recruitment, demonized them, and had overtly racist goals. These have harmed Black Americans generally as well as young people (Washington 259).

Fenfluramine Experiments linked to Feminization of Black Males

Fenfluramine increases extracellular serotonin levels:

Fenfluramine causes an increase in the amount of serotonin, a chemical messenger in the brain, outside of the nerve cells.

Fenfluramine acts as both a serotonergic 5-HT2 receptor agonist and $\sigma 1$ receptor antagonist:

It has two specific effects on certain receptors in the brain:

It activates the agonist, a serotonin receptor called 5-HT2.

It blocks another antagonist, another receptor called $\sigma 1$.

These activities lead to anti-epileptiform activity and therapeutic benefit:

The combined effects of increasing serotonin, activating the 5-HT2 receptor, and blocking the $\sigma 1$ receptor result in a reduction of abnormal electrical activity in the brain associated with seizures (anti-epileptiform activity).

This, in turn, provides therapeutic benefits, meaning it has a positive effect in treating certain conditions, likely epilepsy in this context.

Through an incompletely understood mechanism:

The exact way in which these actions of fenfluramine bring about the anti-epileptiform activity and therapeutic benefits is not fully understood. There is still more to learn about the detailed processes involved.

Fenfluramine appears to impact serotonin levels and specific receptors in the brain, leading to a reduction in abnormal brain activity associated with seizures and providing therapeutic benefits, even though the precise mechanisms are not entirely clear.

The term "fenfluramine experiments" describes a number of investigations and clinical trials carried out to evaluate the effectiveness and safety of fenfluramine, a drug used as an appetite suppressant to aid in weight loss. Fen-phen, a well-known weight-loss combo consisting of phentermine and fenfluramine, was frequently given together. a dispute over New York State Psychiatric Institute doctors who investigated violence among "poor," "non-white," and "inner-city boys" using a fenfluramine-based trial. When the study was published in the Archives of General Psychiatry, critics claimed that it violated federal ethics requirements for research involving children. The researchers argue that the criticism is unwarranted and that they adhered to protocol in their analysis of aggressive conduct, which they view as a serious public health concern.

The chair of the institute's Institutional Review Board (IRB), B. Timothy Walsh, defends the IRB's approval of the study, emphasizing their interpretation of government ethics and rules. The study reported a correlation between fenfluramine-induced serotonin activity and aggressive behavior in 34 boys aged six to ten who were brothers of juvenile delinquents. Fenfluramine, previously part of the diet drug combination Fen-Phen, was withdrawn due to heart valve damage. The study, largely funded by the Lowenstein Foundation, was stopped in 1995, two years before the drug's withdrawal. Recent news articles criticized the study, prompting an investigation by the Office for Protection from Research Risks at the National Institutes of Health (NIH).

Disability Advocates, a law office, filed a complaint alleging that the study subjected children to experiences beyond what healthy children might reasonably expect. The controversy involves interpretation of federal rules regarding research risks and the necessity of generalizable knowledge related to the participants' "disorder or condition." The racial composition of the participant group (44% Black, 56% Hispanic) raises concerns, with critics calling it a "highly disturbing" skew. The researchers attribute this to the demographics of their New York City neighborhood and their efforts to secure funding for wider recruitment before the trial's unrelated halt (Wadman n.p.).

The National Institutes of Mental Health's Center for Crime and Delinquency awarded a three-year $300,000 grant to Digamber Borgaonkar, Ph.D. Under the aegis of Johns Hopkins University, he undertook a large study to investigate whether adolescent boys, many of whom were wards of the State of Maryland's juvenile justice system, gave indications of a genetic anomaly XYY. (Washington 279)

The XYY syndrome was first discovered in 1961 when Dr. Avery Sandberg described a 44 year old, six-foot white male who exhibited no mental or physical abnormalities but who had an unusual chromosomal complement, called an "aneuploidy" or "Jacobs' syndrome." This condition affected not the workaday somatic chromosomes but the sex chromosomes that determine maleness and femaleness. A normal male inherits one X chromosome from his mother and one Y chromosome from his father (women inherit two X's, one from each parent), but this man's karyotype, or chromosome chart, showed that he had one X and two Y's, an accident of reproduction (Hauschka and Sandberg 22).

The trend toward the medicalization of violence in Blacks fed the popularity of genetic violence studies of Black boys, but nature failed to cooperate with politics. Borgaonkar's research and subsequent studies determined that XYY, the supposed marker for violence, is a "white" marker, not a "Black" one, in that it is found more commonly in white men than in Blacks. If the extra chromosome were indeed the "violence gene," white men would be 1.5 to 3 times as likely to harbor a propensity for violence. But it is not. No scientific basis for any propensity to violence or criminality in XYY males was found, and the theory, which was always thin and circumstantial, was discredited. However, the XYY theory of hypermale criminality still thrives in popular culture because the news media, which had widely trumpeted the "criminal gene" controversy, largely failed to publicize the findings that exonerated XYY. As a result, people still think of XYY men as harboring a "criminal gene." Journalists muse on the chromosomal status of the serial killer du jour, and such murderers as Richard Speck and Arthur Shawcross have often raised a supposed XYY anomaly as a defense in murder trials, sometimes successfully." Novels and films celebrate hypermales, such as those in the film Alien 3, whose prison planet is populated by "double Y-chromosome" felons so violent that they require off-world incarceration (Washington 327).

A rarely explored subtext of American experimental history, the use of captive or coerced populations of Black American children was solidified by white supremacist recruitment tactics in the hunt for the "criminal gene," another horrible chapter in American history. This quest stemmed from a psychopathic notion, popularized in the 20th century, that criminal behavior might have a hereditary foundation Exclusively in Black males. The fact that Black American children were forced and held captive for the duration of these trials adds to the problem and illuminates a little-known aspect of the lack of humanity that white supremacists have towards Black people.

Examining this American experimental atrocity subtext makes it necessary to recognize and confront the past injustices done to Black American children in the name of science. We must remain vigilant at upholding ethical standards and supervision to stop the continuation of such abhorrent behavior in contemporary research.

The American Lobotomy: A History of Racism

"African Americans were also victimized by psychosurgery from the 1930s to the 1960s, a process of surgically removing parts of the brain (lobotomy) to treat mental illnesses" (Umeh n.p.).

However, another medical trend that was stoked by the idea that Black boys are "born criminals" puts them in much greater danger right away: invasive, frequently experimental brain surgery to remove the claimed seat of aggression. These procedures were supported by a very elementary understanding of brain function. In the 1950's, Dr. William B. Scoville, a neurosurgeon from Hartford, Connecticut, conducted approximately 750 brain operations at two state hospitals during the peak of the lobotomy era; a majority of these patients were Black. Fast forward to 1980, and Scoville is among a small group of psycho surgeons who, like their predecessors from the 1940s and '50s, maintain the belief that selectively damaging parts of the brain can positively impact human behavior and treat mental illness. Dr. Scoville has advocated for the potential use of psychosurgery to cure violent tendencies in criminals/Black people, and he has even suggested lobotomies for individuals struggling with drug addiction. Notably, the annual number of psychosurgeries in the United States has decreased to somewhere between 200 and 500, a significant drop from the up to 5,000 performed each year in the late 1940s. This was the lobotomy era, which ran from 1936 to 1960 and saw between 40,000 and 50,000 Americans have brain surgeries as part of a widespread, large-scale attempt to treat, or at least manage, the nation's mentally ill (Frankel n.p.).

Psychiatrists and neurosurgeons who engaged in "blind-cut lobotomies" utilized crude tools like the icepick salon. They would indiscriminately sweep these instruments back and forth within the brain, severing all connecting nerves without direct visual guidance. This method of destructive surgery, characterized by its brutality and nightmarish nature, involved the obliteration of critical brain tissue. These acts of surgical hostility, amounting to nothing less than the murder of a child's cognitive center, were tragically imposed on Black boys as young as five.

In the 1960s to the early 1970s, dissatisfaction with the prevalent use of tranquilizers led to a growing interest in brain surgery as an alternative for managing "unruly" patients. Capitalizing on this shift in approach, Dr. Orlando J. Andy, a neurosurgeon at the University of Mississippi, performed various brain ablations, including thalamotomies (the destruction of the thalamus, responsible for emotions and sensory analysis). Shockingly, he conducted these procedures on Black American children as young as six, whom he deemed "aggressive" and "hyperactive." This is evident in his published approach to a child named "J.M."

Andy removed six areas of the boy's brain in five surgeries over three years, areas that were then known to be important to emotion expression and cognitive function. He also implanted electrodes in the child's brain in a vague, unspecified experimental venture. The surgeon did not explain how he arrived at his assessment of J.M.'s behavior disorder and why he thought the extreme remedy of brain surgery was indicated. Therefore, we do not know whether the child had serious behavior problems or whether he was exhibiting the same annoying behaviors displayed by most nine-year-old boys at some point. Andy is not a psychiatrist, and J.M. received no bona fide psychiatric diagnosis. We have no description of the effects or duration of the child's behavior nor what his parents thought of it. Nothing suggests that the parents were notified about the surgery or that their consent was requested. To put it succinctly, Andy did not even bother to persuade everyone that J.M. required any form of medical intervention, much less having portions of his brain removed. In pondering these shocking acts, it is important to know that Andy wrote up this case in medical journals twice because he was proud and considered it an example of his best work (Washington 284–285).

There have always been discussions about diseases and conditions that primarily affect Black people, starting with the antebellum plantations and continuing today. When it comes to healthcare, Black Americans still harbor mistrust and anxiety due to a history of exploitation and abuse. It is evident that racism and white supremacist ideologies have long been the source of health problems for Black Americans. The fact that some of these issues persist to this day is quite regrettable. Black people have disadvantages in all domains, from lower life expectancy to a higher neonatal mortality rate. The racist practices of slavery and segregation, which have defined Black Americans' lives for 400 years, are to blame for these differences.

Unraveling the Enigma: The True History of the Origin of AIDS

The actual narrative of the AIDS Foundation's dark beginnings dates back to the late 1800s, a time when anti-Black prejudice was also prevalent. "The Origin Of AIDS: OPERATION MK-NAOMI" claims. After the United States passed the "Federal Quarantine Act" in 1878, ending slavery, there was an even greater surge in insanity as major research into epidemic diseases began. The historical events that will be discussed in this section must be investigated in order to shed light on the claims that the AIDS virus was developed and spread through a number of government studies and initiatives.

The Early Years: Eugenics and Mycoplasmas: The late 19th century saw the establishment of the U.S. Laboratory of Hygiene in 1887, headed by Dr. Joseph J. Kinyoun, a controversial figure deeply rooted in white supremacist ideologies. By 1889, mycoplasmas, transmissible agents now associated with human diseases, including HIV/AIDS, were identified. The Federal Quarantine Act was strengthened in 1893, coinciding with an outbreak of polio, suggesting a potential link to mycoplasma manipulation.

The Expansion of Biowarfare Programs in the early 20th century witnessed the establishment of the Station for Experimental Evolution in 1902, identifying diseases of ethnic nature. In subsequent years, mycoplasma experiments caused epidemics in horses (1904) and fowl and birds (1910). The Federation of the American Society for Experimental Biology (FASEB) was formed in 1917, reflecting an increasing focus on biological research.

The influenza pandemic and eugenics and the devastating influenza pandemic of 1918, which claimed millions of lives, are alleged to have involved a flu virus modified with a bird mycoplasma. In 1921, Bertrand Russell publicly supported the "organized" plagues against the Black population, revealing sinister eugenics motives. In 1943, the shift to bio-warfare marked the official beginning of the U.S. biowarfare program, culminating in "Operation Paperclip" in 1945, where foreign scientists flocked to the U.S. biological program. The hiring of Dr. Earl Traub in 1946 and the confirmation of a "secret" biological weapon in the same year raised suspicions.

Biological Agreements and the Special Virus Program In 1949, Dr. Bjorn Sigurdsson isolated the VISNA virus, sharing "unique DNA" with HIV. The 1957 creation of the Special Operation-X (SOX) program paved the way for the Special Virus program in 1962. The U.S. and the Soviet Union's 1972 biological agreement signaled collaboration in developing offensive biological agents. The AIDS Epidemic unveiled destruction By 1976, the "Special Virus Program" had allegedly produced 15,000 gallons of AIDS. The AIDS virus was purportedly attached to vaccines sent to Africa and Manhattan, with Batch #751 administered in New York linked to thousands of infections. The covert agenda to kill the Black population gained momentum, as revealed in President Nixon's 1970 memo on "overpopulation."

We attempt to outline a diabolical narrative surrounding the origin of AIDS, implicating various government programs and experiments in the alleged creation and proliferation of the HIV/AIDS virus. While the claims made in this historical account are bold and contentious, they underscore the need for continued scrutiny and investigation into the origins of one of the most devastating pandemics in recent history (Nairaland n.p.).

7

The Mythologizing of Black Awareness

The Reasons for Studying Genuine History

Merely knowing the struggles of our ancestors in the study of history is inadequate. Why we study true history is because we must learn from history and use it to actualize our goals, plan and develop, empower ourselves, and ensure our survival as a community. If we fail to do so, according to Wilson, then Black History Month becomes a narcissistic exercise that distances us from reality. It's ironic that even people who are not our allies join in the celebration, implying that they perceive some benefit in it, potentially at our expense. "We must be instructed by history and should transform history into concrete reality, into planning and development, into the construction of power, and the ability to ensure our survival as a people" (Wilson 13). If they can celebrate our history without feeling threatened, then we are not using it in a revolutionary manner. Therefore, we must study history in a way that challenges the status quo, advances our interests, and does not deceive us. Merely celebrating the struggles of our predecessors in the study of history is inadequate.

I think the term "narcissistic exercise" introduces the notion that the celebration could deviate from its fundamental goal of promoting genuine understanding and awareness. In some instances, the focus may shift towards self-congratulation and token acknowledgment rather than focusing on the historical struggles, achievements, and contributions of the Black community. This interpretation implies a risk of the celebration becoming performative, serving the interests or image of those involved rather than authentically engaging with the essence of Black history.

Furthermore, the assertion that Black History Month might distance people from reality underscores the potential danger of oversimplifying the dangers of white supremacy and its effects on the history of Black people. A superficial or overly celebratory attitude has emerged, leading to a lack of understanding of the ongoing anti-Black race war that we face.

The participation of other races that may be viewed as allies is one of the ironies that Wilson highlights. Dr. John Henrik Clarke notoriously stated that "Black people have no friends" (Clarke, October 29, 2018). Wilson suggests that their engagement can be motivated by factors other than a sincere desire to comprehend and assist the Black community. This could involve actions like virtue signaling, showing inclusivity on the surface without addressing more serious problems, or even using diversity and inclusion as a means of self-interest.

The most critical irony outlined is that other races might perceive a benefit in joining the celebration, potentially at the expense of the Black community. This prompts questions about the sincerity of their engagement and whether their participation genuinely contributes to the goals of Black History Month or aligns with more opportunistic motives. Black History Month must not become a narcissistic exercise that distances us from reality. Ironically, even people who are not our allies join in the celebration, implying that they perceive some benefit in it, potentially at our expense. If they can celebrate our history without feeling threatened, then we are not using it in a revolutionary manner. Therefore, we must study history in a way that challenges the status quo, advances our interests, and does not deceive us. "When courses in college or university are apparently presented "non-politically," "objectively," or "neutrally," they are actually presented in the most political way" (Wilson 13–15).

"Psycho" History and Miseducation

When seeking treatment from a psychiatrist, psychologist, social worker, or psychotherapist, one of the first steps is typically to gather a "case history." They acknowledge that they cannot adequately comprehend us as individuals unless they understand our distinct experiences. It's impossible to take someone else's history and apply psychological principles derived from that history to accurately describe you as a person. That's why each person seeking assistance must provide their own case history and be treated based on their unique situation. The same applies to Black people. It is not possible for us to fix our current state of affairs by applying the psychology of a Caucasoid, which is recognized to be psychotic, savage, and barbarous, based on history.

Applying European psychology to ourselves only leads to confusion, misguidedness, and folly. It is said that "those who forget the past are doomed to repeat it." Adopting European psychology could lead to incorrect decisions since it does not take into account our humanity, our history, or our identity as we handle problems and obstacles. Our psychological make-up is greatly influenced by our cultural background and the knowledge passed down through the generations. If we ignore these influences in favor of outside frameworks, we may miss important opportunities to better understand ourselves and the mental health needs of our communities.

A pressing concern within the realm of education centers on the notable shortage of Black educators taking on the crucial responsibility of shaping the minds of our children, and I suspect that this is by design. This issue is deeply rooted in the historical context and experiences shaped by a white supremacist psychopathic thought process that has permeated the educational landscape. The shortage of Black educators reflects a systemic imbalance that has historical roots in discriminatory practices and a pervasive racial bias within the education system. The enduring legacy of institutional racism has contributed to a dearth of Black role models and mentors in educational settings. This deficiency extends beyond mere representation; it impacts the quality of education and the overall development of Black students.

The historical trajectory of white supremacist ideologies has perpetuated systemic barriers that hinder equitable access to educational opportunities for Black individuals. The pervasive influence of these ideologies has, over time, limited the advancement of Black educators, leading to an underrepresentation that continues to shape the educational landscape today. These educators who support the systematic system of white supremacy will intentionally misguide, mislead, and straight out lie to our Black children. With a debased ideology and psychology that is dedicated to promoting the same white supremacist ideologies that destroyed the greatest African civilization in known history, (KMT) "Kemet."

Mythological Lies as Truths

Europeans comprise around 10% of the world's population; they can only rule over the other 90 percent by lying, deceiving, and using force. The only way that we can be in the condition we are in, as a people, is to believe the destroyer's lies. We accept the falsehood for the truth and the truth for the lie, which has caused our behavior to become backward and our thoughts to be inverted. Telling lies to confuse the beliefs of the majority is the only way a small minority can rule the planet. It renders Black people cognitively backwards by distorting the truth, creating lies, and getting the majority to believe those lies. The history of Europe is multifaceted. Even when it seems to be telling the truth, it lies. An effective white supremacist doesn't want to tell too many big lies or too many obvious lies; he wants to tell the truth in a sort of way that gets him where he wants to go.

We must acknowledge that European history writing is an institution, just like any other discipline. Additionally, institutions in any oppressive society serve to uphold the status quo. Regardless of what institution we may talk about—whether we talk about the family institution, the criminal justice institution, the economic institution, the religious institution, the health institution, or the educational institution—they all have one thing in common in the Eurocentric oppressive system in all areas of activity, and that is to maintain the status quo and to maintain oppression, dominance, and control of Black people worldwide. We must remember this. What they say or don't say is less important than what they represent and do. The important thing is how they operate. As with anything European, the goal of writing about European history is to uphold white supremacy and power. European historiography accomplishes this in a variety of ways. It may achieve this by commission, omission, or outright lies and falsification of history. Wilson refers to it as a "theft of history." Our goal in studying Egypt is to recover the false identities that European history put on the African Egyptian people, as well as the completely stolen and falsified work. Alternatively, we read about Egyptians in historical texts without the complete truth, while obviously lying (Wilson 25).

The truth about Black history is undoubtedly feared by Europeans. European's fear of the truth about Black history implies a potential to rebuild what "The Whiteness of Destruction" has destroyed. Acknowledging the richness of African history and that Black people are the mothers and fathers of all civilizations. This causes a significant disruption to the fragile psyche of the white supremacist. This fear is also rooted in concerns about genetic annihilation. As Dr. Welsing stated, "even though most white people are not consciously understanding their problem in genetics, they are certainly aware that they are genetically dominated by people of color—that's why there's the statement that one drop of Black blood makes you Black. Because people of color have the genetic capacity to annihilate white people" ("White or Black

Superiority? A Controversial Debate: Dr. Francis Welsing vs. Dr. William Shockley").

The impact that a more accurate understanding of Black history may have on current power structures and public attitudes In order to promote a more knowledgeable and equitable global viewpoint, it is imperative that we embrace an open investigation of African history. This involves challenging historical narratives and debunking racist, white supremacist myths. The fact that we are not free today is proof that we still do not know the truth. Wilson opines, "If Eurocentric history and other disciplines are true, then why aren't we free? The knowledge of truth threatens the white supremacists who wish to imprison us back into slavery, keep us in slavery, and keep us dominated. The projection of the European version of history into our minds as mythology is a way of repressing truth within our own minds and within our breasts as a people. European historiography functions to maintain repression" (Wilson 29).

Death is the Result of Historical Amnesia

Amnesia is a condition where a person unintentionally tries to forget certain parts of their past that are painful. They want to erase these memories to rid themselves of the anxieties and fears linked to them. Although these memories are erased from conscious memory, they can still influence how we behave and what we need to do. Diving deeper into the notion that "death is the result of historical amnesia" (Wilson 23), it becomes apparent that our understanding of the past profoundly shapes our present and future. As a Black American man, I see our collective history as a poignant reminder of the interconnectedness between history and the consequences we face in a world of white supremacy. When we forget or do not care about our historical events, we risk neglecting the lessons embedded in our collective experiences. This widespread forgetting has encouraged "The Whiteness of Destruction" both directly and indirectly and has resulted in the recurrence of enormous errors and injustices. It is not merely about re-calling dates and facts but rather understanding what white supremacy is and how it works so that we will not be confused when it comes to the warfare in which the psychopathic white supremacist is, its root causes, and systemic issues that contribute to Black societal sabotage.

Historical amnesia manifests on various levels, from individual memories to societal white supremacist torture methods. This speaks to the danger of selectively remembering parts of the psychopathic history of white supremacy while ignoring Black people, creating a distorted view that justifies harmful actions and perpetuates systematic white supremacy. All Black people, regardless of nationality and cul-ture, are in an anti-Black race war, driven by oppression and social upheavals, which is especially relevant in this context. Without a thor-ough understanding of historical events, white supremacy, what it is, and how it operates in societies, we will struggle to address the deep-rooted issues that lead to loss of life and more. The perpetuation of white supremacist systemic problems, whether in the form of political unrest, discrimination, socioeconomic atrocities, or neglect, that often has life-and-death implications for Black people and our communities.

We have a moral responsibility to our children and our future, not to make the same mistakes that we made yesterday. It is our responsibility to destroy the system of injustice and build a system of justice. We must confront and acknowledge historical injustices. This involves active engagement and effort to change the narratives that have shaped the unbalanced, upside-down, psychopathic worldview mentality. There are those of us who are ashamed of our history of enslavement, who are ashamed of the distorted presentation of Black history (which is why the European distorts and presents it the way he does), who are led to believe that prior to slavery, we were essentially culturally invisible and savage (as the Caucasoid is today), and that we only achieved visibility and civility when the Europeans arrived and gave it to us. "Many of us attempt to repress any knowledge of our American slave experience. But we should heed the fact that a person or people who suffer from social amnesia live lives that are determined by fear, anxiety, terror, and trauma. When we attempt to escape our history because we're afraid of it, when we escape knowledge because it terrifies and makes us feel ashamed, then it is terror, fear, and shame that determine our lives" (Wilson 26).

We then live in terms of what we are afraid of, which includes what we are ashamed of, what we are trying to hide, and what we are trying to avoid facing ourselves with, rather than in terms of our reality and the integration of our reality. After that, people live their lives in denial, escape, and addiction, which appear in many forms. People who try to escape history and live in terror and fear of their own history and reality are largely to blame for the murders, fatalities, and destruction that we see in our communities today. Because of this, I argue that history is not a subject you just happen to take in school; rather, it is directly related to our actual existence. It is an essential part of our everyday existence because, without it, we will be motivated by fear instead of a true knowledge of our own history and identity, which will turn us into monstrosities who virtually mimic the lies, cheating, murder, theft, and other horrible deeds that white supremacists practice.

The Political Ideology of White Supremacists

One extremely unsettling feature of our socio-political environment is the problem of political bias among white supremacists and the deeply ingrained Eurocentric structure in America and around the world. It is a reflection of a system that, at its foundation, frequently works against Black people by prioritizing and upholding a particular cultural viewpoint. This theory makes eurocentric psychopathic psychology seem constrained since it blames the current state of the "Black family" and approaches mental health issues from a white supremacist perspective.

The Eurocentric structure is prevalent in the United States and around the world; this upholds and favors European cultural norms, often at the expense of Black people. This framework, deeply rooted in historical and systemic biases, has contributed to political white supremacist ideologies that reinforce *the "Whiteness of Destruction."* This examines the mother-child relationship as the basis for the personality orientation of brainwashing. However, we must recognize, as non-white people, that this approach is inadequate, primarily because it appears to be relatively non-constructive (Wilson 65).

Contradictions and conflicts are a major way that Black people are kept out of our minds. When faced with what seem to be intractable problems and dilemmas, the mind frequently tries to escape these contradictions by indulging in illness or misbehavior or by grasping onto one of the horns of the dilemma—extreme conformity or extreme rebellion—all of which are ultimately designed to keep Black people in the status quo. For the Europeans to rule the world as they do today, or at least to intimidate it as they do, contradictions must be a chronic part of the lives of the non-European people, as well as those of the Europeans. The imperialist white supremist must essentially function in a very devilish fashion. That is, in a way that makes deception its primary feature. As such, basic beliefs and perspectives about reality have to be changed. The light must now look dark, the good must appear to be the bad, and the truth must be mistaken for deceit. Otherwise, a small group, such as European people, could not continue to keep the rest of the world out of its mind (Wilson 67).

The psyche of European imperialists can be understood by examining their past. As previously stated, history books, not psychology textbooks, contain the psychology of the powerful, especially those who have a Eurocentric worldview. The imperialists themselves have documented their psychology. While they continue to rule the world, their self-documentation proves they are insane. The institutions and beliefs that the European establishments are meant to uphold the status quo because of this history and their desire to continue being the dominant force in the world.

The history books contain the psychology of the world's ruling class, or those who are eurocentrically oriented; all one has to do to understand their psychology is read their history. Of course, neither Black scholars nor I wrote that history. White supremacists wrote it. We have to look at the beliefs that have come from European imperialism if we think its past is traumatizing and terrible. Without confronting the connected ideologies of "The Whiteness of Destruction" in the form of anti-Black racism, we cannot just disregard our people's enslavement, genocide, and wars perpetrated by imperialist anti-Black nations. These events and ideologies are inextricably linked and form an integral part of the same phenomenon. The act of attempting to separate and compartmentalize various aspects of life, including the events and ideologies of imperialism, is a major factor contributing to the mental, physical, and other issues within our community. This is a problem both within our community and within the broader system (Wilson 72).

Compartmentalization refers to the act of dividing complex or multifaceted concepts into smaller, more manageable parts or categories. While this can be helpful in certain contexts, such as organizing information or tasks, it becomes problematic when applied to addressing the system of white supremacy. When we compartmentalize different aspects of life, such as our personal and professional lives, our emotions, thoughts, histories, and ideologies, we risk losing sight of the larger, interconnected picture. "This kind of ideology, of course, is not only an ideology that rationalizes the status quo and removes the responsibility from the social structures developed by Europeans, but it also removes the responsibility from that structure for bringing about the conditions inherent in the community and in individuals" (Wilson 73).

There are major consequences when trying to isolate the beliefs and events connected to imperialism. We miss the more subtle systemic problems at hand if we only see the horrors carried out by colonial powers—such as slavery, genocide, and war—as distinct from the underlying ideas that provided justification for them. Furthermore, this may lead to a lack of responsibility or recognition for the harm done. Self-hatred is not just a personal problem; it is ingrained in the social institutions that influence how we live. People who hate themselves typically feel the same way about other people who are similar to them, even members of their own group. As a result, this causes Black people to doubt the skills and knowledge of other members of the same group. The result is a feeling of collective inadequacy and failure that permeates society as a whole.

The notion of individualism is not just an attack on individual people; it is a tool used by certain communities to maintain dominance over others. Specifically, it is a tool used by Eurocentric communities to assert their dominance over Black communities. If an individual subscribes to the ideology of individualism and believes that their failure to succeed is due to some personal deficiency, they may think that opportunities are available and that they could succeed if they had the right personality traits. However, when they fail to achieve success, they are confronted with a significant contradiction. This contradiction creates what psychologists call cognitive dissonance—a feeling of discomfort when conflicting beliefs or actions are held simultaneously. Such dissonance can be distressing and motivate individuals to resolve the contradictions, often by trying to remove them altogether (Nairaland n.p.).

The Characteristics of Mental Health and Behavior

The discussion at hand revolves around the connection between mental health diagnoses and political and racial dogmatism. If social workers and psychologists fail to consider the political system, they become overly preoccupied with diagnostic procedures. Psychology focuses on predicting behavior and identifying the characteristics and symptoms of mental illnesses. The mental health disciplines are concerned with categorizing behavior and the methods used in this process. "Psychology concerns itself with predicting behavior and with being able to determine to a very fine extent the characteristics and symptomatologies of various mental illnesses. Mental health disciplines concern themselves with the categorization of behavior and the means by which this process is carried out" (Wilson 86). Psychologists and others may believe they are conducting important scientific research while remaining politically apolitical, though, if they place an overly strong emphasis on diagnostic techniques. Problems with one's mental health point to a disturbed psyche, a disturbed individual, and a disturbed individual who disturbs our psyche. When we say that a person is disturbed, we are not only implying that the person may have issues; we are also implying that we are experiencing issues with the person. that the person is not just disturbed, but that the person disturbs (Wilson 86).

When we face racism and anti-Black hatred, it's like a sudden storm that disrupts the very core of my being. It's not just about external words or actions; it's the deep impact it has on my psyche and mental equilibrium. Imagine being assaulted with messages that question your worth and humanity based just on the color of your skin. It is a relentless assault on your sense of self, identity, and place in the world. Every act of racism chips away at my mental well-being, leaving me feeling vulnerable, invalidated, and deeply wounded. It creates a sense of unease, a constant awareness of being under attack simply because of who you are. The psychological toll of racism is profound. It can manifest as anxiety, depression, trauma, and a host of other mental health challenges. It's a constant battle to maintain a sense of dignity and self-worth in the face of such hostility and hatred. Wilson continues:

> "Therefore, the behavior that we are diagnosing may represent a disturbing questioning of our ways of doing things, our values, and the nature of our social relations. The behavior of the so-called sick individual threatens us, threatens to expose our failures, our hypocrisies, our collusion in bringing about the state of mind of the individual who confronts us. So diagnosis is not a one-way street, where only the patient is looked at. It is a two-way street, where both the patient

and the psychiatrist look at each other and work out their problem together, not just the patient's problem" (Wilson 87).

The European, despite causing immense harm by killing people multiple times over, allowing certain individuals to accumulate billions while others suffer from starvation, and engaging in continuous theft, still believes he is entitled to a peaceful night's sleep, a sense of safety in public spaces, and civil treatment. Such beliefs are foolish, for they assume that the rest of the world will not protest against the injustices committed by the Europeans. It is unrealistic to expect victims of such actions to remain silent and not react, even if their actions may be self-destructive.

However, our system demands that the so-called helping professions keep them out of our sight, render them invisible, change their behavior, and make them conform in some way to the system. Give us peace at night by using your abilities to diagnose and treat. Thus, "diagnosis" in this context becomes part of the problem. It becomes the means by which the establishment denies its culpability and becomes a defense mechanism by which the establishment denies its guilt and defends its self-image and prerogatives. In order to project its own criminality and self-insanity onto its victims, the establishment uses diagnosis. In this instance, diagnosis functions as a tool of denial, projection, and repression, serving both psychological and political purposes (Wilson 89).

Who Diagnoses Dr. Frankenstein?

Dr. Wilson describes the act of diagnosis as a prerequisite for legitimizing various forms of repression, including psychiatric, legal, and political repression. It can be seen as a means for establishing state terror, and transforming sadistic practices into those of rehabilitation and correction through psychiatry and social work. The establishment legitimizes its monopoly on the power to incarcerate, torture, harass, maim, and kill in the name of maintaining order and following the correct and bureaucratic execution of procedures. Through careful measurement and testing, Dr. Frankenstein, in the name of science and humanity, labels his creation a monster and deems its behavior as monstrous, even though it may lack social graces and behave loudly on the subway while referring to itself in a degrading manner. The individual in question exhibits behavior that is loud, vulgar, and inconsiderate, engaging in activities such as smoking, drinking, and consuming unconventional foods, all of which align with the criteria established for diagnosis. These actions are deemed brutal, hazardous, egocentric, and petulant, which accurately corresponds with the conditions of their existence .

Thus, Wilson asserts that according to Dr. Frankenstein, if an entity exhibits the characteristics of a monster—appearance, movement, and speech—then it conforms to the monster profile, validating the tests. This parallels the diagnostic process, wherein Eurocentric tools aid in identifying the creation. This holds true for both physical and mental health issues, exacerbated by the prevailing legal and political repression in the global order, contributing to various afflictions. Consequently, Dr. Frankenstein is depicted as the creator, diagnostician, healer, and ultimately the slayer of the monster. However, a critical question arises: who evaluates and diagnoses Dr. Frankenstein? Could the creature's madness be a reflection of the creator's own insanity? The pressing concern emerges—how can Dr. Frankenstein be cured of his ailments, and who will intervene to halt his egregious experiments? (Wilson 92-93)

Navigating the intricate web of legal and political repression within the current global order emerges as a central factor contributing to the physical ailments that afflict our people. This dynamic is reminiscent of the narrative of Dr. Frankenstein, wherein he is not only the creator but also the diagnoser, the healer, and ultimately the slayer of the monstrous creation he brought to life. Yet, the profound question lingers: who diagnoses Dr. Frankenstein? Does the madness inherent in the creature not mirror the underlying madness of its creator? And, more importantly, who will undertake the task of curing Dr. Frankenstein of his afflictions? Who will stand against his heinous experiments and put an end to the cycle of oppression?

Wilson draws a parallel between the global order and the tale of Dr. Frankenstein, unveiling a profound reflection on the interconnectedness of power and its consequences. The metaphorical creation of a monstrous being, burdened with the weight of societal ailments, mirrors the unintended consequences of political and legal repression on Black communities. Dr. Frankenstein's role as the creator and healer serves as an allegory for those in positions of power who craft policies, laws, and systems that have a direct impact on the health and well-being of Black people.

The difficult question arises: who will analyze and investigate Dr. Frankenstein? In the context of our global reality, this question is an urgent call for accountability and scrutiny of those who hold power. It prompts us to question the motives and repercussions of political and legal decisions that perpetuate oppression. The analogy challenges us to look beyond the symptoms and address the root causes of the ailments affecting our society, seeking a diagnosis for the madness that resides within the very structures meant to govern and protect.

The notion that the madness of the creature reflects the creator's madness emphasizes the responsibility that those in power (the psychopathic white supremacists) bear for the consequences of their actions. It compels us to examine the ethical dimensions of governance and the potential repercussions of unchecked authority. If the creation embodies the instability and chaos within its creator, it becomes imperative to scrutinize the motives, biases, and ethical foundations of those shaping the global order.

The pressing need to cure Dr. Frankenstein's sickness underscores the urgency of systemic change and the imperative for a shift in power dynamics. The call for someone to halt his heinous experiments challenges us all to actively engage in dismantling anti-black racism and oppressive systems and start to produce justice. It prompts a collective responsibility to address the root causes of societal ailments, which is white supremacy, and work towards disassembling it.

The Black Consciousness of Political Psychology

Wilson argues that the character and conduct of groups and individuals, however labeled and categorized, whether judged to be good or evil, superior or inferior, are the products of historic intergroup, intragroup, and interpersonal relations and can only be meaningfully understood in terms of these relations. The character and behavior of Black American people, whether labeled "normal" or "abnormal," can only be fully and accurately comprehended, along with the process and purpose of labeling itself, in terms of the historic power relations between dominant European-American and subordinate Black-American groups. In order for whites to gain certain material and non-material benefits, they primarily construct special types of social power relations that involve white dominance and Black subordination. "These social power relations involve social practices and processes that mediate the white American socioeconomic, sociopolitical, and psychological manipulation and construction of Black consciousness and behavior. Under white supremacy, Black consciousness and behavior" (Wilson 101).

Throughout history, the reality of racial superiority and inferiority has been deeply ingrained in societal structures, perpetuating a narrative of white supremacy. This construct, fueled by institutionalized racism, colonialism, and slavery, has facilitated the accumulation of material and non-material benefits for the white population. Economic systems, legal frameworks, and cultural norms have been shaped to reinforce and sustain these power differentials.

The system of white supremacy involves not only the concentration of economic and political power but also the permeation of cultural and social spheres. The construction of social power relations manifests in various forms, from economic to educational injustices to anti-Black biased legal systems and media portrayals. These power dynamics contribute to a pervasive narrative that reinforces the social hierarchy, positioning whites at the apex and relegating Blacks to a subordinate status.

The alleged normality or abnormality of Black consciousness under white supremacy requires that Blacks involuntarily and obsessively deceive themselves. "This collective self-deception, which is the benchmark of oppressed Black consciousness, is the main product of White-Black social power relations, motivated by anxiety and ignorance, founded on the denial and distortion of reality." Both the normalcy and abnormalcy of Black consciousness and behavior, as reproduced by white supremacy's power relations, necessitate that they act against their own best interests in the interests of their white oppressors; that they be self-denying, self-defeating, and, at times, self-destructive, while convincing themselves otherwise (Wilson 103).

Domination and the Mislabeling of Behavior

Through the restructuring of prevailing ideas, sentiments, emotions, driving forces, values, and psychological conditions, a transformation occurs in consciousness and behavior. This process involves the politically strategic application of labels and classifications by the initiators. The act of categorizing and naming the oppressed awareness and behavior by their oppressors functions as a strategy to make the oppressed abnormality and pathology appear "normal," matching it with the universe's perceived natural order. Wilson states "The normalization of pathology is exquisitely functional for oppressive regimes. It is for this productive reason that oppressive white supremacy always attempts to rationalize its oppression of Blacks by normalizing their reactionary, pathological, Eurocentric consciousness and behavior and simultaneously abnormalizing both the reactionary and proactionary, non-pathological, and pathological Afrocentric consciousness and behavior with regard to their political-economic functionality for maintaining white dominance" (Wilson 106). The repressive white supremacist dictatorship seeks to demonstrate, deceptively but persuasively, that subjugated blacks' normative cognition and behavior are the spontaneous, natural, and predictable consequences of the original African character and culture.

Educative Psychotherapy

Wilson establishes a distinction between educational psychotherapy and ethnicized psychotherapy, noting that social power is the key component of both approaches. He claims that ethnicization is the process of using social power to influence people's thoughts and behaviors to conform to social norms. Education includes, among other things, the analysis of social power in order to understand how social power influences people's lives and the lives of social groups.

Educational and therapeutic psychology centered on the Black American experience underscores the importance of critically examining and understanding how individuals, such as therapists and educators, influenced by Eurocentric perspectives, operate within the current global socio-economic context. It highlights the adverse impact on the social and mental well-being of Black Americans. This approach identifies and challenges attempts to conform Black American behavior to Eurocentric standards in the realms of legality, morality, politics, and ethnicity.

A Black American-centered educational approach not only defines specific states of consciousness and forms of behavior in relation to the needs of Black people but also involves clients in a comprehensive analysis of their life goals and methods for achieving them. Simultaneously, it seeks to infuse their endeavors with social meaning, purpose, and creative power. The goal is to cultivate a Black American-centered consciousness and identity, optimizing individuals' capacity to contribute fully to the growth and development of the Black American community and express their inherent humanity in positive ways. The participant in Black American-centered therapeutic and educational encounters learns how he has been unconsciously trained by a Eurocentric system to react habitually and unconsciously to its social cues to Eurocentric authorities and social contexts that cause him "to perceive, think, feel, and behave in certain ways; he has been cued to avoid perceiving, thinking, feeling, and behaving in certain ways" (Wilson 111) and how his Eurocentric awareness forces its Black American hosts to experience dream states akin to somnambulistic wanderers in the dark, killing African-centered consciousness in the process.

Fighting Back

The white power structure vs. Blacks people disadvantages stems from the former's ability to socially manufacture or strongly influence the consciousness and behavior of the latter in favor of maintaining white supremacy. Nevertheless, the only way to stop this trend is to equalize or reverse power disparities by generating justice. This necessary equation or reversal of power relations begins when Black people come to understand the nature of power, its social origins, and its applications; when they recognize that they are as capable of its acquisition and disposition as are their European (and other ethnic group) counterparts; and when we consciously and deliberately choose to acquire and dispose of it in our own interests and in the defense of our own liberty. To achieve this, Black people must first understand the nature and origins of power, recognize their own capacity for acquiring and wielding it, and use it to defend our own [hu]man rights. Developing a logical concept of power, revising reactionary states of "Black American" body politics, upgrading coping resources, neutralizing social stressors, controlling effective coping strategies, and taking charge of labeling and treatment processes are essential steps toward this goal.

In "The Falsification of Afrikan Consciousness," Wilson presents a powerful and compelling analysis of the ways in which Eurocentric values and white supremacy have been used to oppress and marginalize Black Americans. Wilson argues that the education system in the

United States has been designed to perpetuate white supremacy and that Black Americans must reject this system and reclaim their own history and culture in order to achieve true liberation and empowerment.

Wilson's ideas contribute to the understanding that Black psychologists must continue to cultivate a collective consciousness based on historical struggles and a sense of obligation to preserve their collective identity. In the spirit of true liberation, Wilson cautions that Black Americans need to differentiate between religions, ideologies, and esoteric ceremonies that serve them versus those that do not advance their interests or change their political/social situation. Wilson ultimately urges them to dismantle the European social structure and create a new African consciousness and identity that embodies an unwavering will to power. When Black people critically examine the biased perceptions of reality imposed on them by Europeans and seek to understand reality as it is, they will unlock the keys to their own liberation.

One of the key themes of the book is the importance of reclaiming Black American history and culture. Wilson argues that eurocentric values and perspectives have been used to erase the history and culture of Africa and its diaspora and that Black Americans must develop a sense of pride and identity that is grounded in their own history and culture. He shows how the erasure of Black American history and culture has contributed to the oppression of Black Americans and how reclaiming that history and culture is a crucial step in the struggle for liberation.

Another important theme of the book is the need for Black Americans to build their own economic and political power. Wilson argues that Black Americans must reject the structures of power that seek to oppress and exploit them, build their institutions, and support their businesses and communities. He emphasizes the importance of building a strong and resilient Black American community and of working together to challenge the systems of oppression that seek to keep Black Americans in a position of subservience.

Takeaways:

- The education system in the United States has been designed to perpetuate white supremacy and oppress Black Americans.
- Eurocentric values and perspectives have been used to justify the domination of Black Americans and to erase the history and culture of Africa and its diaspora.
- Black Americans must reclaim their own history and culture and reject the eurocentric framework that has been imposed upon them.
- Black Americans must build a strong and resilient community that prioritizes the well-being and success of all its members and challenges the structures of power that seek to oppress and exploit them.
- "If we're going to make a contribution to the world, it's not going to be by imitating somebody else. It's not going to be by copying somebody else. It's going to be by being ourselves and by being the best that we can be as ourselves." (Wilson 60)
- Wilson argues that in order to achieve true liberation, Black Americans must adopt a global perspective and build solidarity with other victims of white supremacy/racism worldwide.

Wilson contends that in order for Black Americans to truly experience emancipation and empowerment, we must recover our own history and culture. He maintains that Eurocentric ideas and viewpoints have been exploited to erase the history and culture of Africa and its diaspora. Developing a sense of pride and identity rooted in Black American history and culture entails acknowledging and appreciating the accomplishments of African civilizations. It is necessary for Black Americans to develop our own economic and political strength in order to confront the systems of dominance that aim to oppress and take advantage of us.

This entails creating our own organizations, assisting Black-owned companies and neighborhoods, and cooperating to confront oppressive structures. Black Americans ought to reject the current non-educational system. The American educational system is set up to uphold white supremacy and obliterate Black Americans and African diasporan history and culture. Black Americans need to reject this educational system and look for other educational options, such as community-based learning programs, movies, and books.

While keeping in mind that white supremacy is the source of all of the problems that Black Americans face and that overthrowing and opposing this system is necessary to achieve independence and empowerment, it is imperative to challenge and confront white supremacy. The criminal justice system, the educational system, and the media are just a few examples of the power institutions that must be challenged in order to end individual acts of racism and dismantle white supremacy. The development of a sense of community is also essential. Wilson stresses the value of creating a sense of community and cooperating to accomplish shared objectives. Black Americans need to abandon individualism and the idea that "every person is for themselves" and instead create networks of cooperation and support for one another.

While doing these strategies, it will help cultivate a sense of spiritual grounding. Having a sense of spiritual grounding is essential for achieving liberation and empowerment. This includes developing a sense of connection to the ancestors, engaging in spiritual practices that are grounded in Black traditions, and recognizing the ways in which the struggle for liberation is connected to the struggle for spiritual awakening.

8
<hr>

Race War/Civil War

FM 6-2003: Ethnic Cleansing Operations

FM 6-2003: Ethnic Cleansing Operations is a manual you can find by doing a simple Google search. It addresses military operations aimed at eradicating the Black population from the contiguous United States, and its disturbing and reprehensible narrative that advocates for racial violence and discrimination. Delving into the text, a reader must acknowledge the inherent racism and hatred that permeate its pages. The blatant disregard for [hu]man life, rights, and humanity. FM 6-2003: Ethnic Cleansing Operations is a blatant example of the psychology of the white supremacist psychopathic behavior and thought. The fundamental principles of this book are deeply unsettling.

This deadly racist hate manual purports to present military strategies but reveals a sinister agenda driven by a toxic ideology that seeks to marginalize, enslave, and eliminate Black people. The language employed not only normalizes racial violence but also attempts to legitimize such heinous acts through distorted historical references and misguided interpretations.

The notion of a coalition aiming to expel an entire racial group, with the confederate battle flag as its unifying symbol, is not only an affront to the principles of unity and diversity but also a dangerous manifestation of white supremacist ideologies. The historical grievances cited to justify such actions are lies and serve as a pretext for advocating a deeply unjust and morally reprehensible cause, Black genocide.

In confronting this manual, it becomes evident that it stands as a testament to the persistence of racism and the urgent need for continuous efforts to combat hatred, discrimination, and systemic injustices. The principles of equality, justice, and human rights must prevail over divisive ideologies that seek to undermine the very foundations of a just and inclusive society. The proposition of ethnically cleansing the country is a grave and reprehensible notion, rooted in distorted perceptions of racial dynamics and fueled by unfounded fears. The argument is built on the premise of escalating crime rates attributed to people of color against whites. While acknowledging the importance of addressing crime, the proposed solution of ethnic cleansing is morally indefensible.

Anecdotes and perspectives shared about racial tensions on city buses and the rationale behind them are presented as evidence for justifying such drastic measures. These narratives, however, perpetuate harmful stereotypes and fail to recognize the diversity and complexity of individuals within any racial group.

The recounting of a conversation with Black men attempting to justify certain behaviors by attributing them to ancestral instincts is both reductionist and perpetuates harmful racial tropes. Such generalizations oversimplify the multifaceted factors that contribute to social issues and undermine the potential for dialogue and understanding.

In this hate-filled anti-Black racist FM 6-2003, the so-called manual denigrates Black culture and promotes anti-Black stereotypes, such as loud car sound systems, using them to project an image of ethnic superiority. This narrative frames these cultural expressions as deliberate acts of aggression, forming part of a supposed campaign of ethnic cleansing. However, interpreting cultural differences as intentional acts of warfare oversimplifies the rich tapestry of cultural exchange and expression in a diverse society.

The author's critique of Black History Month, labeling it as a celebration of a "jungle culture" and an opportunity for self-pity, is a misrepresentation that dismisses the significance of acknowledging historical and cultural contributions. The manual further perpetuates a divisive narrative by asserting that other ethnic groups covet white accomplishments, painting a skewed picture of racial dynamics.

The exploration of gangsta rap is presented in a biased manner, focusing solely on its negative aspects without acknowledging the diversity within the genre or considering the socio-economic factors that may influence its creation. The characterization of Black aspirations based on selective lyrics perpetuates harmful stereotypes and fails to recognize the nuanced experiences and aspirations of individuals within the Black community ("FM 6-2003 Ethnic Cleansing Operations" 9–10).

Economics and Ethnic Cleansing

This so-called book reflects a biased and historically inaccurate perspective. It suggests that gun rights in the Bill of Rights were solely intended to protect the lives and liberties of white people and were not meant for slaves, who were considered not to have rights. The assertion that the federal government and liberal individuals extended rights to former slaves at the expense of white individuals is a misrepresentation of the historical context.

This hate-filled book has a number of different types of weapons, from handguns to assault rifles, and they encourage their white readers to purchase or obtain these weapons in order to fulfill the ethnic cleansing that these white supremacists are attempting. It also discusses a disturbing topic related to ethnic cleansing and acquiring weapons. It suggests that, as ethnic cleansing progresses, individuals may come across modern, high-powered weapons left unattended, possibly obtained from military storage facilities and police evidence lockers. The passage goes on to emphasize the need to equip recruits with these firearms, ranging from machine guns to single-shot shotguns, found in large quantities. It advises inspecting each weapon for functionality and ensuring that psychopathic white supremacists using them in battle have received adequate training. This hate speech book describes a scenario where a breakdown in cooperative order is anticipated, potentially leading to a situation similar to the collapse of Albania's government. It suggests that National Guard units may abandon their posts, leaving armories vulnerable to pillaging. The text then advises that, when the time is right, individuals described as "local whites" should closely monitor the situation and seize any functional equipment that remains in the armories ("FM 6-2003 Ethnic Cleansing Operations" 57).

The passage goes on to mention the varying sizes of armories, ranging from several thousand to several hundred thousand square feet, and suggests that the equipment stored could include items such as armored cars and kevlar helmets, depending on the specific units stationed there. It also mentions the inclusion of images depicting the types of materials one might find in these armories.

It's important to note that discussions or plans involving the illegal acquisition of equipment, especially in the context of potential civil unrest or violence, are not advisable and are against the principles of law and order. Such behaviors can have negative effects on people and communities, as well as legal repercussions if promoted or engaged in. Although it is advised to look for peaceful and legal solutions through the appropriate channels if you are concerned about your safety or security, but white supremacists don't abide by the law.

The forthcoming civil conflict is expected to involve various significant participants, including U.S. Federal Forces, state-controlled National Guard units, State Defense Forces, and unorganized militias. Additionally, militia groups such as the National Socialists, KKK, Skinheads, white street gangs, and Confederate reenactors are anticipated to play a prominent role. These organizations have diligently prepared for potential ethnic cleansing, and it is suggested that their capabilities be fully utilized. Their primary activities are anticipated to involve movement from one neighborhood to another while coordinating with certain extremist white supremacist groups. The pace of their advancement could significantly influence operations in cities. Equip their leaders with radios, global positioning systems (GPS), and accurate maps, and provide them access to artillery, as they are expected to be proficient in its use ("FM 6-2003 Ethnic Cleansing Operations" 61).

Firstly, the insane white supremacists will not confine their murders to armed combatants alone; rather, they will enslave or even kill anyone that is identified as "Black." They will encourage the spreading of fear. They also disseminate dread, which is a "force multiplier." As Black people retreat, they will be reminded of previous lynchings and other crimes committed against them by groups who have rightfully been responsible for beheadings, mutilations, burnings of occupied buildings, and other horrors. Black people will be terrorized and fearful as a result of these memories, which will contribute to their leaving the nation.

According to the hate manual FM 6-2003 Ethnic Cleansing Operations, white folks are generally motivated and don't give a damn about non-whites. Just a small percentage of white supremacists will arm themselves and go on the attack; a severe economic crisis is necessary to pull them out of their depths. Considering that only 12 percent of Americans identify as Black, it won't take many white people to entirely drive Black people out of the country. This hate manual states that there are more than five million Muslims in the United States, with one million of them living in California and roughly a million in New York. Black Americans make up about 42% of the Muslim population in the United States. Despite popular belief, not every member of the Nation of Islam is a fighter; in fact, black military veterans are probably the most proficient shooters. Using scoped rifles or pistols to take out Black people or anybody else deemed a threat will take precedence.

According to this FM 6-2003 terrorist manual, expect street gangs to mostly wield handguns and a few rifles. Black militants, however, are likely to possess high-quality weapons due to dedicated training. Prioritize providing heavy weaponry to Black militants. Artillery spotters should monitor and report when such groups gather. West Coast white racial cleansing groups should be prepared for opposition from "Chicano" and "Black gangs," as well as organized forces like the Brown Berets. Spanish-speaking whites can contribute to psywar broadcasts and papers for white units. Exploit the existing hostility between Chicanos/Latinos and Blacks, utilizing psychological warfare and snipers to heighten gang rivalry throughout the operational spectrum.

The racist so-called "book" identified five key components of ethnic cleansing:

1. Concentration. Surround the area to be cleansed and after warning the
resident.
2. Decapitation. Execute political leaders, lawyers, judges, public officials, writers, and professors.
3. Separation. Divide females, children, and old males from males of 'fighting age': sixteen to sixty years old.
4. Evacuation. Transport females, children, and old males to neighboring territories or country.
5. Liquidation. Execute "fighting age" Black males, disposing of their bodies.

Black people's possessions are to be stolen; disruption and disconnection of phone and cable television connections; the forced labor of Black slaves at gunpoint; the ban on Black women giving birth in hospitals; and "voluntary" property transfers. Local media—TV, radio, newspapers, and so on—must spread fear and hatred toward Black people. Disseminate the names of people who mix races and race traders, as well as harassing phone calls with death threats on them.

Mass deportations, the unjust treatment of Black people in detention facilities and camps, and the targeting and shooting of Black individuals. Detonations and fires of homes and businesses, the desecration of religious monuments and cultural symbols, and the harassment and intimidation of Black people on the streets. The enforced relocation of entire Black communities represents just a few instances of terroristic acts perpetrated by military personnel, paramilitary groups, and armed civilians. This encompasses actions like summary shootings, lynchings, intentional murder, and torture. It also involves strategically pitting Black and Hispanic communities against each other through targeted bombardment of transportation hubs, bakeries, water purification plants, and other means.

The FM 6-2003 terrorist manual states a discernible racial "fault line" exists, and it ought to be fully utilized. Observe that, although there is minimal overlap, the races grow up next to one another. The fact that races prefer the companionship of their own race is revealed here, despite politically forcing Black males into areas populated by Chicano/Latino people. This hate manual stresses that white people are going to face situations that call for the ferocity of barbarians. Every white fighter must possess unadulterated, savage violence. "Barbarians win with cunning, numbers, and courage," the psychopathic white supremacist suggest, immediately killing anyone who has been named, as well as anyone who is not on your Shoot On Site (SOS) list. {This is also a code word, so use extreme caution if you are around suspected white supremacists and you hear this term.} ("FM 6-2003 Ethnic Cleansing Operations," 69–71).

As soon as things truly start to heat up, military and police defections should become more frequent. Place white deserters and their equipment directly into front-line units. Use the equipment right away if they are experienced with using it and have brought big weapons or armored vehicles. Even though things will be quite chaotic, this is a great opportunity to raise money for your cause by charging Black people leaving the area to go south for a "toll." The total amount due should equal the charge. The full amount of money they own, along with all their valuables, should be charged. Black people should also be made to sign a document declaring that all of their property has been abandoned. All of their formal documents, including birth certificates, deeds, automobile titles, and identity cards, should be seized and attached to the form. Elderly Black people are allowed to pass, and all Black people of fighting age are to be exterminated. Cover your tracks and get rid of evidence whenever you can if you want to avoid getting caught. There is minimal concern over combat casualties because they are not considered in war crimes trials, but at least make the effort to remove guns and ammo from the bodies and give them to white recruits who are not equipped.

Many readers of this racist manual will not be members of an organized group, so the book says the first thing you must do is choose your position on white supremacy, or you might find yourself on the list of people to "dance at the end of a rope" if you don't practice white supremacy with your fellow peers.

These psychopaths encourage their white readers to start compiling a list of "niggers" that need to be removed from their neighborhood before you join or form your own organization. The author suggests Black leaders, preachers, legislators, and professionals on this list in addition to non-white people's names and addresses ("FM 6-2003 Ethnic Cleansing Operations" 77). They should also include "race traitors," which include white people who have married Black people and those who have taken on non-white people's customs and characteristics.

FM 6-2003 says that white people who betray other white people should be eliminated alongside the "barbarians they adore" ("FM 6-2003 Ethnic Cleansing Operations"78). The white supremacists are psychopaths who take after their forefathers, who were troglodyte barbarians!

FM 6-2003 terrorist manual states that every white supremacist must understand that the goal of the mission is to eradicate all predatory Black people from the lower 48 states of the United States. They must find, track down, herd, and expel all Black people from the nation. The Confederate battle flag and the sign of death will be combined to create the symbol for this ethnic cleansing effort. All vehicles must fly this design flag from their antennae, and helmet camouflage covers must have patches sewn on the front in muted colors.

This war will be fought in four primary phases:

Phase I. Get them moving;

Phase II. Drive them: Blacks should be driven south toward Florida by armies;

Phase III. Reaching the Racial Fault Lines: Black people should be driven straight to Orlando. Black people should be kept mostly along the major thoroughfares.

Phase IV. On to Mexico: Black people will swarm into areas populated mostly by Chicanos/Latinos, and immigrants from Cuba. This will have an effect on getting the Chicanos/Latinos to finally move to Cuba due to the overwhelming number of Black people. Psychotic warfare forces will use broadcasts in Spanish and leaflet drops to exacerbate the situation. "Prepare the Chicano communities for the Black invasions and allow events to resolve themselves" ("FM 6-2003 Ethnic Cleansing Operations"78).

The idea that the United States disintegrated due to a lengthy racial civil war is a somber but plausible theory offered in the FM 6-2003 terror manual. The nation is returning to pro-white supremacist sentiments, but non-white people will not accept their inferiority. A number of factors, including the political allegiance of white police, the percentage of American combat forces in the country, the level of racial tension, a violent incident (such as the beating of Rodney King or a George Floyd), and a series of coordinated racist attacks on white people who trade races, are suggested by the FM 6-2003 terrorist manual to determine when to launch ethnic cleansing campaigns in the effort to restore the white society this country once was. The authors state that the Black population in the US poses the greatest threat, followed closely by the Chicano/Latino population. When the time comes, whites are encouraged to employ the tactics in this "Whiteness of Destruction" handbook or other similarly effective white supremacist tactics to initiate a broad, coordinated offensive that puts theory into action.

Turner Diaries Template for the Race War

The Turner Diaries, a fictional novel written by white supremacist William Luther Pierce and first published in 1978, acts as a template for how to bring about destruction in America and, above all, practice racism. The book describes a violent, apocalyptic overthrow of the United States government by a white supremacist group known as The Order. The book has been linked to several acts of domestic terrorism, including the Oklahoma City bombing in 1995, which killed 168 people and injured more than 600.

White supremacists use the Turner Diaries as another template or instruction manual for bringing about destruction in America and practicing racism in several ways. First, the book promotes the idea of a race war, where white people must violently overthrow the government and eliminate all non-white people in order to establish a white ethnostate. This concept of a race war is a central tenet of white supremacist ideology and has been used as a justification for violence and terrorism against non-white people.

Second, The Turner Diaries promotes the idea of lone-wolf attacks and decentralized cells of white supremacists. The book describes how small groups of white supremacists can carry out attacks against government and non-white targets without being detected by law enforcement. This strategy has been used by several white supremacist groups, including the Order, to carry out acts of domestic terrorism.

Third, The Turner Diaries promotes the use of weapons and explosives as a means of carrying out attacks. The book describes in detail how to make bombs and other weapons and encourages white supremacists to stockpile weapons and ammunition in preparation for the race war. This has led to an increase in the number of firearms and explosives in the hands of white supremacists in the United States.

Finally, The Turner Diaries promotes the conspiracy theory that the government and the media are controlled by Jews and other non-white groups and that these groups are conspiring to destroy the white race. This idea has been used to fuel anti-Semitic and anti-immigrant sentiment among white supremacists, leading to hate crimes and acts of violence against Jewish and immigrant communities.

In summary, The Turner Diaries is a blueprint for white supremacists to carry out acts of violence and terrorism in the name of establishing a white ethnostate. The book promotes the idea of a race war, decentralized cells, the use of weapons and explosives, and a conspiracy theory of Jewish and non-white control of the government and media. White supremacists have used this book as a template for carrying out acts of violence and terrorism against non-white people in the United States.

Domestic Terrorism and the Assault on America's Electrical Grid

This article talks about the several tactics these terrorists employ, such as physical and computer sabotage. While cyberattacks have garnered a lot of attention, physical sabotage is still a serious threat since it can be hard to detect and result in substantial harm, according to the article. "There were more than 100 attacks on U.S. electrical infrastructure last year—a 72 percent increase over 2021." According to the article, attacks on the electrical infrastructure may be a tactic used by white nationalists, who have a long history of employing violence and sabotage to achieve their objectives. The history of grid attacks is highlighted in the article, including the 2013 attack on a California substation that resulted in severe damage and raised questions about the grid's susceptibility to terrorist strikes. The report also mentions the mounting worry that domestic terrorists—including white nationalists —might attack the grid.

The article also notes the connection between these potential attacks on the grid and the book "The Turner Diaries," which is often cited as an inspiration for white supremacists. The book describes a fictional race war in which white supremacists use violence and sabotage to overthrow the government and establish a white ethnostate. The book includes a scene in which white supremacists attack the electric grid, causing widespread chaos and destruction. "Recently, two neo-Nazis connected to a group called the Atomwaffen Division allegedly plotted to destroy five substations around Baltimore, hoping to cause "cascading failure" in the electric system serving the majority-Black city. This type of sabotage, along with the growing risk of grid cyberattacks, creates real peril as Americans become increasingly dependent on electricity" (Attacking the Grid, n.p.).

The article concludes by emphasizing the urgent need for increased security measures and better coordination between government agencies and the private sector to protect the electric grid from these threats. It notes that while the threat of domestic terrorism targeting the grid is not new, the growing threat from white supremacists makes it more urgent than ever to take action to protect this critical infrastructure (Attacking the Grid, n.p.).

The article discusses the possibility of a second American civil war and argues that it is not an inevitability but a choice of the ruling class. The far-right sees it as an opportunity to create a white ethno-state, while liberals fear it and demand electoral and judicial reforms. Socialists and Marxists argue that the culture wars are a distraction from the class conflict that is emerging between urban and rural capitalists. The article notes that war becomes a means towards capital accumulation when expansion in the market reaches its limit, as evidenced by the "Scramble for Africa" and World War I. Similarly, during the Cold War, capitalists turned against each other and used the culture wars to recruit the working class to fight. As politics becomes more zero-sum and democracy is undermined, civil war becomes more likely.

The article suggests that political polarization in America can be traced back to the collapse of the Soviet Union in 1991, which removed the existential threat that had united the ruling class. Republicans and Democrats shared similar views on issues like abortion before the collapse, but their beliefs diverged afterward. The article argues that class consciousness, rather than electoral and judicial reform, is necessary to prevent civil war. (Attacking the Grid, n.p.)

War on Black History Called "Woke"

Enacted on July 1, 2023, Florida's Senate Bill 266 limits the ways in which elementary, middle, and high school teachers can teach in public schools. Addressing white supremacist racism in any manner that affects Black Americans is now forbidden, and any teachings about systemic racism as ingrained in American institutions are forbidden as well. Critics label it an "educational gag order," comparing it to tactics in illiberal democracies like Israel, Turkey, Russia, and Poland. The law's vagueness allows broad restrictions on teaching topics related to America's racist history, potentially stifling knowledge and information on issues like slavery, Jim Crow laws, and basically anything that addresses injustices that have and continue to affect Black people (Davis and Kane n.p.).

SB 266 also defunds diversity, equity, and inclusion efforts, empowering authorities to take action against violators. This follows Florida's 2022 "Stop WOKE" law, stopping any teachings of America's violent, racist history in K–12 schools. Drawing parallels with international examples, the article warns that such laws may lead to rewriting history, lying, and imposing even more white supremacist ideology.

Governments have laws criminalizing historical facts and truths that expose violators, threatening arrest, imprisonment, and stripping funding. Just like all racist white supremacy ideologues globally, Governor DeSantis aims to rewrite history, undermining calls for reckoning with America's anti-Black history, potentially leading to a greater assault on accurate history and freedom of thought (Davis and Kane n.p.).

Given that white supremacists frequently control historical narratives, I, as a Black man, feel it extremely unjust when they choose to exclude significant historical events that have shaped the current reality for both American history, Black Americans, and all other people. The justifications offered are meant to safeguard the delicate mental health of young white children who experience regret or guilt due to the deeds of their forefathers. Erasing historical and cultural realities not only warps our perception of the past but also helps to sustain systematic racism and inequalities in the modern age. "The Whiteness of Destruction" aims to minimize the hardships, triumphs, and accomplishments of Black American communities by erasing and whitening history, hence sustaining a cycle of subjugation and tyranny. It's imperative to confront and challenge these narratives, ensuring that our Black voices and experiences are acknowledged and respected in shaping our collective understanding of American history.

9

Modern-Day Lynchings

Modern-day lynchings in America have a correlation with the lynchings that occurred in the 1800s and 1900s in terms of the motivation behind the violence, the systemic racism that allowed it to occur, and the impact on Black communities.

Historically, lynchings were a tool used by white supremacists to terrorize and control Black communities. They were often carried out with impunity, with little to no consequences for the perpetrators. These lynchings were typically carried out in public, with the goal of sending a message to other Black people that they were not safe and that any attempts to resist white supremacy would be met with violence.

Today, lynchings are still common; they continue to occur, often in the form of police brutality and extrajudicial killings of Black people. These incidents are often motivated by the same systemic racism that allowed lynchings to occur in the past. They are often carried out with impunity, with little to no consequences for the officers or citizens involved, and they continue to send a message to Black communities that they are not safe and that their lives are not valued.

Another correlation between modern-day lynchings and historical lynchings is the impact on Black communities. Both then and now, these acts of violence and terror have a profound impact on the mental health and well-being of Black people. They can lead to feelings of fear, anxiety, and trauma, and they can also contribute to a sense of helplessness and hopelessness. In addition, they can erode trust between Black communities and law enforcement, making it more difficult to seek justice and feel safe in our own neighborhoods.

While the *"Whiteness of Destruction"* persists, white supremacists are determined to make "America Great Again" and have proposed harsh laws, like in Nashville, where a state legislator from Tennessee proposed including death by hanging as a means of execution in a measure pertaining to the death penalty.

The recommendation was made by Rep. Paul Sherrell, R-Sparta, at a meeting of the Criminal Justice Committee on Tuesday. The lawmakers were debating HB-1245 and an amendment to the measure that would permit death by firing squad as a method of execution in Tennessee. Rep. Paul Sherrell replied, "I was just wondering, could I put an amendment on that, that would include hanging by a tree, too?" Then he made an offer to co-sponsor the bill.

The real question is why are Black children being targeted at an immense rate? White supremacists love soft targets, and Black children are soft targets. There are notable racial differences in the number of child victims of police shootings, according to a recent study by researchers at Children's National Hospital in Washington, DC. The study, which examined national death certificate data from 2003 to 2018, discovered that, in comparison to their white peers, Black adolescents had a six-fold higher risk of being fatally shot by the police, while the risk for Hispanic adolescents was nearly three times higher. The research focused on adolescents aged 12 to 17 who died from firearm injuries due to police intervention, totaling 140 deaths during the 16-year period, with 93% of the victims being Black boys and an average age of 16.

A study published in the Journal Pediatrics, entitled "Black Children Are Six Times More Likely to Be Shot to Death by Police," underscores the alarming and unacceptable racial and ethnic murderous acts documented in police shootings of Black children, mirroring trends seen in adult cases. Dr. Monika K. Goyal, who led the research team, highlighted the potential underestimation of disparities since the study only considered fatal incidents and did not include non-fatal shootings. Dr. Goyal emphasized the profound impact of each child's death on the community, eroding trust in the system and calling for a thorough examination and correction of policies perpetuating these disparities.

In the case of Aderrien Murry, a Black child who suffered serious injuries when police, responding to a call from his mother during a domestic dispute in Indianola, Mississippi, arrived at their home, Aderrien had been asked by his mother to call the police when the father of one of his half-siblings became angry. Upon the police's arrival, Sergeant Greg Capers shot Aderrien in the chest after ordering everyone in the house to raise their hands. Aderrien, running from around a corner toward the door, sustained injuries including a collapsed lung, a fractured rib, and a lacerated liver.

Despite the family's commitment to seeking justice and their lawyer's statement expressing the intent to ensure accountability through the civil legal process, a grand jury determined that there was no criminal conduct by Sgt. Greg Capers in the case. The attorney general's office, led by Lynn Fitch, announced that no charges would be pressed, stating, "As such, no further criminal action will be taken by this office in this matter" ("US Family of 11-year-old Shot by Police Vows to Seek Justice After Officer Gets No Charges").

An article from The Atlanta Journal-Constitution entitled "5 people of color have died in hangings across the country" reports that authorities are investigating a series of recent hangings involving Black and Hispanic individuals in California, Houston, and New York. Five separate incidents, including the deaths of four men and a teenage boy, have raised concerns about the possibility of lynchings, although officials have classified each case as suicide. The incidents fueled fears and suspicions amid ongoing racial tensions following George Floyd's death. In June of 2020, in the case involving a Black 17-year-old teenager found hanged outside a Houston elementary school, the preliminary investigation suggested suicide (as usual), but family members expressed skepticism.

In California, federal agencies, including the FBI and the U.S. Department of Justice's Civil Rights Division, are investigating the deaths of two Black men found hanging from trees: Malcolm Harsch, 38, found in Victorville on May 31, and Robert Fuller, 24, found 53 miles away, hanged on June 10, 2020, at a park near Palmdale City Hall. The families dispute suicide claims and call for independent autopsies.

In New York, 27-year-old Dominique Alexander was found hanging from a tree at Fort Tryon Park on June 9, 2020. The state medical examiner has ruled his death a suicide (as usual).

Ropes tied into nooses, reminiscent of the Jim Crow era's terrorizing symbol of lynchings, have appeared anonymously in various locations nationwide. Law enforcement in Oakland, California, is investigating hate crimes after discovering nooses hanging from trees. The unsettling incidents coincide with heightened racial tensions. Despite the prevailing classification of these cases as suicides, concerns and suspicions persist, prompting calls for thorough investigations and independent autopsies. The context of racial tensions and the history of nooses as symbols of racial violence add complexity to the ongoing investigations (Lee n.p.).

Time is illusionary; no matter if it's in the 17th century or in "modern-day times," lynchings on Black people still happen very frequently, and these are only a few examples; many do not get reported or are covered up by the white supremacist law enforcement and political governmental agencies. While always blaming the victims of psychopathic white supremacists as suicides. Let us not be fooled; we live in an ongoing anti-Black race war.

Racist "Race Soldier Gangs" Masquerading as "Police Officers"

The following is a list of very dangerous police gangs who are actively practicing white supremacy and Black ethnic cleansing and who are "Race Soldiers" who work for the Los Angeles County Sheriff's

Department (LASD). According to press sources, the LASD has struggled with gang activity since the 1970s and currently has about 21
groups.

Banditos, Buffalo Soldiers, Cavemen,
Compton Executioners, Cowboys,
Grim Reapers, Jump Out Boys,
Little Devils, Little Red Devils,
Lomita Lizards, Lynwood Vikings,
Pirates Posse, Rattlesnakes,
Regulators Spartans, Tasmanian Devils,
The Leafs, 3000 Boys, 2000 Boys,
Temple Station, V-Boys, Wayside Whities

Their violent actions and anti-Black sentiment have brought attention to a problem that has long existed inside the 12,000-person LASD.
While police gangs/race soldiers are present in US cities such as New
Orleans, Oakland, New York, and Detroit, other police departments
have anti-Black racist police gangs too. The problem is white supremacy, and in Los Angeles, this anti-Black hatred has persisted since the
police and sheriff departments were created; they used to be called
"slave catchers." Each has its own distinct tattoos and culture, many of
which are reminiscent of the street or prison gangs that the cops have
sworn to oppose as part of their job (Buncombe n.p.).

The "UN International Independent Expert Mechanism to Advance
Racial Justice and Equality in the Context of Law Enforcement" has
released a report stating that systemic racism against Black people
is pervasive in America's police forces and criminal justice system.
Following a country visit earlier this year, the report highlights racial
profiling, police killings, and other human rights violations rooted in
the legacy of slavery and legalized apartheid. Black people in the US
are reported to be three times more likely to be killed by police and 4.5

times more likely to be incarcerated than whites. The report rejects the "bad apple" theory, emphasizing a broader pattern of abusive behavior within law enforcement institutions that needs systemic reform. It calls for alternative responses to policing for issues like mental health crises and homelessness, addressing the mental health impact of racism on police officers. The report condemns the overuse of incarceration, the overrepresentation of Black people in the criminal justice system, and instances of severe punishment, including life imprisonment for children ("Systemic Racism Pervades US Police and Justice Systems, UN Mechanism on Racial Justice in Law Enforcement Says in New Report Urging Reform" n.p.).

Post Traumatic Slave Syndrome or (PTSS)

Post-traumatic stress disorder (PTSD) is a mental health condition that can develop in people who have experienced or witnessed a traumatic or life-threatening event. For victims of white supremacy racism, the trauma experienced can be ongoing and pervasive, leading to a range of symptoms and difficulties in daily life.

One of the most significant ways that white supremacy racism can impact people psychologically is through the experience of racism-related trauma. This trauma can be acute, such as experiencing a hate crime or other violent act, or chronic mistreatment, such as ongoing discrimination, harassment, or microaggressions. This can lead to a range of psychological symptoms, including anxiety, depression, hypervigilance, and avoidance behaviors.

People who have experienced racism-related trauma may have flashbacks or intrusive thoughts about the traumatic event or events, which can be distressing and disruptive to daily life. They may also experience feelings of shame, guilt, and anger related to the trauma, as well as feelings of isolation and disconnection from others.

For many victims of white supremacy racism, the trauma they experience is compounded by the societal structures and institutions that perpetuate racism. This can make it difficult to seek help and support, as well as to feel safe and secure in daily life.

The highly regarded researcher Joy DeGruy, PhD, developed the idea of Post-Traumatic Slave Syndrome (PTSS), which provides a framework for understanding the injustices and persistent multigenerational trauma that Black Americans have experienced. From the time of slavery to the most recent sad events involving Black people dying at the hands of law officers/race soldiers, this trauma has persisted throughout American history.

The concepts of internalized racism and racial indoctrination are central to one unique aspect of PTSS. This includes teaching kids about racism and the complex role that race plays in society through both direct and indirect signals. The intricate web of emotional and psychological issues that the Black American community faces is exacerbated by these messages, which have been genetically imprinted over many generations.

Not only the horrific history that Black people endured up until Juneteenth, but also the terrifying events of Bloody Summer and Black Wall Street, all the way up to the broadcast lynching of George Floyd, are impactful moments in Black American history, but they are also essential parts of the larger saga of American history. It is important to acknowledge the emotional wounds that persist inside our Black worldview and experiences, in addition to the resilience displayed by Black Americans during the trying 400 years of slavery and ill-treatment.

It is clear from thinking back on these historical crimes that the trauma Black Americans endured is intricately woven into the fabric of the country. Therefore, an understanding of PTSS prompts us to recognize the intricate interplay between historical injustices and their enduring impact on the emotional well-being of Black Americans. As we remember these events, it is crucial to honor the strength and perseverance of Black communities while also acknowledging the ongoing need for healing and redress of the historical wounds that persist. Dr.

DeGruy's work explores how trauma impacts people on a biological cellular level, which is genetically infused into DNA and passed on generationally.

Sexual Warfare That Creates Confusion

It is important for victims of white supremacy not to engage in sexual intercourse with members of the dominant society for several reasons. First and foremost, sexual relationships between victims of white supremacy and members of the dominant society can perpetuate power imbalances and reinforce systems of oppression. Such relationships may also lead to confusion and manipulation, as members of the dominant society use sex as a tool to maintain power and control over non-white individuals.

Historically, white people have used sex as a means of domination and control over non-white individuals. This has taken many forms, including rape and sexual assault, forced sterilization, and the exploitation of non-white men and women as sexual objects. In the context of slavery in the United States, for example, white slave owners routinely raped and sexually abused enslaved persons, both as a means of asserting their dominance and as a way of producing more enslaved children. "The American Slave Coast: A History of the Slave-Breeding Industry by Ned and Constance Sublette" is an exploration of this topic.

Even outside of the context of slavery, white people have used sex as a tool of manipulation and control over non-white individuals. This can take many forms, such as the fetishization of non-white bodies, the portrayal of non-white individuals as sexually deviant or exotic, and the use of sex as a means of blackmail or coercion. In addition to the power dynamics inherent in sexual relationships between members of the dominant society and victims of white supremacy, such relationships can also lead to confusion and internalized oppression. For example, victims of white supremacy who engage in sexual relationships with members of the dominant society may begin to internalize beliefs about their own inferiority or worthlessness. They may also experience feelings of shame or guilt as a result of societal messages that suggest that such relationships are taboo or unacceptable.

It is crucial for victims of white supremacy to be mindful of the power dynamics and potential for manipulation that can arise in sexual relationships with members of the dominant society. By avoiding such relationships, victims can work to maintain their sense of agency and autonomy and resist systems of oppression that seek to control and dominate non-white bodies and minds. In the book "The Iceman Inheritance," Michael Bradley states the following about the white race: "Caucasoids have a greater degree of temporal aggression, as reflected in our wars against nature and man. We Caucasoids are also less well-evolved sexually because we have suggested sexual adaptations conflicted with glacial ones." (Bradley 174).

Throughout history, white people have used sex as a tool of domination and control over non-white individuals. For example, during the colonization of Africa, European colonizers used rape and sexual assault as a way to assert their dominance over African men and women. Similarly, during the Japanese occupation of Korea, Japanese soldiers exploited Korean women as "comfort women" for their own sexual pleasure. Even outside of wartime contexts, non-white bodies have been objectified and fetishized, often perpetuating harmful stereotypes and exoticization.

Pedophilia and Homosexual Warfare

> "Well, considering all animal species indulge
> in homosexuality, I'm sure the Neandertals did
> too. Why not? It's just another form of pair
> bonding."
> ~Lorri Robinson

The manifestation and societal structuring of homosexual relationships in the Roman Empire played a pivotal role as the immediate backdrop shaping early Christian and patristic reactions. These responses ultimately paved the way for the widespread suppression of same-sex conduct in subsequent Western civilization. The roots of this suppression were discernible in influential Roman legal texts from the late antiquity period.

While the Roman approach bore some influence from earlier Greek and Etruscan paradigms, particularly in realms such as literature and art, Roman culture underwent its own distinctive evolution in terms of practices and moral perspectives. Unlike the classical Greek elites, who celebrated voluntary pederastic relationships between adult males and freeborn adolescents, contextualizing them within a pedagogical framework, the Romans held a contrasting view.

In this cultural context, there was a distinction made regarding pederastic relationships (relationships involving an adult male and an adolescent). They were only considered acceptable if they were directed towards individuals who were either current slaves, former slaves, or the spoils of war. This implies that this was the Roman mindset and culture; the acceptability of such relationships was the need to have power over victims, with the notion that it was more permissible when the passive role was assumed by someone in a subordinate social position, such as a slave.

To be clear, the Romans were descendants of Neanderthals, just as the current-day white supremacists are descendants of Roman and Greek lineages. This reflects the intersection of their cultural norms, gender expectations, and power dynamics in ancient Rome until this very moment, offering insight into how psychopathically degenerate their everyday behaviors and relationships were within the broader societal framework.

In the classical Greek cultural milieu, the elite members of society held in high regard voluntary pederastic relationships involving adult males and freeborn adolescents. These relationships were not only accepted but were also elevated, being framed within a pedagogical context. This perspective reflected the belief that such associations had an educational dimension, with the older male guiding and mentoring the younger freeborn adolescent (Hubbard n.p.).

Contrastingly, the Roman societal perspective diverged significantly from the Greek model. The Romans, driven by a conquering warrior ethos essential for the expansionist Roman state, viewed any form of passivity as antithetical to the qualities of manliness and unsuitable for individuals embodying the spirit of Roman conquest. As a result, the Roman cultural ethos rejected the celebration of pederastic relation-ships in the same manner as the Greeks. Instead, they deemed such passive roles as unmanly and fundamentally incompatible with the idealized image of the Roman warrior.

In the Roman context, the legitimacy of pederastic attention took a different form. While relationships between adult males and freeborn adolescents were not sanctioned, there was a conditional acceptance when such attention was directed towards individuals who were either current or former slaves. This nuanced understanding of pederastic relations in Roman society reflects the complex interplay between cultural norms, societal expectations, and the militaristic values that underpinned the Roman state's expansionist ambitions (Hubbard n.p.).

In Larissa Peltola thesis entitled "Rape and Sexual Violence Used as a Weapon of War and Genocide," Peltola describes the "strategies of rape" perpetrators of mass rape and sexual violence exhibit during acts of war and genocide that are driven by diverse motivations. She emphasized that rape in these contexts is primarily about power and control. Recent historical events demonstrate that rape can be a calculated method in genocidal campaigns on a massive scale. Genocidal rape is viewed as a direct assault on the ethnic composition of targeted communities, constituting ethnic cleansing. The killing of an unwanted ethnic population is considered an effective method, and rape is utilized as a tool to achieve similar objectives, including forced impregnation, sterilization, and the use of sexual violence to weaken or destroy a community (Peltola 9).

Rape is an attack on the "body-politic" as much as the body, just like all forms of terror warfare. Its objective is to cripple a socio-political process in order to dominate it as a whole, rather than to kill or maim a single person. It is an assault on both cultural integrity and individual identity. The perspective put forth by Peltola underscores the profound and multifaceted impact of rape in the context of warfare, aligning it with other forms of terror warfare. The assertion that rape constitutes an attack on the "body politic" emphasizes that its destructive aim extends beyond the physical body of the victim. Instead, it is a deliberate strategy intended to cripple a socio-political process, seeking to dominate and subjugate an entire community or society rather than merely causing harm to an individual.

In this view, Peltola describes rape as a tool of power and control with broader sociopolitical implications. The objective is not just to inflict physical pain or injury but to disrupt and dismantle the social fabric of a community. By targeting individuals through sexual violence, the perpetrators aim to undermine the cohesion and stability of the entire community or society. It is a form of violence that goes beyond the immediate act, resonating through the collective consciousness of the affected population (Peltola 13).

Racial violence in particular, or sexual assault, was used as a control mechanism. Peltola uses a comparison to the Mayan communities to stifle any possible insurrections or revolutions. This tactic was especially clear under the Rios Montt dictatorship when the army brutalized and tortured its men in an effort to get them ready to commit genocide. Troops were brainwashed into believing that native settlements were a haven for subversives, and they were trained to degrade native people.

The military was told to repress uprisings and keep control by any means necessary, including heinous attacks on civilian men, women, and children (Peltola 77).

Sexual Warfare Against Black Children

Children in America, particularly Black children, are being exposed to toxic beliefs about gender and sexual concepts. This is a warfare tactic waged by state government agencies, local education boards, and new cultural trends found in entertainment and social media. Using cartoons and television shows that encourage and normalize this deceptive and genocidal war tactic. This is designed to warp the children's minds and eliminate families from existence in the future.

The introduction of harmful ideology into K–12 schools and the erosion of parental rights are all being encouraged by the White House and Congress. President Joe Biden signed a polarizing transgender executive order on the first day of his administration, requiring all K–12 public schools in the country that receive federal funding to implement policies regarding gender identity and sexual orientation. According to the New York City Commission on Human Rights, Executive Order 16 mandates that all city agencies guarantee single-sex facilities, like restrooms and locker rooms, to city workers and the general public in city buildings and areas that correspond with their gender identity or expression. These facilities must be accessible to all without requiring proof of identity, medical records, or any other type of gender verification ("Executive Order on Single-Sex Facilities in City Government Buildings and Areas," n.p.).

My last example of the war on our children is the child terror group called N.A.M.B.L.A. This acronym stands for the North American Man-Boy Love Association. It is an advocacy organization that seeks to promote the acceptance of consensual relationships between adult men and underage boys. The organization has been involved in advocating for changes to the age of consent laws and promoting viewpoints that are generally considered harmful and illegal.

The objectives and convictions of NAMBLA, as expressed by its members, consist of changing the age of consent laws. NAMBLA advocates for the reevaluation and alteration of age of consent laws, arguing for a more permissive approach that would allow for consensual relationships between adults and minors. The organization seeks to challenge what it perceives as the societal stigmatization of intergenerational relationships, particularly those involving adult men and underage boys. NAMBLA has been involved in legal defense cases, providing support to individuals charged with offenses related to adult-minor relationships. The organization contends that not all such relationships involve coercion or harm. Ironically enough, pedophiles believe the word "pedohilia" has too negative of a connotation, It gives them a bad rep, and they would now like to be classified as "minor-attracted people"!

Are Caucasoids Liars?

When it comes to dealing with Black people, white supremacists are pathologically and psychopathically liars. All white people in one way or another think of Black people anywhere on Earth as genetically inferior, that all Black people have low IQs, which justifies their practice of deception, abuse, mistreatment, and even murder. White supremacists have used a variety of tactics to deceive and confuse Black people, including lies, half-truths, and misinformation. By manipulating the truth and presenting false information, white supremacists can create a distorted narrative that supports their racist beliefs and agenda.

One way in which white supremacists have used lies and half-truths is through the spread of conspiracy theories. For example, white supremacists have spread the false claim that Black people are genetically and intellectually inferior to white people. This myth has been debunked by scientific research, but white supremacists continue to use it as a tool for promoting their racist ideology.

Another tactic used by white supremacists is the manipulation of historical facts. They may downplay or ignore the role of Black people in history or distort historical events to fit their narrative. For example, white supremacists may claim that the Civil War was not fought over slavery but rather over states' rights, despite overwhelming evidence to the contrary.

White supremacists use half-truths to deceive and confuse Black people. They may present some information that is true, but then twist it to support their racist beliefs. For instance, a white supremacist might note that crime rates are higher in neighborhoods with a higher concentration of Black residents without addressing the underlying causes of these differences, such as a government, state, and local agenda that is "on-code" and intended to perpetuate systemic racism and poverty.

In addition to these tactics, white supremacists also use language in a way that is intentionally confusing and misleading. They may use coded language or dog whistles to communicate racist ideas without being overtly racist. For example, they may use phrases like "woke," "law and order," "welfare reform," "DEI," and "affirmative action" to communicate racist ideas without explicitly mentioning race.

The use of lies and half-truths is a powerful tool for white supremacists to deceive and confuse Black people. Especially terms like "we are all equal," "we are friends," "I don't see color," and "racism isn't a problem these days." By manipulating information and presenting false narratives, they can reinforce racist beliefs and maintain their grip on power. It is important for Black people to be aware of these tactics and to seek out accurate information from reliable sources in order to resist the influence of white supremacist propaganda.

Frequently, victims of white supremacy will suppress and/or ignore upsetting information that could upset their programmed thoughts because they might stand to gain from the lies they tell themselves and other people. For example, the white supremacists promised freedom for Black enslaved victims in the American Revolutionary War (April 19, 1775–September 3, 1783) and the American Civil War (April 12, 1861–May 26, 1865). I'm referring to the false consciousnesses and lies that white people propagate in both themselves and other people. Thus, the thinking of white supremacists is threatened by the truth and an authentic history. They (racist men, women, and child) are able to preserve their sense of self and their perception of who they stand for because they project this mythology onto history.

In the article "10 Pathological Liar Signs and How to Cope with a Habitual Liar," we can compare these 10 signs to any white person that you may have been around to see if my theory is correct. According to this article, pathological lying is linked to distorted thought patterns and beliefs, with the term "pathological" suggesting an underlying pathology or illness. As a result, symptoms of pathological lying are linked to a number of mental health issues. Pathological lying, also known as mythomania and unhealthy lying, is characterized by unusually complex and comprehensive deception that lasts for years or even centuries.

Compulsive lying can also be a sign of narcissistic or antisocial personality disorders, in which people lie to gain sympathy, elevate their social standing, or uphold a false sense of who they are. Lying may be a tactic used by white people with borderline personality disorder (BPD) to avoid rejection or abandonment, which can also show indications of pathological lying ("10 Pathological Liar Signs and How to Cope with a Habitual Liar," n.p.).

Using the article as a template, identifying a pathological liar involves recognizing consistent dishonesty and the weaving of fictional narratives. While suspecting that a person is a white supremacist, noticeable indicators of pathological lying/white supremacists include:

1. Creating elaborate details to support lies.
   Example: The Ancient Egyptians were white.
2. Telling exciting tales that are completely unbelievable.

Example: Christopher Columbus discovered America.

3. Displaying nervousness when conversing.

Example: I can't be racist, my best friend is Black.

4. Being combative when questioned about racism.

Example: What about Black-on-Black crime?

5. Continuously changing their story or remaining evasive when questioned.

Example: A Black man raped me, officer!

6. Acting dishonestly for no apparent reason.

Example: If you decide you are not a boy, you can decide to become a girl.

7. Acting unaffected when exposed as a liar.

Example: George Floyd did not die from an officer's knee on his neck for 9 minutes; he died from a drug overdose!

8. Being filled with excitement after successfully tricking someone.

Example: Organizing research like HR-40, a Commission to Study and Develop Reparation Proposals for Black Americans Act, to figure out whether Black people are deserving to receive reparations for their enslavement from 1776 until 1865.

9. Pretending to be a whole other race of people.

Example: Five Dollar Indians/The Dawes Rolls is a list of people who the Dawes Commission recognized as belonging to the Cherokee, Creek, Choctaw, Chickasaw, and Seminole Indian tribes between 1898 and 1914. People referred to as "Five-Dollar Indians" are another problem on the Dawes Rolls. The practice of white supremacists paying five dollars to government officials to be classified as Native Americans in order to receive land that was allotted for Native Americans. This was a very common practice.

10. Acting in a way that is inconsistent with what they have said.

Example: I'm not racist, but all Black people are lazy.

- Pathological liars are going to maintain their story even when it is visible to everyone that they are lying. You should not expect a white supremacist to acknowledge the truth, even if you can show them to be lying. Above all, remember that you should attempt not to take offense when interacting with a white supremacist. Psychopaths who are pathological liars are unable to stop lying because they have an underlying mental illness.

Since pathological liars are accustomed to lying or may even believe what they are saying, they can easily maintain eye contact while lying, eye contact is not a reliable predictor of authenticity. Remain calm. The more you are around them, the greater the risk of a white supremacist lying to you.

- Instead of listening to what white supremacists say, pay attention to what appears to be their actions to gain an impression of who they are; trust what makes sense, is truthful, and is reality. More information can be gleaned from their body language than from their words. Establish boundaries whenever you are around people who seem to be white supremacists ("10 Pathological Liar Signs and How to Cope with a Habitual Liar," n.p.).

Psychopath white supremacists frequently employ pathological lying as a means of control, manipulation, and maintain trickery over other people, especially Black people. Although psychopaths are sometimes portrayed in the mainstream media as charming, charismatic villains, the truth is usually more ominous. In addition to their propensity for lying, psychopathic white supremacists are also more likely to commit violent crimes, frequently against Black people and even other white people whom they perceive to be "race traders" or "off code." They also pose a threat to everyone nearby because of their tendency toward manipulation and violence, which makes it difficult for others to understand their genuine motivations

There is a complex relationship between pathological liars and psychopathy. Although pathological lying is not solely exclusive to psychopaths, it is a common tendency among those who suffer from mental illness. It's critical to comprehend the fundamental causes of pathological lying. But it becomes important to recognize when pathological liars are motivated by psychopathic tendencies, because not doing so could have dangerous repercussions (Hart n.p.).

In navigating the convoluted terrain of white supremacy and its intricate ties to societal dynamics, I find myself contemplating the intricate interplay of ideologies, biases, and systemic influences that perpetuate this harmful construct. White supremacy, a toxic belief in the inherent superiority of all racial groups, extends its roots beyond mere prejudice, entwining itself with historical narratives, power structures, and cultural perceptions.

Much like pathological lying, white supremacy defies easy categorization. It thrives not only on explicit acts of racism but also on subtle, systemic manifestations embedded in various facets of society. It is a web of distorted beliefs woven into the fabric of historical injustices, perpetuating injustice through a combination of conscious and subconscious actions.

Recognizing the insidious nature of white supremacy within the context of societal structures becomes paramount. It is not confined to explicit acts of hate but manifests in systemic biases, microaggressions, deception, and trickery. The failure to discern these subtleties risks perpetuating a cycle of oppression, undermining the collective well-being of Black people.

The "Ten Best Lies of Black History" were provided by the N.O.I. Research Group. In addition to demonstrating the psychopathic, pathological drive of white supremacists to propagate lies, N.O.I. provides a general summary or beginning point for some of the many lies and deceptions by Caucasoids:

1. The first humans to inhabit Earth were white.
2. Black people in slavery were limited to maids and cotton pickers.
3. Slaves were emancipated by Lincoln.

4. In Africa, Black people ate each other.

5. God cursed Black people.

6. Black people have substantially benefited from government assistance in the US.

7. The pyramids were built by Jews.

8. Black people forced other Black people into slavery.

9. The North was free of slavery.

10. Columbus was the first to discover America.

Lie #1. Mendel's Law is used to expose the myth that white people were the first to emerge on Earth, highlighting the biological concept that states that Black skin is dominant and white skin is recessive. It emphasizes the genetic evidence that Africa is the [hu]man ancestor's home, which is corroborated by recent University of Chicago tests that show a major genetic shift 6,600 years ago. Contrary to the claim that whites were the initial [hu]mans, the genetic alteration that Dr. Francis Cress Welsing spoke about aligns with Elijah Muhammad's teachings about the birth of the white race. Additionally, it discusses the advanced civilization of Black-skinned Egyptians predating Neanderthals, highlighting the lack of skills in the latter despite their curiosity about Egyptian structures like pyramids. The encounters between Egyptians and the nomadic Tamahu, marked by white skin, resulted in disruptive consequences for the Egyptians. Overall, the statement debunks the historical inaccuracy of whites being the first [hu]mans while providing biological and genetic evidence supporting Africa as the cradle of humanity.

Lie #2. Challenges the misconception that Blacks in slavery were limited to "cotton pickers" and "maids." Contrary to this stereotype, historical evidence reveals that whites coveted Black people for their skills, with many being skilled artisans, engineers, architects, carpenters, mechanics, brick masons, nurses, blacksmiths, seamstresses, and bakers. The narrative emphasizes the significant contributions of Black slaves to America's infrastructure, buildings, roads, bridges, and railways, dispelling the notion that their role was confined to menial tasks.

Lie #3. Debunks the myth that Abraham Lincoln freed the slaves with the Emancipation Proclamation. While commonly believed, a closer examination of the proclamation reveals that it only applied to slaves in rebellious states, allowing loyal states to retain their Africans as slaves. The statement exposes Lincoln's prejudiced views toward Black people and challenges the idealized image of him as a liberator of slaves, asserting that such perceptions were created by historians and Hollywood myth-makers.

Lie #4. Addresses the false claim that Blacks in Africa practiced cannibalism. Historical accounts, including Captain John Smith's writings, provide evidence that early European settlers, not Africans, engaged in acts of cannibalism. The statement highlights how accusations of cannibalism were often used as a justification for the subjugation of indigenous populations. While the white supremacist murderers of Nat Turner consumed his flesh.

Lie #5. The historical lie that Blacks were cursed Black by God is commonly known as the Curse of Ham or Hamitic Myth. It traces the origins of this racial belief system to the Biblical story of Noah (Genesis 9:21–27) and its distortion by Talmudic rabbis. The narrative involves God supposedly cursing Noah's son Ham and his descendants with Black skin. The statement highlights the economic motivation behind the creation of this racist myth by Jewish traders dominating the early slave trade. Initially, race played no role in selecting victims, but over time, Africans' perceived skills, intelligence, and strength led to their marketability, justifying the racial focus on the "God-cursed" African. This distortion of the Noah story served to sanctify the African-centered slave trade and was widely adopted by major religions to assert white supremacy throughout the centuries.

Lie #6. Challenges the belief that the U.S. government has actively supported the success of Black individuals. By pointing to the FBI's actions against civil rights organizations during the civil rights era and its suspected involvement in the murders of Black leaders, it asserts a long history of government oppression against non-white communities.

Lie #7. Is the notion that Jews built the pyramids, clarifying that scholars have discredited this claim. The statement argues that the pyramids predate any mention of Hebrews in history and suggests that the ancient Egyptians kept meticulous records, which contain no mention of the supposed Jewish involvement in pyramid construction.

Lie #8. Addresses the misconception that Africans sold other Africans into slavery. The statement exposes the role of European slave merchants, particularly Portuguese and Jewish slave traders, who manipulated mixed-race individuals to infiltrate African communities and facilitate the capture and enslavement of native Africans.

Lie #9. Challenges the belief that while slavery was just as prevalent in the northern parts of America as well as the southern regions, it was still practiced in the northern states during the colonial and early American periods. However, by the early 19th century, northern states began to abolish slavery through gradual emancipation laws. These laws were supposed to provide for the gradual freeing of enslaved people. By the time of the American Civil War in the 1860s, slavery had been abolished throughout the Northern States. So while the Northern part of America became free of slavery earlier than the South, it was not entirely free of slavery during earlier periods.

Lie #10. Disputes the idea that Columbus discovered America by highlighting his prior involvement in the African slave trade and his lack of originality in the so-called "discovery." The statement points out that Indigenous peoples had already established trade relationships with Africans, and Columbus himself encountered evidence suggesting prior visitors to the Americas (N.O.I. RESEARCH GROUP n.p.).

Other lies that the dominant white supremacist society promotes are:

- Intellectual Inferiority: One of the most pervasive lies is the false notion that Black individuals are intellectually inferior. This stereotype has been used historically to justify discriminatory practices and policies.
- Stereotypes in the Media: The media has aided in the continuation of negative stereotypes about Black people by portraying

them in limited and oftentimes unfavorable roles. Insensitive depictions of Black people in films, TV series, and other media consist of making them into "The Big Bad Black Boogie Man."

- Minimization of Achievements: Achievements of Black peoples in various fields, including science, literature, arts, and politics, have been minimized or overlooked. This perpetuates the false idea that significant contributions were only made by whites.
- Criminalization and Stereotyping of Black Men: Black men are often extremely criminalized in media and society, contributing to negative stereotypes. The disproportionate portrayal of Black men as criminals reinforces harmful biases and can lead to discriminatory practices.
- Denial of Historical Wrongs: The dominant society habitually downplays or downright denies historical wrongs such as slavery, segregation, and systemic racism. This denial destroys efforts to address ongoing issues related to racial injustices.
- Monolithic Representations: Viewing the Black community as a single, homogenous entity, or "One Big Negro," and approving of other groups mistreatment of Black people while downplaying the diversity that exists within it.
- Black people are dirty: "Coprophilia, the love of filth," refers to a specific fetish or paraphilia where some Eastern Europeans derive sexual pleasure or arousal from feces or the act of defecation. The term "coprophilia" is derived from two Greek words: "copro," meaning feces, and "philia," meaning love or strong affinity. People with coprophilia may find the smell, sight, or thought of feces sexually stimulating. In 1957, a young microbiologist named Stanley Falkow started asking sick people to swallow their own feces. Read the book entitled "Dirt" by Terence McLaughlin.

10

The Coon's Mental Dilemma, Also Known As "The Jesus Gene"

Religion is the organization of spirituality into something that became the handmaiden of conquerors. Nearly all religions were brought to people and imposed on people by conquerors, and used as the framework to control their minds.
~John Henrik Clarke

The word "Raccoon" or "coon' has a negative, degrading meaning. Like the caricature of the "Sambo" negro, the coon was portrayed as lazy, easily startled, uninterested, uninspiring, and a clown. The coon and sambo were comparable, yet they were also very different. While the coon, while displaying juvenile behavior, was recognized as an adult, albeit one of limited worth, racist white people believe that all Black people are "Sambos," incapable of forever living independently. In contrast to Sambo's depiction as a devoted and happy worker, the coon's persona supported segregation and slavery.

By the 1900s, Sambo had come to be identified with older, sub-missive Black people who followed social mores and Jim Crow rules. On the other hand, Coons were more frequently associated with young Black people living in urban ghetto areas who showed disrespect for white people. Put another way, the Coon was perceived as a departure from the Sambo stereotype, which was initially docile. Pure Coons were portrayed as being worthless, untrustworthy, mentally unstable, lazy, and subhuman; they were good for nothing and only interested in gambling, parlor games, and eating watermelons. They were also depicted as being unable to speak clearly, mispronouncing words, and misusing the "good white men's" English language.

They said that Black people were foolish, hedonistic children who were destined for indolence, or worse, if left to their own devices. White people used to differentiate between negroes (Toms, Sambos, and Mammies) and niggers (Coons and Bucks). something that prevents you from moving forward. Toms, Sambos, Mammies, Coons, and Bucks were known to "sell you down the river." This expression has a more sinister past, but now it connotes a deadly betrayal. In the 1800s, Black slaves were essentially sold down the river. Slave traders traveled down the Mississippi River, selling Black people into slavery to plantation owners further south. There would be horrible working conditions and often deadly labor.

Some Black people have reclaimed the term "Coon," repurposing it as an intraracial slur directed at a specific type of Black person perceived to betray their own race. In contemporary usage, a "Coon" aligns closely with the concept of an "Uncle Tom." This term characterizes a Black individual who deliberately performs in a manner pleasing to white people, saying or doing things to win their favor and receive social rewards. It involves a quid pro quo, where the individual conforms to certain expectations that uplift and maintain the system of white supremacy while denigrating and sabotaging their own Black race in exchange for benefits from the white community. For instance, a Black radio host, Jesse L. Peterson, expressing gratitude for slavery and defending Jim Crow, illustrates this behavior. The damage caused by "Cooning" extends to its public visibility, as the Black individual's actions are witnessed by many.

Cooning is characterized as a public act that either accepts blatant instances of racism white supremacist behavior in exchange for a favor. Individuals who identify as Black and those who interact with others in public while demonstrating a quid pro quo behavior that denies racism are considered to be Cooning. As a collective, Black people are interested in surviving and resisting white supremacy, as well as attempting to find happiness in a society where anti-Black racism is prevalent and committed to depriving Black people of their basic needs.

A Coon's treachery can take many forms, like supporting anti-Black racist policies, choosing legislation against Black people and families, actively taking part in activities that negatively impact Black communities and families, and supporting and cooperating with systems of white supremacist structures for oppression. A Coon is essentially a trader to their Black race. With only personal gain, only to desire close proximity to white people, and the desire to use any means necessary to gain acceptance within the dominant group, trumping the constructive interests of Black people collectively and the well-being of their Black communities.

Words like Coon, sellouts, Oreo's, whitewashed, et cetera serve as a warning to other Black people, who do not practice the same ideology, informing them that certain actions that harm the group's interests will not be accepted and will result in consequences. Excommunication and harsh criticism are appropriate responses for Black individuals who support white supremacist policies, as this will benefit the larger group of Black victims of racism and white supremacy.

However, Black people must be permitted to defend themselves against individuals who jeopardize the welfare of their race. A Coon is any Black person who has the chance to support our communities or other Black people but decides against it since doing so maintains the racist, white status quo. A Coon is also a Black person who white people use as a token and are put into positions to be the racist white supremacist mouthpiece.

The Jesus Gene

In the Bible, Jesus says if someone hits you, then you are to "turn the other cheek." Meaning let the person hit you on the other side of your face, to love and pray for your enemies, and to forgive those who persecute you. I say stop defending white people, who have historically been Black people's natural enemies. Similar to the lion and the gazelle's relationship. Black people are easily manipulated and are offered false promises for their loyalty, and the only loyalty that Black people get in 2024 is the hope for white acceptance, which is equivalent to being next to white Jesus. African tribes that sold Black people into slavery got trinkets; they literally received trinkets for selling Black people out. Those who are "selling out" today receive only white validation and a pat on the head for their treachery. We have to wake up from our useless slumber. Some are given money, fame, or close proximity to whiteness; more often, these are non-tangible hopes and dreams received for selling their soul.

Black people have been beaten down to become the way we are, our strength striped away in order to benefit the white supremacist psychopath. Starting from a Black person's childhood (possibly conception), they only give us lies, misinformation, ignorance, imprisonment, and death. And in turn, we reward them with our loyalty by believing anything and everything that they say. The white supremacists' goal is domination and control over their Black objects. Most Black people will read this and think about it for a few moments and go right back to sleep or back into a submissive position to be dictated to, while others, which is only a small few, will heed these words and become the God's the universe intended you to be.

The Jesus Gene has been environmentally and genetically introduced to all colonized-minded Black people, first through extreme brutality, violence, starvation, and horrific sexual abuse. The pairing of the colonization process and the implantation of Christian ideology causes Black people to reject any sound teaching and always defend the white master's programming. This psychological dysfunction has lasted in Black people for hundreds of years. So here lies the question: why? Why is it that, through fear and terror, this genetic modification and very much abnormal modification has occurred? According to William Lynch, if you use certain methods, the slave owner can accomplish this genetic mutation of mind manipulation for hundreds or even thousands of years. "I guarantee every one of you that if installed correctly, it will control the slaves for at least 300 years" (William Lynch 1). Dr. Joy DeGruy discusses studies that prove that a generation exposed to trauma has genetic and behavioral changes that pass down to subsequent generations.

Black folks have gotten into the bad habit of relying on every word that "white mommy" and "white daddy" tell us, mostly at our own peril. Every habit, as it turns out, originates from a psychological sequence known as a "habit loop," a three-step process. Initially, there is a cue or trigger signaling the brain to switch to automatic mode and initiate a particular behavior. The second component is the routine, which encompasses the behavior itself, constituting what we typically associate with habits. According to Duhigg, the third and final stage is the reward—a pleasing outcome that reinforces the "habit loop" in the brain for future reference. Our reward (Black people) is white "acceptance,"validation and a pat on the head.

Neuroscientists have identified the basal ganglia in the brain region, which are responsible for our habit-forming behaviors. This area, integral to emotions, memories, and pattern recognition, plays a crucial role in the development of habits. Decision-making, on the other hand, occurs in a separate part of the brain called the prefrontal cortex. Once a behavior becomes automatic, the decision-making section of the brain essentially enters a rest mode.

"In fact, the brain starts working less and less," explains Duhigg. "The brain can almost completely shut down. And this is a real advantage because it means you have all of this mental activity you can devote to something else" ("Habits: How They Form And How To Break Them," n.p.). Unconsciously, certain habits arise from stress, either internal or external. These are typically negative or dysfunctional habits. The most common method of control in modern life is punishment, seen in various forms such as physical force, legal consequences, religious sanctions, and educational measures like wipes and beating rods. Punishment aims to reduce undesirable behaviors, contrasting with reinforcement, which seeks to strengthen desired tendencies. The extent to which punishment is employed appears to be constrained only by the level of power attainable for enforcement (Skinner 182).

The recessive "Jesus Gene" allows Black people to escape personal responsibility for their actions and remain in a constant state of blaming others. The "Jesus Gene" allows all Black people to participate in their own personal destruction. Black people who have the "Jesus Gene" will support family members to sell crack and deadly drugs to other family members, while the children and any observer who may be witnessing can see behavior that is non-constructive, full of debauchery, self-hatred, and immoral filth. The common response is to say we must forgive as Jesus forgave us, supporting the destruction of their family. And in the same breath, wondering why there are so many funerals and defective families. Often, the only solution that they can come up with is "I will pray for you." This is the "Coon Minded Status Quo." The Latin term "status quo" refers to the current situation, especially when it comes to social, political, religious, scientific, or military matters. The term "status quo" in sociology describes the existing social structure or ideals.

Those who possess the "Jesus Gene " will always forgive and defend the killers of our Black people who are in the white dominant society. For example, in Botham Jean's case in 2018, after work, Amber Guyger, a Houston police officer and suspected white supremacist, entered Jean's apartment when the 26-year-old was eating ice cream. Because Guyger, a white woman, believed Jean, a Black accountant from St. Lucia who lived one level above her, was a burglar, Guyger shot and killed Jean. Jean's brother was at the sentencing as he turned to face the judge on the witness stand, Brandt Jean's voice broke, and he begged to embrace the person who had slain his brother. "I don't know if this is possible, but can I give her a hug, please?" he asked. "PLEASE?" "Yes," District Judge Tammy Kemp said. Brandt was raised in the Church of Christ in St. Lucia "I think giving your life to Christ would be the best thing that Botham would want you to do," Brandt Jean said. "Again, I love you as a person, and I don't wish anything bad on you," he told Guyger. He wiped a tear from his eye and stepped off the witness stand to hug her. Sobs could be heard in the courtroom as the two hugged. Kemp (the Black judge) hugged and wiped Guyger's tears from her eyes and gave her a Bible: the "Jesus Gene."

The "Jesus Gene" Is always accompanied by "Stockholm Syndrome" and "Cognitive Dissonance." This cognitive dissonance is a mental conflict that occurs when your beliefs don't line up with your actions. An example is a Christian who reads the Bible and believes fully and wholeheartedly in it, who attends church, and still will justify homosexuality and the killing of Black babies (abortions). Although the mass majority of Black people will not practice homosexuality or get an abortion, they will vote for politicians who support these destructive policies.

Stockholm syndrome is a psychological response wherein a captive begins to identify closely with his or her captors, as well as with their agenda and demands (Lambert). The same example above applies to this syndrome as well. "It's an uncomfortable state of mind when someone has contradictory values, attitudes, or perspectives about the same thing," says psychiatrist Grant H. Brenner, MD. Individuals involved in cults may exhibit behaviors indicative of Stockholm syndrome. They may defend or support the leader, even in the face of harmful or dangerous actions.

Merriam-Webster offers five definitions for the word 'cult,' three of which I have included:

1: a system of religious beliefs and rituals.

2: formal religious veneration; worship (correcting 'warship' to 'worship').

3: a system for the cure of disease based on dogma set forth by its promulgator.

Black people who possess this "Jesus Gene" exhibit this behavior and participate in cult-like activities, beliefs, and actions. Black American slaves suffered this for hundreds of years, and now the descendants of slaves in the so-called "modern times" experience psychological trauma generationally, which is a more subtle and refined form of Stockholm syndrome. Cues and triggers include internalized racism, economic dependency, cultural alienation, educational disparities, and influence.

- Internalized racism is one facet where Black people internalize societal attitudes and white supremacist structures that perpetuate racism, aligning with the dominant culture even if it contradicts their own interests.
- Economic disparities contribute to a situation where Black people are economically dependent on systems that sustain inequality, potentially influencing attitudes that appear to align with the dominant culture.
- Cultural alienation and displacement have led to the adoption of norms and values outside one's heritage and culture, seen as a survival strategy amid societal expectations aligned with systematic white supremacy.
- Educational barriers also hinder knowledge of past wrongdoings and cultural legacies, which encourages acceptance of stories that minimize structural injustices. Another factor that shapes views and reinforces unfavorable stereotypes that affect how people view themselves is how they are portrayed and represented in the media. Systemic oppression and generational trauma have a very substantial negative influence on Black people's psychological health that should not be disregarded or undervalued.

Religion is the tool often wielded by white conquerors to establish dominion. Across diverse cultures, religions haven't organically emerged but rather been introduced and enforced by those in positions of conquest. This imposition serves a dual purpose: to bring a semblance of order and control to the conquered and to shape the narrative that governs their minds. The symbiotic relationship between white conquerors and religious frameworks underscores the role of spirituality as a means of governance. It operates as a handmaiden to those in power, offering a structured avenue to channel beliefs, values, and behaviors. By molding religious narratives, conquerors can effectively mold the minds of the conquered, creating a framework that serves their interests. This historical pattern prompts critical reflection on the origins and intentions behind widely practiced religions. Understanding the entwined history of conquest and religious imposition reveals the power dynamics at play. It encourages a discerning approach to spirituality, urging individuals to scrutinize the origins and manipulative potential inherent in the religious frameworks handed down through generations.

What Qualifies a Person to Be a White Supremacist?

There is a little bit of Hitler in all white people.
~Khalid Abdul Muhammad

First of all, you have to be white and/or be classified as white in order to be a qualifying member and be allowed to be a participant in white supremacy. White supremacy is an ideology, and this thought process entails intentional participation and engagement for all who are racially classified as "white." The only way for a white person to be considered a white supremacist is if they actively participate in and practice the ideology of white supremacy. In addition to neglecting to conduct the most effective anti-racist actions to help replace the system of white supremacy with a system of justice, tiny acts of racism can range from planning the complete elimination of an entire nation or group of Black people.

Those white people who should not be considered white supremacists are infants who can't decipher color, and/or those white people who are blind, mute, deaf, wheelchair-bound, and invalid cannot be white supremacists; those who lack the cognitive awareness and/or mental faculties that hinder them from engaging in racial ideologies and practices cannot be an active white supremacist. An infant, for instance, is incapable of discerning between colors or comprehending racial concepts, while a severely disabled person may have diminished cognitive abilities that prevent active participation in such ideologies.

This emphasizes that conscious engagement in white supremacist ideology and behavior is necessary, with a focus on action. This viewpoint promotes the idea that those who identify as white should undoubtedly uphold white supremacist views, arguing that the term should only be applied to those who actively support and engage in the ideology. White supremacy is an innate quality founded only on racial identification, and it is a purposeful and intentional decision. So I have concluded that those white people who do fit into the aforementioned categories cannot be white supremacists. A white person who is classified as white should always be suspected of being a "suspected white supremacist" until that person practices white supremacy in any form, whether subtle or extreme. Remember that all it takes to be identified as a white supremacist is one action; one does not have to practice white supremacy 500 times to qualify as one. At that point, he or she is now verified as a white supremacist based on their actions, not just "suspected" of being one at that precise moment. Just one act of practicing white supremacy qualifies a white person to always be a white supremacist and no longer a suspected one. Black people who suffer from the *"Jesus gene"* cannot or will not be able to recognize a white supremacist unless it is in extreme cases, such as Derek Chauvin kneeling on George Floyd's neck for nine minutes. Most (but not all) Black people would agree that Chauvin is a racist white supremacist.

The main tools used by white supremacists collectively and individually are lies, misinformation, and being deceitful. This action further widens the power imbalance resulting from their untruthfulness. Lies are very powerful and deadly, and the white supremacists are the greatest liars of all time. The white supremacist lies embodied "*The Whiteness of Destruction"* and killed countless thousands of black people over the centuries because of lies that were and are used to deceive and control Black people. The main effects of this growing power imbalance are that it produces an atmosphere where the victim of deception is more vulnerable to the choices and actions of the power hierarchy. As this power differential widens, so does the impression of dependence on the powerful individual for information, resources, and services. The person who has been duped feels less powerful and self-sufficient, which makes them easier to manipulate and take advantage of. Under the system of white supremacist racism, members of the white majority have the potential to exert tremendous harm merely by lying to Black people.

All of this is said because there is a method for identifying potential white supremacists. It occurs when someone who is white tells you something that is not true. No matter how big or tiny the lie, this is the first indication that the person you are speaking with is a white supremacist. Many Black people have lost their lives and towns like Tulsa, Oklahoma, Rosewood, and thousands of other Black towns worldwide because of white lies.

Passive-Aggressive Racism White Supremacy

Passive-aggressive racism refers to a form of white supremacist discrimination or bias where people in the dominant society express their racism indirectly or subtly, often through non-verbal behaviors, microaggressions, or covert actions. Unlike overt or explicit racism, passive-aggressive racism may not involve explicit racist language or actions but manifest in ways that are insidious and harder to identify. This form of racism can be more subtle and may include behaviors such as:

- **Microaggressions**: Microaggressions are subtle, often seeming unintentional, comments or actions that communicate derogatory messages about a person's race or ethnicity.
- **Stereotyping:** Employing stereotypes about a particular racial or ethnic group in a seemingly harmless manner, but with negative implications.
- **Exclusion:** Engaging in exclusionary practices that may not be overtly racist but have the effect of isolating or marginalizing individuals based on their race.
- **Withholding Opportunities:** Discriminating against Black people by withholding opportunities, resources, or benefits based on their race, often without explicitly stating the discriminatory intent.
- **Undermining Achievements:** Discrediting or downplaying the achievements of Black people from a specific racial or ethnic background, either directly or indirectly.
- **Color Blindness:** Ignoring or dismissing the experiences of Black people by claiming not to see or acknowledge racial differences, which can invalidate the challenges we face.
- **Jokes and Humor:** Using racial jokes or humor that may appear harmless on the surface but perpetuate stereotypes and contribute to a hostile environment.
- **Backhanded Compliments:** Offering compliments that seem positive but contain an underlying negative or patronizing message related to a person's race.

Identifying passive-aggressive racism proves challenging since it often operates beneath the surface, rendering it elusive for both Black people who are directly affected and bystanders. The covert nature of these discriminatory behaviors makes them less apparent and, consequently, harder to spot. As Black people navigate this systematic white supremacist landscape, I find it not too difficult to recognize these subtle manifestations of racism, as they might be veiled in seemingly innocuous actions or comments. This inherent invisibility underscores the insidious nature of passive-aggressive racism.

White Supremacist Tattoos, Haircuts, and Clothing

Self proclaimed white nationalists, neo-Nazis, and white supremacists planned the 'Unite the Right' demonstration in Charlottesville, Virginia, in 2017 to protest the removal of a Confederate monument. Attendees and counter-protesters engaged in physical altercations when the gathering turned violent. Heather was killed when a car driven by a white nationalist crashed into a crowd. The demonstration brought attention to radicalism and racial problems in the US. White nationalists are people or organizations that support the upholding of a perceived white identity and frequently advance racially discriminatory views. They might back laws that discriminate against multiculturalism and favor white people.

The Ku Klux Klan, according to Cam Wolf's article "The New Uniform of White Supremacy," resurrected as a predominantly white supremacist organization beginning in 1915. It adopted the now-iconic white robes for two purposes: to terrify and to conceal. Many white supremacists wearing khakis and well-fitting polos turned the business-casual dull uniform into a refined statement of white supremacist fashion. According to Susan Campbell Bartoletti, author of "Hitler Youth Growing Up in Hitler's Shadow and They Called Themselves the K.K.K.: The Birth of an American Terrorist Group," what we see in a lot of images coming out of Charlottesville are these very clean-cut-looking young men (Wolf n.p.).

In addition to exposing the defects and rotting of American society in a plethora of other ways, that weekend also made clear: that vigilantes with cloaks and daggers no longer carry out the work of white supremacy. It is carried out during the day. And it's carried out by individuals (mainly young, white men) dressed in khakis and polos, the most stereotypically American outfits. Today, the uniform of white hatred is commonplace, unremarkable, and a part of daily American life (Wolf n.p.).

Following the development of white supremacist organizations' attire, particularly that of the Klan, reveals that they appear to have completed a long-term image makeover. Although racism has always been a part of both historical and contemporary America, the victory of Donald Trump gave legitimacy to a minority that previously felt it was necessary to hide. As a result, white hate's attire has evolved and is now more widely accepted. Things that gave away the wearer's affiliation with any given white supremacist organization, such as suspenders, a shaved head, Doc Martens, and a long list of tattoos (Wolf n.p). Even though these marks were tiny, they weren't typical. You could probably identify a white nationalist goon if you spotted a man with a shaved head wearing suspenders and Doc Martens with red or white laces. Proud Boys and other groups have tried to brand Fred Perry polos, which the company has strongly condemned.

Since the Proud Boys have long been associated with skinheads, groups like them have tried to claim ownership of Fred Perry polos (the brand has vehemently repudiated the group). The widespread use of khakis and polos is the result of white nationalists' persistent effort to change their image from that of the other to that of the mainstream (Wolf n.p.).

"We support wearing casual attire, as seen in most offices or at church. Please don't wear 'biker' or camouflage [sic] apparel" (Wolf n.p.). The sheet forbade the use of weapons and profane language. "If I didn't know I was at the Klan meeting, they would have seemed like very ordinary people that I would see in the supermarket where I live" (Wolf, n.p.). The Klan is reorienting itself in terms of both attire and philosophy. The Klan today professes to be about a perverted form of "love"—"love for the white race," according to Bartoletti, despite the fact that its initial iterations were established on hate. This is, at least in part, the reason behind the increased readiness of white nationalists to appear in public on video. "They think that promoting whiteness and the virtues associated with it is their goal" (Wolf,n.p.).

According to Wolf, style is a propaganda tactic for the alt-right; individuals like Richard Spencer, who espouse overtly racist views, dress in what is referred to as "dapper" ways to give them an air of respectability. They were attempting to fit in. And in the process, they've given our closet's most boring objects a dog whistle. Does your neighbor have on khakis and a polo shirt? It's also important to note how strikingly similar President Trump's off-duty attire is to the new white nationalist outfit. A protester wearing khakis, a white polo shirt, and a Make America Great Again (MAGA) cap doesn't seem to be much different from one another (Wolf n.p.).

The choice of khakis, a polo shirt, and a MAGA cap by some white nationalists reflects a deliberate effort to present a more mainstream and ordinary image. This clothing combination is associated with a casual, everyday style that aims to blend in with mainstream American fashion. By adopting such attire, white nationalists attempt to appear non-threatening and relatable, contrasting with traditional extremist symbols. Additionally, the MAGA cap signifies political alignment with the Trump administration, and the overall ensemble serves as a subtle means of expressing support for nationalist and conservative ideologies while attempting to normalize their extremist views in broader society (Wolf n.p.).

The MAGA phrase frequently conjures up nostalgic memories of an era in American history marked by pervasive and widespread systematic racism, segregation, and discrimination against Black people. The phrase refers to historical eras that were considered "great" by white supremacists, like the Jim Crow era, the freedom to hang or lynch black people, destroy families, and burn down towns without facing any consequences from the law. Along with countless other instances of racial injustice.

My concern, among many others, is that the term unintentionally and deliberately harkens back to a period before significant advancements in civil rights. During these and earlier times, racial injustices became institutionalized, and Black Americans continue to face systemic oppression in public spaces, voting rights, education, and other areas of daily life. I argue that by not explicitly addressing historical anti-Black racism/white supremacy, the slogan is perceived as dismissive of the struggles faced by Black communities.

11

Get Ready and Stay Ready

"Intelligence is a game of imperfect information. We can guess our opponent's moves, but we can't be sure until the game is over."
— *Khalid Muhammad, Agency Rules: Never an Easy Day at the Office*

"The white race is absolutely disagreeable to get along with in peace. No other people on the face of the earth have been able to get along with white people since white people have been on our planet."
—*Khalid Muhammad*

In a world increasingly marked by uncertainty and unrest, preparing for a spectrum of potential crises becomes not just a choice but a responsibility. My journey toward readiness begins with acknowledging the unpredictable nature of natural disasters that can strike without warning. Establishing a comprehensive emergency plan, from evacuation routes to communication strategies, becomes the foundation for navigating these challenges.

Beyond the forces of nature, the specter of potential uprisings, economic disruptions, and civic unrest looms on the horizon. Adapting to these volatile scenarios requires a dual focus on financial preparedness and community engagement. Diversifying assets and maintaining an emergency fund become essential tools for navigating economic storms, while building connections within our community fosters a sense of collective strength.

A serious response is required in light of the possibility of civil unrest and the dire possibility of a civil war/race war. It becomes crucial to implement self-defense techniques, home security systems, and legal compliance. In addition to ensuring our personal safety, we also want to strengthen the bonds that bind our families and communities together. The combination of resource management, planning, and self-defense appears in this multifaceted pattern of preparedness as a comprehensive reaction to the various problems that our always-changing world may bring. As I commit to this journey, it becomes a means of protecting not only myself but also the Black community's overall well-being in the face of an uncertain future. These tools ought to be accessible to all Black individuals and families in an emergency. Here are some broad pointers to get you ready:

A bug-out bag, often abbreviated as BOB, is a portable kit that contains essential items to help an individual or family survive and sustain themselves during an emergency or disaster situation. The primary purpose of a bug-out bag is to provide the necessary resources for a short-term evacuation or survival scenario. It is designed to be easily carried and readily accessible, allowing individuals to quickly "bug out" or leave their current location to reach a safer place.

Key components typically found in a bug out bag include:

- **Basic Survival Gear:**
    - First aid kit
    - Multi-tool or knife

- ○ Fire-starting tools (lighter, waterproof matches, or fire starter)
- ○ Emergency whistle

- **Shelter and Clothing:**
  - ○ Lightweight, compact tent or tarp
  - ○ Weather-appropriate clothing (including a hat and gloves)
  - ○ Mylar emergency blankets for warmth

- **Food and Water Supplies:**
  - ○ Non-perishable, easy-to-prepare food items (energy bars, dried fruits, etc.)
  - ○ Water purification tablets or a portable water filter
  - ○ Collapsible water containers or water pouches

- **Navigation and Communication:**
  - ○ Compass and maps of the local area
  - ○ Battery-powered or hand-crank emergency radio
  - ○ Glow sticks or flashlights with extra batteries

- **Tools and Equipment:**
  - ○ Duct tape and zip ties
  - ○ Paracord or nylon rope
  - ○ Small folding shovel
  - ○ Compact, lightweight cooking utensils

- **Personal Hygiene Items:**
  - ○ Travel-sized toiletries (toothbrush, toothpaste, soap, etc.)
  - ○ Hand sanitizer or wet wipes
  - ○ Feminine hygiene products (if applicable)

- **Important Documents:**
  - ○ Copies of essential documents (identification, insurance, medical records)
  - ○ USB drive with important digital information
  - ○ Emergency contact information

- **Cash:**
  - ○ Small denominations of cash in case of banking system disruptions

- **Self-Defense Items:**
    - Multi-tool or pocket knife
    - Pepper spray or personal safety alarm
    - Depending on local laws, a small firearm
- **Additional Items:**
    - Notepad and pen
    - Spare batteries for electronic devices
    - N95 masks or face coverings
    - Prescription medications

It's important to customize a bug-out bag based on individual needs, the specific environment, and the potential risks in the area. Regularly reviewing and updating the contents ensures that the bug-out bag remains relevant and ready for use in case of an emergency.

Natural Disasters

A well-thought-out emergency plan and necessary supplies are necessary when preparing at home for natural catastrophes or food shortages. Water, nonperishable food, a first aid kit, a flashlight, batteries, and critical documents are among the necessities. For a full preparedness strategy, consider including tools, pet supplies, and prescriptions in your kit customization, depending on your specific needs.

- Emergency Food Supplies:
    - Non-perishable food items (canned goods, dried fruits, nuts, and granola bars)
    - Ready-to-eat meals or MREs (Meals Ready-to-Eat),
    - Shelf-stable snacks
    - Freeze-dried foods
    - Emergency food rations
- Water and Water Purification:
    - Bottled water (at least one gallon per person per day)

- Water purification tablets or drops
- Portable water filter or water purification system
- First Aid Kit:
  - Adhesive bandages and sterile gauze
  - Antiseptic wipes and ointments
  - Pain relievers
  - Tweezers and scissors
  - First aid manual
- Emergency Shelter and Warmth:
  - Mylar emergency blankets
  - Compact, lightweight tent or tarp
  - Sleeping bags or blankets
  - Hand warmers
- Lighting and Communication:
  - Flashlights with extra batteries
  - Battery-powered or hand-crank emergency radio
  - Glow sticks or candles
  - Whistle
  - Solar-powered chargers for electronic devices
- Personal Hygiene and Sanitation:
  - Travel-sized toiletries (toothbrush, toothpaste, soap, etc.)
  - Hand sanitizer or wet wipes
  - Feminine hygiene products (if applicable)
  - Plastic bags for waste disposal
  - Portable toilet or disposable toilet liners
- Clothing and Footwear:
  - Weather-appropriate clothing (including rain gear and sturdy shoes)
  - Extra socks and underwear
  - Hats and gloves
  - Thermal layers for cold weather
- Tools and Equipment:
  - Multi-tool or knife
  - Duct tape and zip ties

- Small folding shovel
- Work gloves
- Manual can opener
- Important Documents:
  - Copies of essential documents (identification, insurance, medical records)
  - USB drive with important digital information
  - Emergency contact information
  - Maps of the local area
- Self-Defense Items:
  - Personal safety alarm
  - Pepper spray
  - Whistle
  - Firearms
  - Knive, machete
- Additional Supplies:
  - Notepad and pen
  - Entertainment items (books, games, or playing cards)
  - N95 masks or face coverings
  - Prescription medications
  - Pet supplies (if applicable)

Remember to customize your emergency supplies based on the specific needs of your household, the local environment, and potential risks in your area. Regularly review and update your emergency kit to ensure that it remains current and ready for use in case of a natural disaster or food shortages.

The need to develop "Counter-Racist War Tactics" is because articles like the Anti-Defamation League's (ADL) findings entitled "White Supremacists Embrace Race War" discusses the growing popularity of the concept of a "race war" among white supremacists. The article highlights instances where the phrase "Race War Now" has appeared in racist graffiti and license plates. White supremacist groups such as Atomwaffen and the Feuerkrieg Division openly claim to be preparing for a "race war." The historical context of the term is explored, originating from fears of slave revolts in antebellum American South. The article details various ways white supremacists discuss and approach the concept, including passive preparation, viewing a closing window of opportunity, and actively embracing the idea. The article also connects discussions of "race war" to criminal activities, citing examples of white supremacists engaging in violent plots with the intent of sparking racial conflict ("White Supremacists Embrace "Race War " n.p.).

Preparing For a Civil/Race War

It is a serious and vital matter to prepare for a possible civil war driven by white supremacists, and the possibility of a situation like this is quite alarming. Even so, it's critical to be ready for any potential societal disputes. The following general advice is offered for people's personal safety in potentially explosive situations:

1. Stay informed:

Reliable News Sources:

- National Public Radio (NPR)
- BBC News
- The New York Times
- Reuters
- Associated Press (AP)
  Monitoring Tensions:
- Monitoring local government announcements and press releases
- Follow credible journalists on social media for real-time updates
- Subscribing to emergency alert systems
- Participating in community forums for shared information
- Checking reputable fact-checking websites for accuracy verification

2. *Develop a safety plan:*

Evacuation Routes:

- Identifying primary and alternative routes to exit the neighborhood
- Designating meeting points outside the neighborhood for family members
- Establishing communication protocols for quick coordination
- Rehearsing evacuation drills periodically
- Keeping emergency contact information accessible

Meeting Places:

- Designating a nearby park or community center as a central meeting point
- Coordinating with neighbors for mutual support
- Creating a neighborhood contact list
- Establishing a virtual meeting point through a shared online platform
- Considering local businesses or schools as meeting places

3. *Emergency Supplies:*

Essential Stockpiles:

- Storing canned goods, dry foods, and bottled water for at least two weeks
- Maintaining a supply of prescription medications
- Having a well-equipped first aid kit
- Including hygiene items and toiletries
- Stockpiling batteries, flashlights, and portable chargers

Extended Necessities:

- Adding long-lasting, non-perishable items like rice and pasta
- Including extra medications beyond immediate needs
- Ensuring a backup power source, such as a generator
- Having water purification tablets or filters
- Storing blankets, warm clothing, and sleeping bags

4. *Communication:*

Reliable Plans:

- Establishing a family group chat for quick updates
- Creating a contact list with phone numbers and email addresses
- Having a designated spokesperson for external communication
- Testing various communication channels regularly
- Exploring secure messaging apps for sensitive information
Alternative Devices:
- Investing in two-way radios with a sufficient range
- Purchasing a satellite phone for communication in remote areas
- Having a battery-powered or hand-crank emergency radio
- Exploring mesh networking apps for offline communication
- Using signal flares or flags for visual signaling

5. Home Security:

Reinforced Defenses:
- Installing reinforced doors with heavy-duty locks
- Adding window security film to deter break-ins
- Upgrading to impact-resistant windows
- Installing security bars or grilles
- Utilizing smart doorbell cameras for remote monitoring
Surveillance Measures:
- Setting up security cameras at key entry points
- Implementing motion-sensor lighting around the property
- Installing a monitored security system
- Using window sensors and glass break detectors
- Employing a video doorbell for package security

6. Maintain Neutrality: On white-on-white issues/conflicts

- Examples of Avoiding Inflammatory Discussions:
  - Refrain from participating in heated political debates on social media.
  - Steer clear of controversial topics in workplace conversations.
  - Choosing neutral language when discussing sensitive issues.

- ○ Avoid confrontations during public events or gatherings.
- ○ Politely redirecting conversations away from potentially divisive subjects.
- Examples of Keeping a Low Profile:
  - ○ Limiting public disclosure of personal opinions on contentious issues.
  - ○ Minimizing social media presence to reduce visibility.
  - ○ Choosing understated attire to avoid drawing attention.
  - ○ Using privacy settings on social platforms to control information access.
  - ○ Participating in community activities without seeking the spotlight.

  ### 7. Legal Understanding:

- Examples of Understanding Self-Defense Laws:
  - ○ Researching state and local laws on the use of force for self-defense.
  - ○ Consulting legal professionals for clarification on specific scenarios.
  - ○ Attending workshops or seminars on self-defense legalities.
  - ○ Staying informed about any recent changes in legislation.
  - ○ Joining community forums to discuss legal aspects of self-defense.
- Examples of Being Aware of Rights and Responsibilities:
  - ○ Understanding the obligation to retreat before using force in some jurisdictions.
  - ○ Being aware of legal limits on the use of certain self-defense tools.
  - ○ Knowing when and how to report incidents to law enforcement.
  - ○ Familiarizing oneself with the legal consequences of excessive force.

- Seeking legal advice for a comprehensive understanding of individual rights.

8. Personal Protection:

- Examples of Considering Self-Defense Training:
    - Enrolling in martial arts or self-defense classes.
    - Participating in workshops on situational awareness and personal safety.
    - Regularly practicing self-defense techniques to build proficiency.
    - Attending seminars on de-escalation tactics and conflict resolution.
    - Joining community groups focused on personal protection education.
- Examples of Exploring Non-Lethal Protection:
    - Carrying pepper spray or personal alarms for immediate self-defense.
    - Investigating legal options for non-lethal weapons in the local area.
    - Learning about effective non-lethal tools such as tasers or stun guns.
    - Seeking advice from security professionals on non-lethal protection.
    - Attending community safety workshops that cover non-lethal defense.

9. Financial Preparedness:

- Examples of Keeping Cash on Hand:
    - Maintaining a small emergency cash fund at home.
    - Withdrawing extra cash before anticipated disruptions.
    - Designating a secure place to store emergency cash.
    - Periodically reviewing and replenishing the cash reserve.
    - Educating family members on the location and purpose of the cash fund.
- Examples of Diversifying Assets:
    - Allocating investments across various asset classes.

- Exploring investment options beyond traditional stocks and bonds.
- Considering precious metals as a part of the diversified portfolio.
- Seeking advice from financial professionals on diversified strategies.
- Regularly reviewing and adjusting the asset allocation based on market conditions.

10. Mental Health:

- Examples of Seeking Support:
  - Talking to friends or family about emotional challenges.
  - Joining support groups or online communities for shared experiences.
  - Seeking guidance from religious or spiritual leaders.
  - Engaging in activities that promote emotional well-being.
  - Reaching out to mental health professionals for counseling or therapy.
- Examples of Considering Professional Counseling:
  - Scheduling regular sessions with a licensed therapist.
  - Exploring teletherapy options for convenience.
  - Attending group therapy sessions for shared support.
  - Participating in stress-reduction workshops or programs.
  - Being proactive in seeking mental health resources when needed.

11. Evacuation Plan:

- Examples of Knowing Multiple Routes:
  - Mapping out primary, secondary, and tertiary evacuation routes.
  - Familiarizing oneself with backroads and alternative paths.
  - Considering different modes of transportation for flexibility.
  - Practicing evacuation routes during non-emergency times.
  - Collaborating with neighbors to share information about routes.

- Examples of Being Prepared to Leave at Short Notice:
    - Having a "ready-to-go bag" with essential items ready for quick departure.
    - Keeping important documents and identification easily accessible.
    - Maintaining a list of emergency contacts and essential phone numbers.
    - Regularly updating and reviewing the evacuation plan

It's crucial to emphasize that preparing for civil unrest involves a balance between being cautious and maintaining a sense of community and empathy. Additionally, this advice is general in nature, and the specific circumstances and legal considerations in your region should guide your actions. Seek guidance from local authorities, law enforcement, and community leaders for more specific and up-to-date information.

12

The Illegal Immigrant War on Black People

It appears that there is a genocidal plan against Black people.
~Louis Farrakhan

Weaponized Invasion

There is an organized warfare movement that is designed to destroy the few remaining vestiges of security and hope that Black people in America have, and this also threatens the continuity of the United States as a whole. This involves the so-called "migrant crisis," or illegal immigrants that started crossing the border by the tens of thousands into the United States of America in 2021 and that will further undermine and reduce the quality of living standards for Black people as well as all Americans. The recent surge of migrants at the US-Mexico border has led to an extreme crisis that has monumental and significant implications for various aspects of American society, especially for Black people, families, and communities nationwide. The statistics reveal an unprecedented level of illegal migration, marking the highest monthly total in over two decades. Black communities are under tremendous pressure as a result of this increase, which is depleting their few resources and necessitating urgent talks with local government representatives to address the worsening situation.

With approximately 10,000 illegal immigrants entering the country every day on average, this influx of migrants is another manifestation of *"The Destruction of Whiteness."* This is blatant proof that the nation is deliberately collapsing in order to drive out and replace Black Americans. With the help of the white supremacist government, this is exploited to establish a sizable buffer class of anti-Black Latinos who are migrating into Black communities, further maintaining the status of Black Americans as a permanent underclass that never goes away. The result is more competition for jobs, which impacts Black people's employment prospects, especially if they are already dealing with a systemic racial labor market.

The analysis, which makes use of data from Fair and Yale University, estimates that there are between 16.8 million and 29 million undocumented immigrants living in the country at the moment. Based on the data, about 3.8 million such immigrants entered the country during the Biden administration. "A new report from House Republicans suggests that the migrant crisis currently affecting the border and America's major cities could end up costing taxpayers up to $451 billion" (What They Are Saying: Homeland Majority's Fourth Interim Report on the Financial Cost of Secretary Mayorkas' Border Crisis. Homeland Security, 16 Nov. 2023., web).

The terrible atrocities committed against Black Americans throughout the Jim Crow and slavery ages remain unaddressed in America. The way things are going, it looks like the status quo will continue, with Black communities suffering. It seems that despite spending large sums of money to support illegal immigrants, the federal government is not doing anything to support Black families and communities.

I find that the word "atonement" speaks to a moral need to right historical wrongs and institutional injustices. There seems to be a clear disconnect between this illegal immigrant crisis and how the government is currently allocating resources, which gives the problems that

Black communities face a sense of disregard or apathy. The possibility that the goals do not correspond with the urgent need for justice and equality worries me. This statement expresses my opinion that, in order to guarantee equitable treatment and assistance for Black communities across the country, reparations in the form of cash payments need to be allocated to descendants of American slaves in order to start correcting America's wrongs.

U.S. authorities encountered more than 142,000 migrants at the border during the first half of September 2023, according to CBP figures. That's slightly more than half of the August 2023 total of 232,000 (Collins n.p.) This migrant dilemma has effects on Black communities in American cities that go beyond the border regions. A number of cities mayors, including those in Chicago, Los Angeles, Denver, and New York City, have voiced worries regarding the pressure on regional economies. Black communities and neighborhoods are left devastated by a lack of resources as a result of the extreme expenditures connected with providing shelter and assistance for migrants, with some towns having to devote a sizable amount of their budgets to addressing the situation.

Republican and Texas Governor Greg Abbott is transporting migrants to states controlled by Democrats by bus and airplane. Mayors of receiving cities contend that this policy puts an unsustainable load on their local economies, despite his office's defense that it offers relief to overburdened border areas.

They emphasize that if the existing state of affairs is not resolved, it will cause destabilization and financial strain, which might have an effect on vital services like law enforcement, school programs, and senior citizen resources. Due to the persistent racial disadvantages that Black people currently face on a daily basis, these acts will undoubtedly have the biggest impact on Black communities.

President Joe Biden's administration is responding by increasing financing for grants that support migrant hosts and taking steps to speed up the issuance of work permits for qualified illegal immigrants. The administration's dedication to carrying out more destruction of the nation while ignoring the issue is indicative of the administration's unique brutality and inhumanity.

The recent wave of migrants at the US-Mexico border has had direct and deliberate repercussions on Black Americans. Thousands of illegal immigrants are bussed in and placed in mostly Black communities, taking over local churches, police stations, airports, closed or shuttered schools, and converted spaces for housing. Even if the percentage of Black people who are homeless in Chicago and New York is over 60%, Black people are forced to sleep on subway trains in the winter in order to remain warm.

Over 7,000 migrants were apprehended by border officials in a single day along the US-Mexico border, according to a Homeland Security official. Although this number is less than the daily total of over 10,000 apprehensions that was recorded earlier in December 2023, it does provide some respite for border officials. There has been a noticeable decrease in border crossings daily, a top administration official reported. The seven-day average of daily interactions increased from 6,800 in late November 2023 to approximately 9,600 in early December 2023. According to the most recent Customs and Border Protection (CBP) figures, more than 2.8 million migrants have interacted with authorities thus far this fiscal year, down from more than 2.7 million migrants in 2022, as reported by USA Today. August is included in the current migration estimate, but September—the final month of this fiscal year—is not (USA Today n.p.).

We are navigating the beginning of a dangerous new period in the field of strategically controlled migration, one that seems to be characterized by a created catastrophe. The root cause of this dilemma is forced migration, a phenomenon intricately linked to massive population shifts designed to achieve militaristic, export-oriented, or possessive goals. I think that the deeply embedded and often hidden nature of this migration method has led to a widespread underappreciation and, thus, an undervaluing of Black people.

It is comparable to an intricate puzzle that is hidden from view, making it difficult for many viewers to completely understand. As I struggle with this insight, it becomes more and more clear that this is a strategically designed migration that functions on several levels, each with unique ramifications and outcomes. Anyone wishing to comprehend the profound effects of this phenomenon on the impacted Black communities and the larger global scene must have this sophisticated perspective on how this particular type of warfare is waged. I realize that in order to have a more intelligent and perceptive conversation, it is critical to clarify the complicated aspects of strategically designed migration.

Within the intricate domain of this manufactured warfare, migration can be effectively utilized as a tool to further military, political, or economic objectives. Several strategies come to light under this paradigm, each with its own set of implications. In order to increase the vulnerability of the United States, deliberate mass migration is used to overwhelm resources, disrupt economies, and strain social institutions. The demographic composition of the United States is altered via engineered migration. By orchestrating the deliberate displacement of Latino populations, crafting humanitarian crises, and applying pressure on cities and states, the infiltration of covert military operatives, camouflaged as migrants, becomes a method for gathering intelligence, executing subversive activities, or laying the groundwork for future military attacks. Exploiting asylum and refugee systems becomes a tactic to infiltrate agents or sympathetic individuals into the United States, while migrants are strategically deployed as proxies in conflicts, serving as a pressure tactic or aligning with a broader strategy to advance the interests of a third-party nation.

Let's look at the effects of the immigration war that is occurring in Chicago, primarily in the Black community. As of December 2023, 1.7 million immigrants resided in Chicago, or 18 percent of the total population. With roughly 21,000 migrants arriving in Chicago from Texas, moves to reduce or revoke the city's sanctuary status could pose difficulties. A coalition of Black community organizations is demonstrating and addressing the Chicago City Council, drawing attention to the overt political racism that the city tolerates while giving illegal immigrants priority over Black Chicagoans.

The City Council's actions jeopardize long-time residents, while the Council's Rules Committee won't allow the city's voters to vote whether Chicago should remain a sanctuary city, further eroding and denying Black people's democratic rights. Notably, Chicago's sanctuary city status, focused on protecting illegal immigrants, does legally involve encouraging immigrants to move to the city and allocating taxpayer funds for their care. However, some Council members, including Ald. Anthony Beale and Ald. Raymond Lopez, advocates for a nonbinding referendum on the sanctuary city's status, criticizing Mayor Brandon Johnson's (a Black man) support for migrants, another example of "Coon behavior." Despite projected costs of $361 million to care for illegal migrants, concerns and criticisms persist, while racism and illegal migrants are committing crimes in Chicago.

It's crucial to remember that white supremacist beliefs support the marginalization and subjection of Black people as well as our communities in order to further the interests of white people. As I discussed in Chapter 7's Section FM 6-2003: Ethnic Cleansing Operations Manual and the Turner Diaries, white supremacist organizations have deliberately used illegal immigration in specific situations to weaken Black communities. In addition to escalating racial tensions and resource competition, white supremacists are utilizing illegal immigration to further weaken Black communities. Aiming to displace Black people from their homes, jobs, and social services through illegal immigration, which will exacerbate hostility between immigrants and Black communities. By deflecting attention from the structural problems of racism and inequality that both groups face, this strategy seeks to undermine any potential coalitions and acts of solidarity between both groups. Advancing their goal of destroying Black people by using illegal immigrants as a buffer to prevent Black people from directly opposing the institutionalized racism system.

Illegal immigration is a tool used by white supremacists. In January 2021, President Joe Biden told the Congressional Black Caucus, "It is doomed not just because of African Americans but because by 2040, this country is going to be a minority white European. Hear me, minority white European. And you guys are going to have to start working with Hispanics, who make up a larger portion of the population than y'all do" (Reuters, 2021). In my view, President Joe Biden is a white supremacist, and it is obvious that he took advantage of the chance to address the Congressional Black Caucus to talk down to Black people, just like a plantation owner would talk down to his slaves.

Illegal immigration is a tool used by white supremacists to reinforce negative stereotypes about Black communities. By presenting immigrants as hardworking people who merely want a better life, especially those from Latin America, this further solidifies unfavorable stereotypes of Black people and gives illegal immigrants the opportunity to establish themselves as champions of white interests, turning them into de facto white supremacists. This strategy maintains racial hierarchies and divisions by demonizing Black people and Black communities. Illegal immigration is deliberately encouraged by white supremacist organizations in an effort to weaken the political clout and influence of Black people. Their goal is to undercut Black communities' political clout and hamper their capacity to speak up for themselves by bringing in more illegal immigrants to Black neighborhoods. This tactic, which tries to maintain white supremacy in political structures, can be implemented through gerrymandering, attempts to suppress the Black vote, or other political manipulation techniques.

It's critical to understand that white supremacist organizations' support for illegal immigration is motivated more by their desire to forward their racist goals than by a sincere concern for immigrants or their rights. To uphold white supremacy by displacing and ethnically cleansing Black people. Their aim is to strengthen their privilege and power by taking advantage of current racial tensions and disparities, which also affect Black communities. Although it may appear contradictory given their anti-immigrant position, white supremacists frequently promote illegal immigration for strategic reasons aimed at harming Black communities and maintaining injustice and division.

They aim to keep their power and influence over Black people by taking advantage of racial tensions, promoting stereotypes, and influencing the political processes.

13

Counter-Racist Code and Action

"If you don't understand racism/white supremacy, then everything else that you do understand will only confuse you."
Neely Fuller Jr., 1971

Nelly Fuller Jr.'s book "The United-Independent Compensatory Code/System/Concept: A Compensatory Counter-Racist Code" offers a codified analysis of racism and a proposed solution for eradicating it. The book presents a "code" or "concept" based on a system of principles designed to counteract racism and provides a practical framework for achieving justice, equity, and peace.

"The United-Independent Compensatory Code/System/Concept: A Compensatory Counter-Racist Code" outlines guidelines for identifying and combating racism in all its forms. The book offers a unique perspective on the nature of racism and how it operates in society, and it has become a key resource for those seeking to combat racism and promote social justice.

Fuller argues that racism is a system of oppression that is designed to dominate and exploit non-white people and that it is upheld by a system of beliefs, attitudes, and practices that are deeply ingrained in society. He suggests that the only way to eradicate racism is to develop a new system of beliefs, attitudes, and practices based on principles of justice, equity, and peace.

His work outlines a code of conduct that is based on a set of principles, including the principle of "balance," the principle of "compensation," and the principle of "universal law." These principles are designed to promote justice, equity, and peace and to counteract the system of racism.

One of Fuller's key themes is the idea that racism is a global problem that can only be eradicated through collective action. Fuller argues that everyone, regardless of race or ethnicity, has a role to play in eradicating racism and that it is only through collective action that we can achieve a world free from racism.

The UICC/SC includes several core principles, including:

1. The principle of justice: This principle emphasizes the importance of treating all Black people with respect and civility, regardless of their race, gender, or other characteristics.
2. The principle of balance: This principle emphasizes the importance of maintaining balance in all areas of life, including relationships, work, and personal growth.
3. The refinement principle emphasizes the importance of constantly refining one's thoughts, speech, and actions to promote greater understanding and effectiveness.
4. The principle of priority: This principle emphasizes the importance of focusing on the most important issues facing Black people and communities and taking action to address them.

Overall, the UICC/SC is a comprehensive system designed to help Black people understand and counteract the effects of racism and promote justice and righteousness. It contributes to the ongoing struggle for the eradication of injustice and erasing the hierarchy of those who do not possess melanin or non-white characteristics based on skin color.

The "Ten Stops"

These "Ten Stops" are key areas where Black people can make changes to counteract the effects of racism and promote justice and civility Fuller Jr. recommends:

1. *Stop "Snitching:"* Making negative remarks about individuals who shouldn't be hurt. To knowingly and voluntarily "snitch" on someone in order to collect praise or favors from white supremacists or other direct or indirect personal favors.

2. *Stop "Name-Calling:"* Name-calling is a small but significant behavior that encourages significant conflict among non-White individuals. Name-calling frequently sparks violent altercations that end in death.

3. *Stop "Cursing:"* To use foul language against someone in a way that could be interpreted as aggressive or disrespectful frequently leads to the fostering of antagonism, which frequently has no positive outcome.

4. *Stop "Gossiping:"* Speaking to someone else about someone you wouldn't be willing to speak to directly at the same time and location while those other people are listening is known as gossiping about that individual.

5. *Stop being Discourteous*: When someone does or says something in a way that betrays a lack of regard for what they are saying, doing, or attempting to accomplish in order to advance understanding of their thoughts,speech, and/or actions, it is considered inappropriate.

6. *Stop Stealing:* Stealing from someone for any cause constitutes the advancement of injustice. Even stealing for one's survival is an act of injustice. Promoting injustice means continuing to deal

with someone who has stolen from you. To create injustice is to remain neutral toward an adversary. Even stealing from a white supremacist who is racist is an act of injustice.

7. ***Stop Robbing:*** To rob someone is to take anything from them unfairly, using either direct physical harm or the fear of such harm, and then to use the stolen items to satisfy one's desires or to make one's own body more comfortable.

8. ***Stop Fighting:*** As long as people can communicate with one another and reduce conflict, justice will be served more effectively; there should be no fighting. People should take all reasonable steps to reduce or end contact with one another when they are unable to communicate with one another without attempting to maim or inflict other physical harm.

9. ***Stop Killing:*** Exception: when required to act in the immediate and proper defense of oneself, others, or significant property, or when required to act by enacting "Maximum Emergency Compensatory Action."

10. ***Stop Squabbling:*** One of the main unjust practices of racist white supremacists is creating circumstances that lead to or encourage internal strife among non-white individuals. Racists want to keep using non-white people as their objects of desire and victims. Particularly when employing non-white people as victims, racists urge non-white people to quarrel with one another and then come to them for help in resolving the differences. This is one of the main strategies used by races to hold onto their dominance. They also use this to amuse themselves, stroke their egos, and demonstrate their dominance. For "fun," "glory," and "material comfort," they engage in this.

The "Ten Stops" reflect Neely Fuller Jr.'s belief that Black people must take responsibility for their actions and work towards creating a more just and civil existence with each other, and as a result of this behavior, our children, families, communities, cities, and states. Which will change the world. By avoiding negative behaviors and promoting positive values, Black people can counteract the effects of white supremacy racism and work towards a world system free of oppression, injustice, and inequality.

Codification

Neely Fuller Jr. developed the concept of codification as a way to organize and systematize information related to the dynamics of racism and white supremacy. In his work, Fuller's codification refers to identifying patterns that work and organizing information into a comprehensive system that can be used to understand and counteract the effects of racism.

Codification is essential because racism is a complex psychopathic system that operates in all areas of human activity, including: Economics, Education, Entertainment, Labor, Law, Politics, Religion, Sex, and War. In order to effectively counteract the effects of racism, Black people must have a comprehensive understanding of how the system works and how to respond to it.

In order to do this, Fuller created the United Independent Compensatory Code/System/Concept (UICC/SC), a comprehensive framework for thought, speech, and action. Developing thought that aims to combat racism's impacts and advance righteousness and justice. The UICC/SC comprises particular directions for Black people to act in a way that advances the values of justice, balance, refinement, and priority in their lives and the environment around them. As stated by our esteemed instructor and elder, Dr. Claud Anderson, "No one wants to bring up Black problems with Black solutions. It is more palatable for society to suggest general minority answers for problems that are actually unique to Black people" (Anderson).

Through the process of codification, Fuller sought to create a comprehensive code system that could be used by Black people to understand and counteract the effects of racism/white supremacy in all areas of [hu]man activity. By organizing information into a systematic and comprehensive framework, he believes that Black people could better understand the dynamics of racism and work towards a world system where "nobody is mistreated" and whoever needs the most constructive help, gets the most constructive help (Fuller Jr. 23).

Nine Areas of Activity

Neely Fuller has explored the concept of the "Nine Areas of Activity," encompassing economics, education, entertainment, labor, law, politics, religion, sex, and war. This framework delineates the diverse spheres of [hu]man activity where racism and white supremacy exert influence. According to Fuller, racism is pervasive across all nine areas, emphasizing the importance of comprehending its workings in each domain to effectively address its impact. The "Nine Areas of Activity" framework offers a thorough and organized approach to examining the intricacies of racism, enabling the development of strategies aimed at fostering justice and equality within each distinct area (Fuller Jr. 1).

In examining Fuller's concept of the "Nine Areas of Activity," I find that the influence of white supremacy permeates various aspects of human life.

1. In Economics, the allocation of time and energy is manipulated to perpetuate racial disparities.
2. Education becomes a tool for disseminating misinformation and maintaining control over institutions, contributing to the confusion and programming of non-white individuals.
3. Entertainment serves as a distraction, with movies, music, and sports diverting attention from the practices of white supremacists.
4. Labor, involving the production of goods and services, reflects the unequal exchange for wages and salaries.

5. Law is utilized to exert control, sustaining the systematic implementation of white supremacy.
6. Politics operates in ways that disproportionately impact non-white individuals, with laws often creating destructive consequences while granting privileges to white individuals.
7. Religion is employed to subdue and control non-white individuals, fostering docility and fear and justifying acts of genocide and war.
8. Sex is wielded as a weapon to destabilize families and manipulate minds, promoting debasement and harm.
9. War and Counter-War acknowledge an ongoing struggle against an unjust and psychopathic opponent who has the power and is practicing systematic white supremacy.

Destroying the widespread effects of racism requires an understanding of and attention to each of these issues. Gaining this insight can help one grasp why white supremacy can be easily understood and, in the end, defend Black individuals, Black families, and Black communities.

Constructive Use of Black Dollars

In navigating the realm of money, Fuller advises Black people to refrain from engaging in activities solely for financial gain or utilizing money in ways that lack constructive purpose. While recognizing the utility of money, it is crucial not to worship it but rather to view it as a precision tool, utilizing it only when necessary for constructive goals. Ethical considerations come into play, emphasizing the importance of not stealing, robbing or using others' possessions without permission. A prudent approach involves saving portions of acquired money.

Anticipating the tactics of white supremacists, individuals should be prepared for obstacles they might create, such as financial losses through deceit and theft. Given the prevailing white supremacy, borrowing or lending money is discouraged unless it is indispensable for a constructive purpose. When lending to non-white individuals, it is suggested not to exceed one's capacity to donate. The acquisition of money should be accompanied by judicious spending, with an emphasis on increased investment and a cautious approach to avoid financial setbacks (Fuller Jr. 56).

It is acknowledged that, under white supremacy, these financial dynamics are controlled by the white supremacists, influencing who has access to money, the amount, the means of acquisition, permissible actions, and the perceived value of money. Consequently, blame for financial insufficiencies is directed towards the structural inequalities imposed by the white supremacists, hindering constructive comfort, survival, and progress. While simultaneously extorting their power and control over non-white people in every area of activity (Fuller 74).

"Power is the ability to get things done despite the resistance and opposition of others. Economics is the production, distribution, and consumption of goods and wealth. PowerNomics then is the ability of Blacks to pool resources and power to produce, distribute, and consume in a way that creates goods." Dr. Claud Anderson

Racism can only be overcome through a sustained effort to promote justice and equality. "If you do not understand racism and how it works, everything else that you understand will only confuse you" (Fuller Jr., 39). Fuller Jr.'s statement on racism underscores the profound impact that an understanding of racism has on an individual. This speaks to the foundational nature of racism in shaping societal structures, interactions, and power dynamics. This claim highlights how crucial it is to comprehend racism in order to make sense of it in a variety of contexts. Individual viewpoints, societal structures, and interpersonal relationships are all shaped by racism, a complex social phenomenon with roots in historical and systemic biases

White supremacist racism has a significant negative influence that must be acknowledged in order to address the multifaceted nature of the world controlled by white supremacy. It becomes next to impossible to try to make sense of other problems without this understanding. Racism is ingrained in institutional structures, policies, and historical legacies and is not limited to personal prejudices. Its operation can be interpreted incorrectly, which can cause misunderstandings regarding justice, inequality, and Black communities' experiences.

More broadly, the remark suggests that understanding racism provides a lens through which to view complex problems. It emphasizes how social dynamics are interconnected and shows how racism is deeply ingrained in communities all around the world, rather than being a singular issue. Ignorance of this basic fact can lead to distorted views on a range of issues, impeding attempts to rectify social inequalities and promote a more just and equal society. Therefore, it is vital to recognize that racism has a pervasive influence on social institutions, power relations, and personal prejudices, in addition to just acknowledging its existence. It is a crucial first step in developing a holistic perspective and actively working to undermine institutional white supremacy.

The assertion implies that racism is not merely a peripheral issue but a fundamental force that permeates various aspects of human existence. Without a comprehensive understanding of how white supremacy racism operates, Black people will find it Next to impossible to make sense of social, economic, and political dynamics. In essence, racism becomes a lens through which one must view and analyze broader societal issues. By promoting justice and correctness, it becomes a counteractive force against racism. It involves challenging discriminatory policies, advocating for humane opportunities, and fostering a societal environment where all individuals have access to the same rights and privileges, regardless of their racial background.

Our great teachers, people of our wonderful lineage, are called by many names, such as "Freedmen", "Descendants of American slaves", or "Foundational Black American" (FBA). I encourage Black people to recognize the pivotal point that we are at and the role of racism in shaping societal conceptual thought rooted in psychopathic aggression. So we must actively engage in efforts to dismantle the system of white supremacy and its ideology. Understanding racism becomes a prerequisite for having a sound mind, which will create social change. Having knowledge and information about the dangers (that concern Black people) of white supremacy should be our objective to help us navigate through an anti-Black, racist system. Black people need to and should champion a system that is "Just" and "Upright."

Dr. Claud Anderson's definition of racism/white supremacy is as follows: "Racism is wealth and power-based competitive relationship between Blacks and non-Blacks. The sole purpose of racism is to support and ensure that the White majority and its ethnic subgroups continue to dominate and use Blacks as a means to produce wealth and power. True racism exists only when one group holds a disproportionate share of wealth and power over another group and then uses those resources to marginalize, exploit, exclude, and subordinate the weaker group" ("10 Quotes From PowerNomics Pioneer Dr. Claud Anderson," n.p.).

Dr. Claud Anderson's definition of racism/white supremacy goes beyond individual prejudice or discriminatory attitudes. It analyzes the structural and systemic dimensions of white supremacy, emphasizing the aggressive relationship between Blacks and non-Blacks based on disparities in wealth and power. According to Dr. Anderson's viewpoint, the deliberate use of resources to dehumanize, exploit, exclude, and enslave a weaker group is what sets racism apart from bigotry. The dynamics of racism are most evident when a more privileged group—in this case, white people—actively seeks to maintain and increase its control over a less privileged group, despite having amassed a disproportionate amount of wealth and influence.

This definition implies that racism is not just about personal prejudices or discriminatory acts but about the structural mechanisms that enable one group to maintain control over another. It underscores how economic and social disparities are not accidental but are intentionally engineered to sustain the existing power dynamics.

Dr. Anderson's framework encourages a deeper examination of the historical and ongoing systems that perpetuate racial inequalities. It prompts individuals to consider the broader structural issues embedded in wealth distribution, access to resources, and the exercise of power. By focusing on the systemic nature of racism, Dr. Anderson provides a lens through which individuals can analyze and address the root causes of racial disparities in society.

Neely Fuller Jr. Quotes

Racism is a system of power that operates to maintain social control and dominance over Black people. "Racism is the local and global power system and is dynamic, structured and maintained by persons who classify themselves as white, whether consciously or subconsciously determined; which consists of patterns of perception, logic, symbol formation, thought, speech, action, and emotional response, as conducted simultaneously in all areas of people's activity (economics, education, entertainment, labor, law, politics, religion, sex, and war); for the ultimate purpose of white genetic survival and to prevent white genetic annihilation on the planet Earth" (Fuller Jr., 38).

Racism can only be overcome through a sustained effort to promote justice and equality. *"If you do not understand racism and how it works, everything else that you understand will only confuse you." (Fuller Jr., 1984, 39)*

Self-respect and self-determination are essential for Black people to overcome racism. *"In order to replace white supremacy with justice, it is necessary that each and every black person begin the task of self-reconstruction, and self-respect is an absolute necessity for self-reconstruction." (Fuller Jr., 1984, 74)*

"The white supremacy system is a political and economic system and is the only functional system of racism, which is maintained by violence against non-white people" (Fuller Jr., 1984, 54).

"If you do not understand racism (white supremacy), what it is and how it works, everything else that you understand will only confuse you." (Fuller Jr.)

"Racism (white supremacy) is the local and global power system and dynamic, structured and maintained by persons who classify themselves as white, whether consciously or subconsciously determined; which consists of patterns of perception, logic, symbol formation, thought, speech, action and emotional response, as conducted simultaneously in all areas of people activity (economics, education, entertainment, labor, law, politics, religion, sex, and war)." (Fuller Jr.).

"The only true solution to the problem of racism is a complete universal system of justice." (Fuller Jr.)

Nelly Fuller Jr. said, "In the system of white supremacy, the victim is never responsible for the actions of the oppressor" (Fuller Jr.). The core message is that, within this systemic framework, the victims—those who are oppressed and subjected to discriminatory practices—bear no responsibility for the actions of the oppressors, who wield power and perpetuate inequality.

To elaborate further, the "system of white supremacy" refers to a socio-political structure in which white individuals or groups hold disproportionate power and control, often at the expense of non-white individuals and communities. This system is characterized by institutionalized racism, discrimination, and the perpetuation of unequal social, economic, and political conditions.

The victim of white supremacy is not responsible for the actions of the oppressor. Any tendency to assign blame or culpability to those who suffer under the system of white supremacy should be looked at as incorrect thinking. It acknowledges the inherent imbalance of power within the system of white supremacy and asserts that the oppressed should not be held accountable for the injustices imposed upon them but rather that the architects and sustainers of this unjust system who cause Black people to become monstrosities should be held responsible and the only ones held responsible for the actions of their subjects.

By no means does this relinquish our responsibility as victims of white supremacy to be willfully ignorant and be participants in foolishness, destructiveness, unproductiveness, and degenerate behaviors. It is our duty to remain diligent to fix our problems, and it is also our duty not to create more problems.

In practical terms, this perspective rejects victim-blaming, a tendency that may arise when individuals or groups face discrimination. Victim-blaming often involves attributing the consequences of systemic oppression to the behavior or characteristics of those who are oppressed. This statement, however, emphasizes that the responsibility for discriminatory actions lies squarely with the individuals or structures perpetuating the system of white supremacy.

This principle encourages a shift in focus from scrutinizing the behavior or responses of the oppressed to examining the root causes of systemic injustices. By doing so, it directs attention toward dismantling the structures that uphold white supremacy rather than placing the burden on those who are victimized by it.

One key benefit of a codified system for victims of white supremacy is that it can help to provide a sense of community and solidarity. By sharing a common understanding of the ways in which racism operates, victims can come together to support one another and to work towards common goals. This can be particularly important in the face of the isolation and alienation that many victims of white supremacy experience.

A codified system can also help to provide victims with a set of guidelines and best practices for avoiding further mistreatment. For example, victims may be encouraged to document instances of racism, to report incidents to appropriate authorities, and to seek out supportive communities and allies. Such guidelines can help empower victims and give them a greater sense of agency and control over their lives.

In terms of specific ideas for a codified system, some potential elements might include:

- ***Education and awareness-raising:*** Victims of white supremacy may benefit from education and training in the ways in which racism operates, as well as strategies for recognizing and responding to racist behaviors.
- ***Community building:*** Providing opportunities for victims to connect with one another and to build supportive networks can be essential in countering the isolation and marginalization that many experience.
- ***Advocacy and activism:*** Victims of white supremacy may benefit from opportunities to engage in advocacy and activism efforts aimed at challenging racist policies and practices.
- ***Legal support:*** Victims may benefit from access to legal support and guidance in navigating the legal system and seeking redress for instances of discrimination and mistreatment.
- ***Mental health support:*** Given the potential psychological impacts of racism-related trauma, victims may benefit from access to mental health services and support groups.
- Self-care practices: Encouraging victims to engage in self-care practices such as mindfulness, exercise, and stress reduction techniques can help to promote resilience and well-being in the face of ongoing mistreatment.

Lastly, a codified system for victims of white supremacy would serve as a valuable resource for those who are seeking to counter racism and avoid further mistreatment. By providing a shared language, set of tools, and community support, such a system can help empower victims and promote a more just and correct society. This ideal challenges individuals to question and resist any narrative that places blame on the victims of racism/white supremacy. It prompts a deeper understanding of the power imbalances inherent in systems of oppression and advocates for collective efforts to dismantle these systems of white supremacy and work towards a more just and correct society.

"The most powerful form of change is individual change. Each individual must change their own thinking, speech, and actions in order to counteract the effects of racism." ~Neely Fuller Jr.

"Racism is a global system of white supremacy that operates in all areas of human activity, including economics, education, entertainment, labor, law, politics, religion, sex, and war" (Fuller Jr. 14).

"All human beings are born with the potential to be equally intelligent and creative, regardless of their race or ethnicity" (Fuller Jr. 27).

"The concept of 'codification' is the process of identifying patterns and organizing information into a comprehensive system that can be used to understand and counteract the effects of racism" (Fuller Jr. 73).

"The white supremacists use propaganda to promote and maintain their system of racism, which includes messages that reinforce negative stereotypes and encourage division among non-white people" (Fuller Jr. 83).

"The ultimate solution to the problem of racism is the replacement of the system of racism/white supremacy with a system of justice" (Fuller Jr., 98).

"The primary goal of all counter-racist activities should be to promote the principle of justice and to eliminate racism in all areas of human activity" (Fuller Jr., 118).

14

Conclusion

White people are potential humans; they haven't evolved yet.
~Louis Farrakhan

In reality, white people are the original mixed people and the most confused. A worldwide research team examined the genomes of eighty-three ancient people from European archaeological sites, according to Gyanendranath Mitra. According to their research, populations from three different races that moved to Europe in different waves over the course of the last 8,000 years have blended to become modern Europeans. I suspect that Caucasoids have more Neanderthal genes than reports suggest. Caucasoids project their genetic mutations, as well as their disconnection from humanity, onto Black people.

In 1787, white supremacists added to the United States Constitution included a provision known as the Three-Fifths Compromise, outlined in Article I, Section 2. This compromise determined that enslaved Black Americans would be counted as three-fifths of a person.

My suspicion is that Black people, who have the highest melanin concentrations, are the "missing link" that scientists purportedly cannot find. This explains how homo sapiens and many different species of hominids evolved, having sexual reproductive organs that would be suitable for the "God Gene" (melanin), which created mankind with recessive genes. The caucasoidal "recessive gene" has an expiration date, so to speak, and what allows those who possess this recessive gene to prolong life is by having offspring with people that have melanin, which can only be found in Black men and women. Because of this, the birth rate of Caucasoids is gradually dropping and is predicted to remain nearly zero in the not-too-distant future. " Thus, all animals have an internal core of melanin in their brains. All humans possess this Black internal brain evidence of their common Black African origin. The "All Black" neuromelanin nerve tract of the brain is profound proof that the human race is a Black race, with many variations of Black, from Black-Black to White-Black" (King 36).

In this book, I'm introducing a new term that seeks to redefine the narrative surrounding white racial identities. I've coined the term "The D.O.N.'s," which stands for "Descendants Of Neanderthals," to refer to the Caucasoid people on Earth. This term is a deliberate departure from traditional racial terminology, aiming to provoke thought and challenge established norms. Throughout history, Black people have faced oppression and discrimination at the hands of those I refer to as "The D.O.N.'s." These white supremacists have abused their status and influence, frequently at the expense of underprivileged Black people.

By employing this new phrase, I hope to draw attention to the systemic injustices that have endured over time as well as the historical background of the interactions between races. They are a reflection of Black people's historical struggles and relationships with authority. The natural enemies of Black people (the D.O.N.'s.) invented every word used in this book because we speak English. The terminology employed is a reclaiming of language, a way to assert agency and challenge the narratives imposed by dominant white society. While some may view these terms as controversial or confrontational, they serve a purpose in sparking dialogue and fostering a deeper understanding of racial dynamics. By acknowledging the historical context and power dynamics inherent in language, we can begin to dismantle the systems of oppression that have long plagued our society.

White Birth Decline

Examine Italy, CNN.com reports that it is presently handling an extraordinary crisis. Official predictions for 2022 show that, for the first time, the annual birth rate fell below 400,000, or an average of 1.25 babies per woman. The replacement rate is currently negative because there are currently more deaths than births (12 deaths for every 7 births). With a little under 60 million people living there, Italy has the eighth largest economy in the world. The Italian National Institute of Statistics (ISTAT) reports that in 2022, the country in southern Europe reported a mere 393,000 births—the fewest since records date back to 1861 (Nadeau, n.p.).

Fertility rates have significantly declined across Europe, a trend observed in all European regions. In 1960, Estonia was the sole European country with a total fertility rate below two. As of the latest data, only Iceland and Albania maintain fertility rates above two within Europe.

The article "Latin America's Fertility Decline is Accelerating" claims that. Nobody Is Sure Why. The country's population, according to a recent census, is 203 million, a substantial decrease from the 208 million expected by Brazil's National Statistics Institute and even less than the 216 million forecast by the United Nations. These differences are caused by a shortage of births rather than people migrating or disappearing. With the COVID-19 epidemic postponing the 2022 census, it was shown that Brazil's population growth in the 2010s was only 0.52% yearly, half that of the 2000s and the lowest since 1872. Rafael Rofman, an Argentine economist and demographer, noted that his country's fertility declined more in the last six years than in the preceding six decades. Consequently, he predicts a 30% decrease in 4-year-olds entering Argentine preschools in 2024 compared to 2020. Luis Rosero-Bixby, a renowned demographer from the University of Costa Rica, describes the decline in births in his country as "vertiginous," with fertility among native-born women nearing just one child per woman. In their recent paper titled "The Great Decline," Wanda Cabella and three other Uruguayan demographers highlight that Uruguay's total fertility rate plummeted from 2.0 to 1.27 children per woman in just seven years (Constance n.p.).

Also in the article "White Deaths Exceed Births in a Majority of U.S. States," In 2016, twenty-six states in the U.S. experienced more deaths among non-Hispanic whites than births, marking the highest occurrence in American history. These states were home to approximately 179 million residents, which accounts for around 56% of the total U.S. population. By contrast, in 2004, only four states and as recently as 2014, seventeen states witnessed this phenomenon. Moreover, in 2016, the nation as a whole experienced more deaths than births among non-Hispanic whites for the first time. This shift, known as "natural decrease," occurs when deaths outpace births and can only be offset by migration gains. Notably, in seventeen of the twenty-six states with white natural decrease, the white population decreased overall between 2015 and 2016.

The increasing occurrence of white natural decline carries significant implications for the demographic future of the United States. While much attention has been given to the influence of growing minority populations on diversity, the rising incidence of white natural decrease is also a significant factor. Factors such as aging and below-replacement fertility among the white population contribute to this trend. The aging baby-boom population, primarily white, is expected to grow substantially by 2060, leading to an increase in white mortality. This, coupled with a decline in white births, heightens the likelihood of more instances of white natural decrease. In contrast, the Latino population, which experiences a surplus of births over deaths, contributes to the increasing diversity of the U.S. population.

Although demographers have observed a growing occurrence of natural decrease in the overall U.S. population, less attention has been paid to its prevalence among racial sub-groups. To address this gap, we analyze data from the National Center for Health Statistics to examine trends in births and deaths among whites from 1999 to 2016. Our findings indicate a significant rise in the number of states experiencing white natural decrease in recent years. Despite this trend, only three states experienced more deaths than births in their total populations, highlighting the increasing importance of minority natural increase in overall U.S. demographic trends.

Between 1999 and 2016, the number of white births declined by 10.8%, while white deaths increased by 9.2%. These demographic shifts contributed to a decline in natural increase and the onset of white natural decrease. The pace of decline in white births intensified from 2007 to 2016, partly due to the impact of the Great Recession on U.S. fertility. As a result, natural increase ceased in 2016, marking the first time in U.S. history that white deaths surpassed white births. The declining birth-to-death ratio among whites contrasts with higher ratios among minority populations, accelerating the diversity of the U.S. population (Sáenz and Johnson n.p.).

White Skin

"Skin fairness is a better predictor for impaired physical and mental health than hair redness" (Flegr,Sýkorová n.p.). About 2 percent of individuals with European/D.O.N ancestry have red hair. The study found that red-haired women tend to have higher pain thresholds and an increased risk of certain diseases. Furthermore, a negative correlation exists between the intensity of red hair and aspects such as fertility, sexual desire, and overall physical and mental health, based on a study that involved 4,117 participants. Positive correlations were identified between red hair and the quantity of medications prescribed, reported mental health symptoms, and several neuropsychiatric conditions, notably general anxiety disorder in women and learning difficulties in men. However, when skin pigmentation was considered, these correlations largely disappeared, suggesting that skin fairness, rather than hair color, maybe a more significant factor in these health outcomes. And when melanin levels increased, these connections almost vanished (Flegr,Sýkorová n.p.).

The study looked into a number of possible causes, such as folic acid deficiency among fair-skinned (white) people, including a subgroup of redheads, and vitamin D inadequacy brought on by sun avoidance. The findings underscore the need for empirical studies examining vitamin D and folic acid concentrations in relation to skin and hair pigmentation (Flegr,Sýkorová n.p.). If you have red hair and pale skin that doesn't "tan" easily and are unable to get a "nice tan", you might be at a higher risk of developing melanoma, a type of skin cancer. This tendency is often linked to a specific gene called the melanocortin 1 receptor (MC1R). When this gene is not working properly, it affects the production of pigments in your skin, making you more susceptible to skin cancer (Flegr,Sýkorová n.p.).

What is melanoma? Melanoma is a type of skin cancer that originates in the pigment-producing cells called melanocytes. These cells are responsible for producing melanin, the pigment that gives color to the skin, hair, and eyes. Melanoma is considered more dangerous than other types of skin cancer because it can spread to other parts of the body (metastasize). The connection between melanin and melanoma lies in the fact that melanocytes produce melanin, and excessive exposure to UV radiation from the sun can damage the DNA in these cells. This damage can increase the risk of melanoma development. People with fair skin, which contains less melanin, are generally more susceptible to the harmful effects of UV radiation and have a higher risk of developing melanoma compared to those with darker skin tones.

The primary cause of melanoma is often exposure to ultraviolet (UV) radiation from the sun, which damages the DNA in the skin cells. However, genetic factors, such as certain gene mutations like those in the melanocortin 1 receptor (MC1R) gene, family history of melanoma, and a weakened immune system, can also contribute to the development of melanoma.

Just as the "D.O.N" race is the enemy of Black people and also the enemy of the world and all living creatures on planet Earth, the Sun is the D.O.N's natural enemy. The Sun kills people who lack pigmentation, or melanin. Excessive sun exposure without proper protection, such as sunscreen and clothing, increases the risk of sunburn, premature aging, and skin cancer. Some white people believe that if they don't obtain melanin through their offspring, they could face extinction in the future. All things in the universe have melanin and need melanin to survive, including caucasoids.

Melanin is a common pigment found in living things—in bacteria, fungi, plants, animals, and even in outer space. "Melanin is a ubiquitous biological pigment found in bacteria, fungi, plants, animals, and interstellar space" (Herrera and Arias). In nature, it performs a number of functions, including boosting color, shielding the body from the sun, purifying the body, and attaching itself to metals in the bloodstream to aid in the conversion of electricity and/or energy.

Melanin exhibits such resilience that it often remains preserved in fossils, where most other substances would typically degrade. In living cells, whether they're more complex (eukaryotic) or simpler (prokaryotic), melanin mainly acts like a built-in sunscreen, shielding the cells from harmful sun rays; it's like a natural protector found all over the living world.

Eumelanins, which are a type of pigment found in things like hair and skin, have interesting features like reacting to light, grabbing onto certain metal ions, having special properties related to chemical reactions (redox properties), and having these persistent free radical centers in their structure. However, scientists are not exactly sure why these features are so important in living things.

We now discover an interesting relationship between melanin and interstellar chemicals in space when we gaze out into space. Melanin, which is mostly made up of atoms of carbon, hydrogen, nitrogen, and oxygen, is essential for both light absorption and UV radiation protection. In a surprising turn of events, researchers have found complex compounds in interstellar space, some of which are comparable to melanin. Carbon is another component of these interstellar molecules' makeup. This discovery suggests that the fundamental components of melanin—a biological pigment essential to life on Earth—have cosmic origins.

The article "Why are Europeans white? A genetic study" investigated and identified two forms of melanin: eumelanin and pheomelanin. While eumelanin is a dark brown-black pigment, pheomelanin is a reddish-pink pigment. Greater pheomelanin content results in lighter skin, whereas the amount of eumelanin determines the skin's blackness. Over the course of mankind's/D.O.N's development, hairy, four-legged forebears gave way to upright walkers. Mankind/D.O.N's started to walk upright and shed their body hair, which exposed their skin to UV rays from the sun. This adaptation made it possible for humans to control body temperature, along with the emergence of sweat glands. Two theories explain the origin and migration of [hu]mans: the 'Out of Africa theory,' which postulates that contemporary [hu]mans evolved in tropical Africa before spreading globally, and the multi-regional hypothesis, which suggests evolution occurred in many locations. One theory is that water sources dried up during a mega-drought that occurred between 135,000 and 90,000 years ago, which is likely to have caused [hu]man migration (Mitra n.p.).

According to Mitra, genetic studies, including DNA analysis, support an African origin for modern mankind/D.O.N's around 200,000 years ago. Pale skin and lactose tolerance evolved as solutions to the need for efficient UV absorption and the ability to digest vitamin D in milk, respectively. Early Europeans/D.O.N's, however, had darker skin. The introduction of fairness genes, SLC24A5 and SLC45A2, through interbreeding with Near Eastern farmers 7,800 years ago, led to the lighter skin of modern Europeans/D.O.N's. Genetic studies show that Europeans, due to generations of limited intermingling with other racial groups, have maintained genetic integrity and distinctive skin colors (Mitra n.p.).

Melanin and the Unconscious Mind

One of the keys, in my opinion, to bringing about justice and dismantling the racist system of white supremacy can be found within our melanin, or "The Black Dot." The book "African Origins of Biological Psychiatry" by Richard D. King, M.D., provides extensive information on the subject of melanin and how it is connected to our unconscious minds. Dr. King states that the brains of all animals include an intrinsic melanin core. Because of this shared Black African origin, all humans have this Black internal brain evidence. The brain's "All Black" neuro-melanin nerve tract provides compelling evidence that [hu]mans are a Black race with numerous Black subraces, ranging from Black-Black to White-Black, all of which are inherently based on a vast sea of brain blackness.

The presence of intense blackness, the neuromelanin pigmentation of the locus coeruleus, also known as the "Black Dot," the uppermost pigmentation center, the doorway leading into an entirely black hall of blackness, and the neuromelanin " Once again, an expanding body of biological research emphasizes how the collective unconscious is imprinted in our minds, with a significant connection to our brains. The evolutionary history of the [hu]man brain may be methodically followed, starting with animal ancestors and continuing through primates, mammals, reptiles, amphibians, fish, and single-celled organisms. An important point about the embryonic period is that all animal embryos, including human embryos, show remarkable similarities as they evolve from fish to mammals through ancestral forms. The black nerve pathways are located in the brain stem, which is the oldest part of the brain. Anomalies throughout this black neuromelanin tract may manifest as ancestral-like behaviors.

Considering melanin's biological features, its memory storage, its presence in ancient brain centers, heightened brain pigmentation in advanced species, and numerous reports of detailed memory images of historical concepts, the cumulative evidence is compelling. Rapid Eye Movement (REM) sleep, recognized as the dreaming phase, involves historical memory images derived from the collective unconscious memory banks in the brain stem's black neuromelanin (Amenta) nerve tract, passing through the locus coeruleus doorway.

The "Akhet" or "Akhet hieroglyph" is the symbol for the horizon in ancient Egyptian mythology. It represents the line that separates both the celestial and terrestrial domains, where the sun emerges and sets. The sun rising or setting on the horizon is visually represented by the Akhet hieroglyph, which represents the everlasting cycle of day and night, life and death, and the sun's endless regeneration.

The Akhet represents the rising or setting sun and appears as two mountains or peaks surrounding a partially concealed solar disk. Ra, the sun deity, was strongly linked to this emblem, which represents his nighttime descent into the underworld and dawn rebirth, thereby completing the circle of life. Melanin at higher levels bridges the gap between the unconscious and conscious minds, leading to Amenta/ Duat, the Universal Mind or Knowledge. This is how Amenta, Akhet, and melanin are directly related.

Amenta & The Unconscious Mind

The comparison between Amenta's symbolism and the concept of the unconscious mind reveals intriguing insights into the depth and complexity of [hu]man psychology. In a broader context, the un-conscious mind, a subject explored by renowned psychologists such as Sigmund Freud and Carl Jung, unveils a vast expanse encompassing thoughts, memories, desires, and instincts that operate beyond imme-diate conscious awareness.

Amenta, with its depiction as a realm of hidden knowledge, symbols, and mysteries in Egyptian mythology, aligns with the notion of the unconscious mind. Much like Amenta, the unconscious mind serves as a repository for concealed aspects of ourselves—those elements that elude our conscious perception. This includes repressed memories, emotions that haven't been fully acknowledged, and instinctual drives that influence our behavior.

Deep connections can be seen between the process of exploring the unconscious mind and the study of Amenta. Both paths entail discovering undiscovered facts and obtaining access to psychological components that might not be immediately obvious. People discover layers of complexity inside themselves when they explore their unconscious, which develops self-awareness and encourages personal development.

Just as Amenta holds symbolic significance in Egyptian mythology, representing a gateway to hidden realms and knowledge, the unconscious mind serves as a gateway to understanding the intricate workings of the [hu]man psyche. The exploration of both realms offers a transformative journey—one that can lead to a deeper understanding of oneself, enhanced personal development, and a more profound connection with the complexities of the [hu]man mind. It is here in the Amenta where we can find answers to our problems by communicating with our ancestors, tapping into energy sources to give us heightened levels of awareness and physical abilities, and opening up a door to commune with nature and even harness its powers. Every cell in our body has memory, and this memory is directly connected to our melanin.

Dr. King claims that the Black Dot, which symbolizes the all-black neuromelanin (Amenta) brain nerve tract led by the locus coeruleus, is essential to the unconscious memory image's development into consciousness. Harvard psychiatrists J. Allan Hobson and Robert McCarley describe the brain as a dream state generator with a dynamic flow of memory images. Melatonin, the pineal hormone released at night, influences the dream system, enhancing the movement of sensory images from the brainstem to the cortex.

Serotonin, which is released during the day, helps memories move from the conscious (mind centers) to the unconscious (stored memory). The substantia nigra is the twelfth-pigmented nucleus that is rich in melanin. A surge of upward memory images into awareness is generally reflected in increased melanin intake, which also frequently causes heightened dream experiences, hallucinations, and confusional psychosis.

Melanin plays a complex role in consciousness, as evidenced by its interactions with stimulants, hallucinogens, and tranquilizers.

Emotional states and consciousness are influenced by natural opiates and opioid peptides associated with the locus coeruleus. The complicated link between physiological processes, awareness, and memory systems is further highlighted by the interplay of melatonin, dopamine, and melanin (King 43–44). Our nerve tracts are essential characteristics that set man apart from all other animals. King contends that the presence of the brain's all Black neuromelanin nerve tract offers compelling evidence for the assertion that humans constitute a Black race with various subraces, encompassing a spectrum from Black-Black to White-Black. This racial categorization is said to be fundamentally grounded in a vast realm of brain Blackness.

Key features supporting this distinction include the intense blackness associated with the neuromelanin pigmentation of the locus coeruleus, commonly referred to as the Black Dot and considered the uppermost pigmentation center. This pigmentation is symbolically portrayed as a doorway leading into an entirely black hall of blackness. Additionally, the neuromelanin "Amenta" nerve tract is highlighted as another crucial characteristic that distinguishes [hu]mans from all other animals. King employs symbolic language and metaphorical descriptions to underscore the uniqueness and significance attributed to neuromelanin within the [hu]man brain.

Dr. King explores the concept of the Black Dot Black Ectoderm, which is the Doorway to the Temple, asserting that there is only one [hu]man race on Earth, the Black Race, with various nuances of Black. Drawing parallels between written and geological records of [hu]man history and biological and mental records of [hu]man origin, he delves into the process of [hu]man development after fertilization. Following the union of male sperm and female egg, a blastula forms, consisting of three layers: outer ectoderm, inner endoderm, and mesoderm. Dr. King emphasizes that melanin is present throughout the outermost layer of the ectoderm.

Around the 28th hour post-conception, the ectoderm begins to invaginate, forming a neural tube critical for the development of the spinal cord. The end of this tube, known as the neural crest mid-point, evolves into the brain, while cells along its length give rise to various components, including melanocytes and endocrine glands such as the pineal, pituitary, adrenal, mast cells, hypothalamus, thyroid, parathyroid, pancreas, and others. This narrative provides a detailed account of [hu]man development and the role of melanin in various physiological processes (King 36–38).

Melanin is not only found in the skin but is also present in the inner ear nucleus. Research indicates that melanin in the fetal inner ear plays a crucial role in guiding the growth of inner ear nerves, specifically the projections of the retinogenic-clostrate nerve. These projections extend from one ear to the opposite ear, facilitating coordinated hearing and vision. However, certain birth defects are associated with a lack of inner ear melanin, including human ocular albinism, sex-linked ocular albinism, and autosomal recessively inherited ocular albinism.

King cites research conducted in 1980 by Donald Creel that revealed that congenital deficits in visual acuity (20/400 to 20/50) and diminished pigmentation of different eye tissues (retina, ciliary body, and iris) occur in people with ocular albinism. As a result, those who are albino have a 20-degree blind patch in their temporal fields, nystagmus (a persistent fluttering of the eyes), and weak neural connections that cause them to lose coordination between their ears and eyes. According to King, inner ear melanin is essential for defining the correct pattern and direction of growth for the eyes and nerves, just as the melanin seed blueprint in the ectoderm defines the evolution of the brain, spinal cord, and endocrine glands (King 40).

The Black Dot, also referred to as the Memory Doorway to the temple, signifies the entrance into the African temple, a symbolic representation of birth or creation within the [hu]man mind-body. Descriptions from various sources outline the features of this entrance, including two columns and obelisks, both crowned with black pyramidions. These obelisks at the African temple entrance symbolize fundamental opposites in nature, embodying concepts such as male and female, active and passive, or positive and negative.

According to research by M. A. Pathak and D. L. Fanselow, exposure to sunlight causes melanin pigmentation, which is caused by two different photobiological processes: melanogenesis, which is the creation of new pigment, and instantaneous pigment-darkening, or tanning. Melanin's distinctive physical characteristics, which enable it to work as a superior electrical conductor or semiconductor, are responsible for its black hue. Melanin has threshold and memory switching in response to an applied electrical field, and it absorbs light, colors, and energy.

Threshold switching occurs when the electrical field triggers a shift from low to high conductivity and back to low when the field is removed. On the other hand, memory switching involves a sample that can be returned to the low conductivity state by bigger electrical fields, but it also involves a sample that remains in the high conductivity state long after the field is withdrawn. The Black Dot is conceptualized as the doorway to the collective unconscious, allowing the passage of chaos, the hierarchy of energies, God, and the macrocosm to manifest into the individual [hu]man mind, or as Dr. King terms it, the "Ptah Macrocosm." Melanin's role in memory pool operation is exemplified by its direct linkage to DNA, a crucial biological blueprint for life. King underscores the intricate relationship between melanin, consciousness, and memory within the context of African temple symbolism (King 41-42).

Once again, an expanding body of biological research emphasizes how the collective unconscious is imprinted in our minds, with a significant connection to our brains. The [hu]man brain's evolutionary journey is systematically traced from animal ancestors, progressing through primate, mammal, reptilian, amphibian, fish, and one-celled organisms. A pivotal observation is made concerning the embryonic stage, where all animal embryos, including [hu]mans, exhibit striking similarities, passing through ancestral forms from fish to mammals. The oldest layer of the brain, the brain stem, houses the black nerve tracts. In my opinion, these defects in this black neuromelanin tract can reveal behaviors reminiscent of neanderthal hostility and aggression (King 42).

King continues, The cumulative evidence is compelling when one considers the biological properties of melanin, memory storage, its presence in ancient brain centers, heightened brain pigmentation in advanced species, and numerous reports of detailed memory images of historical concepts. The dream phase, known as Rapid Eye Movement (REM) sleep, is characterized by historical memory images that pass through the locus coeruleus doorway and originate from the collective unconscious memory banks in the black neuromelanin (Amenta) nerve tract in the brain stem.

The Black Dot, representing the all-black neuromelanin (Amenta) brain nerve tract led by the locus coeruleus, plays a critical role in the path of unconscious memory images ascending to consciousness. Harvard psychiatrists J. Allan Hobson and Robert McCarley describe the brain as a dream state generator with a dynamic flow of memory images. Melatonin, the pineal hormone released at night, influences the dream system, enhancing the movement of sensory images from the brainstem to the cortex.

Serotonin, released during daylight, facilitates the flow of memory images from the brain centers (consciousness) to unconscious memory storage. The substantia nigra, an eleventh pigmented nucleus rich in melanin, is crucial; its depigmentation leads to Parkinson's disease. Increased melanin intake often results in heightened dream experiences, hallucinations, and confusional psychosis, reflecting a surge of upward memory images into consciousness.

The interaction of melanin with various substances, such as stimulants, hallucinogens, and tranquilizers, underscores its intricate role in consciousness. Natural opiates and opioid peptides linked to the locus coeruleus influence emotional states and guide consciousness. The interplay of melatonin, dopamine, and melanin further emphasizes the intricate relationship between biochemical processes, consciousness, and memory systems (King 42–44).

These issues are important in understanding our present-day relationships between Blacks and Caucasians/D.O.N's. Frances Cress Welsing, author of "The Cress Theory of Color Confrontation and Racism

(White Supremacy), has said of such relationships, "The Theory of Color-Confrontation states that the white or color-deficient Europeans responded psychologically with a profound sense of numerical inadequacy and color inferiority upon their confrontations with a massive majority of the world's people, all of whom possessed varying degrees of color-producing capacity" (Welsing). Her theory explores the complex psychological interactions that arose during historical exchanges between varied tribes around the world and white or color-deficient Europeans.

Dr. Welsings theory posits that these encounters triggered a profound psychological response characterized by a sense of numerical inadequacy and color inferiority among the Europeans. The presence of a vast majority of individuals with diverse skin tones heightened these psychological dynamics, leading to intricate and complex responses. The theory suggests that the Europeans, faced with the numerical dominance of people with varying degrees of color-producing capacity, grappled with a fundamental challenge to their self-perception. This challenge was deeply rooted in the external appearance of individuals, reflecting an intricate interplay between consciousness and unconscious reactions. As a result, an uncontrollable sense of hostility and aggression emerged, persisting throughout the historical epoch of mass confrontations between whites and Black people.

In essence, the Theory of Color-Confrontation provides a framework for understanding the psychological complexities that arose during historical interactions, shedding light on how perceptions of numerical inadequacy and color inferiority influenced the dynamics of these encounters. This psychological response, whether consciously or unconsciously expressed, struck at the core of their identity—their external appearance. In the context of modern psychological theories, this deep-seated inadequacy triggered an uncontrolled surge of hostility and aggression. These intense emotions became pervasive and persisted throughout the historical epoch, marked by mass confrontations between white populations and people of color. The "Color Confrontation" theory suggests that these psychological dynamics played a significant role in shaping historical interactions and conflicts between different racial and ethnic groups. The initial defensive hostility and aggression came from whites and are recorded in innumerable diaries, journals, and books written by whites. It is also a matter of record that only after long periods of great abuse have "non-whites" responded defensively to any form of it's action (King 87).

Final Thoughts

This text aims to identify the true enemies of Black people world-wide. To understand that the programming is real! We are currently in 2024, and if we don't stay educated and vigilant, Black people will slowly be forced back into Jim Crow and eventually the slave fields. The white supremacists have the technology and the weapons to destroy the entire planet. The white supremacists are dedicated to maintaining and practicing anti-Black racism and hell bent on keeping control over all Black people on the planet. As our dear freedom fighter, who is now in the realm of the ancestors, Khalid Muhammad, eloquently said, "The white race is absolutely disagreeable to get along with in peace. No other people on the face of the earth have been able to get along with white people since white people have been on our planet" (Khalid Muhammad).

It is not impossible to coexist peacefully with white supremacists/racist individuals who adhere to destructive ideologies. White supremacy is deeply rooted in hatred toward Black people; this has indeed been the main source of Black people's conflict and problems throughout history. The impact of white supremacist ideologies is evident in the historical atrocities and ongoing systemic inequalities. To address this severe problem, it is crucial to fully understand and not be confused about what white supremacy is and how it operates when it comes to dealing with people with color in their skin. It is extremely difficult and/or next to impossible to get along with those who support white supremacist ideologies. In an effort to confront and replace the system of white supremacy, I attempt to promote dialogue and education. This corrupt system needs to be replaced with one based on justice. Social activities that challenge white supremacist notions, promote inclusivity and prevent prejudice are crucial for Black people.

Toxic racist ideology, fueled by racial prejudice, has spawned a multitude of societal problems and tensions. Attempts at harmonious cohabitation face an inherent obstacle, as the very core of white supremacy contradicts the principles of equality, justice, and humanity. I've discovered that the first stage in influencing the Black American population is to influence their self-perception and how they relate to their own history and culture. I have discovered this during my journey through the several tiers of white deceit and my education of white supremacists. This is also significant to give insight and emphasize how psychological control worked well in slavery. There is less need for physical restraints like prison walls or chains when those in positions of power are successful in instilling shame and contempt for the cultural identity and historical history of Black people.

The proliferation of toxic racist ideology, driven by racial prejudice, has given rise to a myriad of societal issues and tensions. The endeavor for harmonious cohabitation is not possible, as the very essence of white supremacy stands in stark contradiction to the fundamental principles of equality, justice, and humanity.

In my journey through the layers of white deception and control, I have come to recognize that influencing the Black American population begins with manipulating their perception of themselves and their connection to their own history and culture. This revelation underscores the potency of psychological manipulation as a tool of enslavement. The insidious impact of this psychological control becomes evident as it permeates the consciousness of the oppressed, shaping their self-perception and distorting their understanding of their cultural heritage. This strategic manipulation serves to perpetuate a cycle of subjugation, and Black individuals become complicit in their own oppression by internalizing the degrading narratives imposed upon them. Thus, the conquest of minds proves to be a formidable weapon in the arsenal of white supremacy, further complicating the pursuit of a society built on principles of equality and justice.

The essence of this wisdom lies in recognizing that a people stripped of pride in their culture and history become vulnerable to manipulation and domination. It emphasizes the complex relationship that exists between mental freedom and the capacity to fend against injustice. Because of this, the fight for liberation is not just fought on the ground but also in the hearts and minds of individuals whose lives have been shaped by white supremacist influences. By comprehending this paradigm, we may retake control over our ideas and identities by resisting attempts at cultural erasure.

Understanding this plea resonates as a rallying cry for the unity of Black individuals in our nation, urging them to embrace and celebrate their rich heritage while fostering a collectively just spirit. It extends beyond a mere call for unity, emphasizing the need for Black communities to forge a distinct identity and to construct a communal bond that transcends historical challenges. At its core, this call advocates for self-determination, urging Black individuals to take charge of their destinies by defining their aspirations and assuming leadership roles within their organizations.

The essence lies in empowerment—the empowerment to shape goals, aspirations, and organizational trajectories from within. It's an invitation to reclaim agency over narratives, rejecting external impositions, and charting a course guided by shared values and experiences. This call acknowledges the strength embedded in a unified front, recognizing that a collective, self-directed approach is pivotal for the progression and upliftment of Black communities. Ultimately, it echoes a vision where Black people stand as architects of their own fate, crafting a future imbued with purpose, unity, and self-determined success.

In my perspective, Black individuals who steadfastly reject the shackles of oppression pose a perceived threat to white society, not due to any inherent danger but because they emerge as beacons of hope for their fellow brothers and sisters. By boldly resisting systemic oppression, we transcend mere slaves, transforming into symbols that inspire others within their community to defy injustice and join in the pursuit of justice. It's not about inherent danger but the transformative power of resilience and the refusal to accept subjugation.

These Black individuals, standing as symbols of hope, become catalysts for a collective awakening, encouraging the world to follow suit in our journey toward liberation. Our refusal to succumb to oppression sparks a ripple effect, instigating a sense of empowerment and solidarity within the Black community. The perceived threat lies in the potential to dismantle oppressive structures of white supremacy through unity and collective action.

In essence, this underscores the transformative power of Black individuals who, through their courageous defiance, become catalysts for a broader movement. Their resistance becomes a rallying point, inspiring others to envision a future liberated from the constraints of systemic oppression. From my perspective, the deliberate suppression of Black history within American education, specifically in schools and history books, orchestrated by white America, has obscured the courageous narratives of our ancestors. The valor and resilience demonstrated by hundreds of Black men and women who actively participated in slave rebellions have been obscured and lost in the mists of time. Plantation owners, motivated by their own interests, took measures to eradicate written accounts of these uprisings, perpetuating a historical silence that echoes through generations.

An incomplete and skewed knowledge of our shared history is perpetuated by the deliberate removal of these narratives from mainstream education. The broader story is left unfinished by omitting to mention the struggles and defiance of those who opposed the atrocities of slavery, such as Gabriel Prosser in Virginia in 1800, Denmark Vesey in Charleston, South Carolina, in 1822, and Nat Turner's Slave Rebellion in Southampton County, Virginia, in 1831. It is essential to recognize the concerted efforts to suppress these stories, as they are integral to understanding the complex tapestry of Black history and resilience. In light of this historical erasure, it becomes crucial to actively seek, preserve, and share these untold stories, ensuring that the bravery and resistance of our ancestors are not relegated to obscurity. Through a collective effort to unearth and amplify suppressed histories, we reclaim a more comprehensive and accurate narrative that reflects the full spectrum of Black experiences in America.

I think it's important to address the belief—held by some—that fighting fire means employing more fire. But I really think that using water to put out a fire is a more efficient method than continuing the aggressive cycle. This idea also applies to how we fight racism; we support using justice and the truth to oppose racism rather than imitating white supremacists. The concept is based on the conviction that reacting to hatred with retaliatory hostility only serves to continue a damaging cycle. We can eradicate racism's underlying origins and work together to overthrow systematic white supremacy by enacting justice.

Through a commitment to solidarity, we strive to build bridges, foster understanding, and create a society where the bonds of shared humanity triumph over the divisive forces of racism. The pursuit of justice has seldom been achieved by appealing to the moral sensibilities of those who perpetrate oppression. Depending only on persuasive morality and appealing to the guilt of oppressors is erroneous when dealing with a psychopath when structural injustice is involved. History attests that oppressed individuals or groups rarely attain liberation solely through moral appeals to their oppressors. While moral arguments may play a role in shaping public opinion, substantive change typically requires a more direct confrontation with oppressive forces. Movements for freedom and equality have historically thrived on resilience, collective action, and a unified commitment to challenging the status quo. Freedom is often secured through determined and strategic actions that challenge the oppressive structures and systems in place.

I believe that we must become instruments of mass productivity and constructiveness as Black people; this is a fundamental call to go beyond traditional ideas of activism and bring about social change. The transformation of today's society requires not just changes to the structures already in place but also an internal, simultaneous metamorphosis within ourselves. In order to be weapons of mass constructiveness, one must actively contribute to the building and strengthening of a world that produces "Maat," which stands for Truth, Justice, Harmony, Balance, Order, Propriety, and Reciprocity. It involves more than just criticizing the systems as they are now; it involves actively participating in projects that elevate, develop, and cultivate a collective consciousness. On the other hand, being weapons of mass productivity involves the transformative power of productivity as a force that may break down barriers, promote unity, and develop understanding.

The idea that changing the system is insufficient without a concurrent transformation of ourselves, and the interconnectedness of personal and societal evolution. It suggests that sustainable and meaningful change requires introspection, consciousness, and a genuine commitment to embodying the values we seek to instill in the broader social fabric. This perspective advocates for a holistic approach to societal transformation, where individuals become active agents in both deconstructing oppressive systems and constructing a world grounded in truth and justice. This strikes a deep chord with me personally because it highlights how subtle and ubiquitous oppression is, alerting us to the dangers of growing acclimated to its unceasing presence. It describes a psychological phenomenon in which the capacity to bear the burden of oppression increases as one's awareness of it decreases. Over time, oppression becomes an ingrained, unchangeable aspect of one's world rather than an outside force.

Wisdom emphasizes the necessity of raising consciousness about Black people's subjugation in order to achieve true emancipation. The path to liberation requires a conscious and acute recognition of the shackles, rejecting the idea that tyranny is natural and should be an unavoidable part of life. This increased consciousness serves as a spark, inspiring people to take up resistance and revolutionary causes.

The aforementioned statement highlights the importance of acute awareness and encourages Black people to challenge the normality of our own subordination. It challenges the risky complacency that results from accepting oppression as the standard and promotes a watchful and critical viewpoint that is essential for destroying structural injustice. It basically asks for the development of a conscious mentality that actively encourages people to seek freedom and to demolish oppressive systems in both their individual and societal lives.

Envisioning a scenario where Black people earnestly organize and arm themselves for the pursuit of justice, it is anticipated that the sheer weight of guilt and fear might lead to an astonishing outcome. The notion that some white individuals may succumb to their own fear and guilt, resulting in untimely deaths, underscores the profound impact of systemic injustices on both oppressors and the oppressed. It serves as a stark commentary on the psychological toll of institutionalized racism and the potential consequences when marginalized communities actively assert their right to self-determination and justice.

Based on my personal experience, there is an intrinsic duty to stand up for a righteous cause once it has been identified as just. I know deep down, in my bones, that when we give up on something that is truly ours, it is the first step toward a slow and inevitable descent toward literal physical death. It's a phenomenon in which a large number of Black people, even if they are physically present, move through the world like dead bodies, driven only by their capacity to be consumers of material possessions and indulge in incorrect behaviors.

The contradictory situation in which a great number of brothers and sisters choose to remain silent or act indifferently while admitting that an unjust cause is legitimate. The idea of talking about justice while surrounded by walking corpses highlights the glaring inconsistency between declared moral principles and the inability to put them into practice. It makes one reevaluate their commitment to justice and calls into doubt the sincerity of views in the absence of steadfast advocacy and defense. This is a powerful call to reflection which urges Black people to live up to their stated principles. Highlighting the importance of actively participating in the defense of just causes and serves as a reminder that remaining silent in the face of injustice is equal to spiritual decay.

It is clear from challenging the popular narrative that opposition to a powerful force like the white supremacist empire is sane and that history has been gravely misinterpreted. Despite popular belief, history demonstrates that even the strongest civilizations ultimately crumble and burn to the ground due to the unstoppable march of time. The empires of white supremacists are ephemeral in nature. To not resist, as asserted, is to passively surrender to one's own oppression, acquiescing to a force that seeks to repress and stifle the indomitable spirit inherent in every human being. The notion of resistance, then, becomes a manifestation of profound sanity—an act of preserving one's autonomy and defending the intrinsic essence of humanity. We will continue to challenge the status quo, recognizing the impermanence of oppressive systems and the inevitability of their downfall.

The call to resist is a call to assert one's agency in the face of oppressive forces, aligning with the historical truth that no empire endures indefinitely. It is an affirmation of the enduring resilience of the [hu]man spirit and a refusal to succumb to the illusion of eternal dominance wielded by empires throughout history. It is a sentiment that is beyond description to realize that a system of white supremacist oppression is a living hell. It alludes to a terrifying world painstakingly created and maintained by an anti-Black world system. Torment, the embodiment of the American living of death, that permits the D.O.N.s to observe justice while prohibiting direct and tangible justice for [hu]mans. The American continent is considered a figurative representation of Hell. It conveys a feeling of being in a state similar to hell, devoid of human warmth or connection, and lonesomeness.

This version of hell, where most of the inmates are Black urbanites, emphasizes the spatial and racial aspects of structural oppression. In this particular context, the portrayal of hell offers a poignant commentary on the institutionalized cruelty that is supported by a system that, in spite of its claims to justice, confines Black people to a place where the harsh reality of physical separation and isolation is cruelly juxtaposed to a system of justice.

It's imperative to transmit the lessons of our ancestors that resonate with all generations with a profound sense of responsibility. It calls for a concerted effort to weave the threads of our collective wisdom into the fabric of our people's minds and lives. This commitment to legacy-building becomes a sacred duty, an undertaking that transcends Black individual existence and extends into the continuum of our shared heritage.

The nature of racism is undeniable; it is an insidious force that permeates the very air we breathe and infiltrates every facet of Black people's existence. From subtle and often overlooked microaggressions to the horrifying specter of violent acts, the impact of racism is an ever-present reality that shapes our daily lives. Racism is omnipresent, its influence is both ubiquitous and inescapable. It operates as an invisible force, subtly shaping interpersonal interactions, institutional structures, and societal norms. In this environment, racism permeates every aspect of our lives, impacting everything from intimate relationships to more significant institutional injustices. It can take many different forms, from subtle slights to overt instances of terror.

The recognition that racism extends across a spectrum, from the seemingly mundane to the profoundly brutal, highlights the multifaceted nature of the challenge we face. It is not confined to isolated incidents but manifests in a continuum of experiences that collectively contribute to the complex tapestry of racial injustice. This acknowledgment is a call to confront racism in all its manifestations, demanding a comprehensive and sustained effort to dismantle its deeply ingrained roots and foster a society where equity, understanding, and justice prevail. I've come to recognize the paramount importance of empowering young minds, especially in today's world, with the ability to independently observe, listen, and think critically. The foundational lesson is learning to rely on one's own senses and cognitive faculties to form intelligent and informed decisions. This emphasis on self-reliance encourages individuals to break free from the influence of external opinions and societal expectations.

Encouraging a habit of self-directed inquiry is a call to intellectual independence. It advocates for a mindset that actively seeks knowledge, questions assumptions, and navigates the complexities of life based on firsthand experiences. Young people can chart their own paths, navigate the multitude of influences around them, and, ultimately, develop a sense of autonomy that is essential for genuine understanding and personal growth in a world rife with white supremacist values by being given the opportunity to think for themselves.

I pose a question: Is the cockroach aware that the homeowner is attempting to destroy it? Based on my investigations, I've come to the conclusion that the roach, aside from its occasional victims, is unaware that it is being eradicated while the homeowner buys every kind of poison and pesticide to eradicate the infestation. If you've ever had cockroaches, you know that the goal is to eradicate the cockroach at its nest and at its heart. And I assert that Black people are experiencing this seven days a week, 24 hours a day, by a system of white supremacy in perpetuity. The white supremacists are trying to exterminate Black people, and just like the cockroach, we have no idea that this extermination is taking place on a grand scale.

Does the gazelle try to befriend the lion? And if the lion is friends with the gazelle whose life is in jeopardy, if the gazelle trusts the lion, then whose life is in jeopardy? If the gazelle believes whatever the lion says, whose life is in jeopardy? We, as children of the Sun, have a natural enemy in the form of those who can and do practice white supremacy, and in the system of white supremacy, those who possess dark skin are the "gazelle." The white supremacist of this planet with weapons of destruction is the "lion." We,as people with dark melanated skin, or [hu]mans, are unaware that mankind/D.O.N. is in an active war against [hu]man beings. And unfortunately, D.O.N. are Africa's offspring/children. It's time to rear the children. The only way to accomplish this mission is to practice Sankofa, "Go back and retrieve what was lost in order to move forward." We must employ our ancient natural connections to the Earth, the universe, and our ancestors. The European style of thinking must go, and we must reject and discard their ideologies like trash. The concept behind white supremacist ideology is one of sexual immorality, depravity, self-destruction, and hatred founded in envy.

HTP.

Works Cited

"Autosomal Dominant Inheritance." Britannica.Com, www.britannica.com/science/human-genetic-disease/Autosomal-dominant-inheritance.

Alexander, M. The New Jim Crow: Mass Incarceration in the Age of Colorblindness. The New Press, 2010.

"Almendron.com." *Https://Www.almendron.com*, 2019, www.almendron.com/tribuna/wp-content/uploads/2019/10/african-origin-of-civilization-complete.pdf.

Anderson, C. Powernomics: The National Plan to Empower Black America. Powernomics Corporation of America, 2001.

Ani, Marimba. Yurugu: An African-Centered Critique of European Cultural Thought and Behavior. Trenton, NJ: Africa World Press, 1994.

Baradaran, Mehrsa. The Color of Money: Black Banks and the Racial Wealth Gap. Hardcover, Harvard University Press, 2017.

"Benign neglect." Merriam-Webster.com Dictionary, Merriam-Webster, https://www.merriam-webster.com/dictionary/benign%20neglect. Accessed 30 Nov. 2023.

Ben-Jochannan, Y. Black Man of the Nile and his Family. Black Classic Press, 1989.

Berry, Henty. "ABOLITION OF SLAVERY." *US.Archive.Org*, 11 Jan. 1832, ia600209.us.archive.org/11/items/speechofhenryber00berr/speechofhenryber00berr.pdf. Accessed 6 Nov. 1832.

"Black Children Are Six Times More Likely to Be Shot to Death by Police." *Equal Justice Initiative*, 2 Dec. 2020, eji.org/news/black-children-are-six-times-more-likely-to-be-shot-to-death-by-police/.

Blakemore, Erin . "Who Were the Moors?" *National Geographic*, 12 May 2019, www.nationalgeographic.com/history/article/who-were-moors. n.p.

Bradley, Michael. The Iceman Inheritance: Prehistoric Sources of Western Man's Racism, Sexism, and Aggression. Toronto: Stoddart Publishing Co., 1991.

Brown, Dan. The Da Vinci Code. Doubleday, 2003.

Buncombe, Andrew. "WsWorldAmericas The Battle to Root Out Police Gangs like The Executioners from LA County Sheriff'S Department." *Independent*, 21 June. 2021, www.independent.co.uk/news/world/americas/police-gangs-la-sheriff-executioners.

Censer, Jane Turner. Review of They Were Her Property: White Women as Slave Owners in the American South, by Stephanie E. Jones-Rogers. The Journal of the Civil War Era, vol. 9 no. 4, 2019, p. 633-635. Project MUSE, https://doi.org/10.1353/cwe.2019.0077.

Clarke, J. H. Christopher Columbus and the African Holocaust: Slavery and the Rise of European Capitalism. A & B Books Publishers, 1992.

Collins, Terry. 'New Normal': High Number of Migrants Crossing Border Not Likely   toSlow."USAToday,30,Sept.2023,www.usatoday.com/story/news/nation/2023/09/30/how-many-migrants-crossed-the-border-2023-mexico-venezuela-.

Constance, Paul . "Latin America'S Fertility Decline Is Accelerating. No One'S Certain Why." *Americas Quarterly*, 4 Feb. 2024, www.americasquarterly.org/article/latin-americas-fertility-decline-is-accelerating-no-ones-sure-why/.

Cooper, Thomas, and Spencer James McMorris. Address to the Graduates of the South Carolina College: At the Public Commencement, 1830. Printed by S.J. M Morris, 1831.

"Cult." *Merriam-Webster.Com*, www.merriam-webster.com/dictionary/cult.

Curry, Tommy J. The Man-Not: Race, Class, Genre, and the Dilemmas of Black Manhood. Temple University Press, 2017.

Davis, Rochelle A., and Eileen Kane. "DeSantis' 'War on Woke' Looks a Lot like Attempts by Other Countries to Deny and Rewrite History." *The Conversation*, 24 Jul. 2023.theconversation.com/desantis-war-on-woke-looks-a-lot-like-attempts-by-other-countries-to-deny-and-rewrite-history-204884.

Diop, C. A.The African Origin of Civilization: Myth or Reality. Lawrence Hill & Company, 1974.

Dorwart, L. (2023, October 18). How to Tell If Someone Is a Psychopath. Verywellhealth. https://www.verywellhealth.com/psychopath

"Feb 5, 1885 CE: Belgian King Establishes Congo Free State." *National Geographic*, 19 Oct. 2023,www.education.nationalgeographic.org/resource/belgian-king-establishes-congo-free-state/.

Festinger, and Carlsmith. "Festinger and Carlsmith Cognitive Consequences of Forced Compliance."1959,www.age-of-the-sage.org/psychology/social/festinger_carlsmith_cognitive_dissonance.html.

Flegr, J., Sýkorová, K. Skin fairness is a better predictor for impaired physical and mental health than hair redness. *Sci Rep* 9, 18138 (2019). https://doi.org/10.1038/s41598-019-54662-5

"FM 6-2003 Ethnic Cleansing Operations." *Jr. Books Online*, www.jrbooksonline.com/PDF_Books_added2009-2/FM_6-2003_Ethnic_Cleansing_Operations.pdf.

Foster, T. A. Rethinking Rufus: Sexual Violations of Enslaved Men. University of Georgia Press, 2019.

From Atlantis To the Sphinx. 1st ed., vol. 1, *Virgin Publishing*, 1994. pp. 196, 222-223.

Frankel, Glenn . ""Today's Psychosurgeons Defend Techniques"." *Washington Post*, 8 Apr. 1980, www.washingtonpost.com/archive/politics/1980/04/08/todays-psychosurgeons-defend-techniques. Accessed 8 Apr. 1980.

Fuller, Neely Jr. The United-Independent Compensatory Code/System/Concept: A Compensatory Counter-Racist Code. Washington D.C.: Institute for Independent Education, 1984.

Gates Jr., Henry L. "How Many Slaves Landed in the U.S.?" *PBS*, 2003, www.pbs.org.

"Habits: How They Form And How To Break Them." *NPR.Org*, 5 Mar. 2012, www.npr.org/2012/03/05/147192599/habits-how-they-form-and-how-to-break-them.

Hanchard, Neil A. "Mendelian Autosomal Dominant Disorder." *National Human Genome Research*, www.genome.gov/genetics-glossary/Autosomal-Dominant-Disorder. Accessed 7 Nov. 2023.

Harris, Kelley , and Rasmus Nielsen. "The Genetic Cost of Neanderthal Introgression." *National Library of Medicine*, 2016, p. 881–891, https://doi.org/10.1534/genetics.116.186890.

Hart, Christian L. Ph.D. "Psychopaths and Pathological Lying." Psychology Today, 30 Mar.2023,www.psychologytoday.com/us/blog/the-nature-of-deception/202303/psychopaths-and-pathological-lying#.

HAUSCHKA,, THEODORE S., and AVERY A. SANDBERG. "An XYY Man with Progeny Indicating Familial Tendency to Non-disjunction." *National Institute of Arthritis and Metabolic Diseases,*, 1958, p. 22, https://doi.org/n.a.

Herrera, Arturo S., and Paola E. S. Arias. "Einstein Cosmological Constant, the Cell, and the Intrinsic Property of Melanin to Split and Re-form the Water Molecule." *MedCrave*,27 Aug.2014,medcraveonline.com/MOJCSR/einstein-cosmological-constant-the-cell-and-the-intrinsic-property-of-melanin-to-split-and-re-form-the-water-molecule.html.

"A History of the Slave-Breeding Industry in the United States." *Civil War Talk*, 17 Sept. 2019, www.jggscivilwartalk.online/index.php?threads/a-history-of-the-slave-breeding-industry-in-the-united-states.428/.

Hobson, John. *Imperialism: A Study.* James Pott and Company, 1902.

Hornblum, Allen M. *Acres of Skin: Human Experiments at Holmesburg Prison.* Routledge, 1998.

"Hue." Merriam-Webster.com Dictionary, Merriam-Webster, https://www.merriam-webster.com/dictionary/hue. Accessed 12 Nov. 2023.n.p.

Hubbard, T. K. (2020, March 31). *Historical Views of Homosexuality: Roman Empire.* Oxford University Press. https://oxfordre.com/politics/display

"Hyperaggressiveness."Cambridge,University,dictionary.cambridge.org/dictionary/english/hyper-aggressiveness.

King, Richard D. M.D. *African Origins of Biological Psychiatry. African World Books,Inc.,* 1987. pp. 36, 37.

Lambert, Laura. "Stockholm syndrome". Encyclopedia Britannica, 16 Oct. 2023, https://www.britannica.com/science/Stockholm-syndrome. Accessed 20 December 2023.

James, George G.M. Stolen Legacy: Greek Philosophy is Stolen Egyptian Philosophy.SanFrancisco: Julian Richardson Associates, 1992.

"Jim Crow Laws." *Jim_crow_educational_resource_.Pdf*, www.gcsu.edu/sites/files/page-assets/node-2213/attachments/jim_crow_educational_resource .pdf.n.d.

Jones-Rogers, Stephanie E. They Were Her Property: White Women as Slave Owners in the American South. New Haven, CT: Yale University Press, 2019.

Lee, ArLuthe. "5 People of Color Have Died in Hangings across Country." *The Atlanta Journal-Constitution*, 24 Jun. 2020, www.ajc.com/news/people-color-have-died-recent-string-hangings-across-county

Lincoln, Abraham . "Fragment of Speech regarding Sectionalism, [23 July 1856]." *Papers of Abraham Lincoln.*, 23 July. 1856, papersofabrahamlincoln.org/documents/D200898. Accessed 23 July. 1953.

LOVE, VICTORIA C., and LORELEI SHANNON. *Mad Madame LaLaurie 'New Orleans Most Famous Murderess Revealed".* The History Press, 2011.

Longrich, Nicholas R. ""War in the Time of Neanderthals: How Our Species Battled for Supremacy for over 100,000 Years"." *The Conversation*, 2 Nov. 2020, theconversation.com/war-in-the-time-of-neanderthals-how-our-species-battled-for-supremacy-for-over-100-000-years.

Luckman, Sol . "Pedophilia Quotes." *Good Reads,* www.goodreads.com/quotes/tag/pedophilia.n.p. , n.d.

Lynch, Willie. *Willie Lynch Letters & Making of a Slave.* 41400th ed., *African Tree Press,* 2011.

Mark, Joshua J. *"'IMHOTEP'."* *World History Encyclopedia,* www.worldhistory.org. n.p, n.d.

Martineau, Harriet. Retrospect of Western Travel, vol. 1. Saunders and Otley, 1838.

Mitra, Gyanendranath . "Why Are Europeans White? A Genetic Study." *Daily Pioneer,* 16,Nov.2018,www.dailypioneer.com/2018/state-editions/why-are-europeans-white--a-genetic-study.html.

Morcan, James, and Lance Morcan. *The Orphan Conspiracies: 29 Conspiracy Theories from The Orphan Trilogy. Sterling Gate Books Limited,* 2020.

Nadeau, Barbie L., et al. "'Low Fertility Trap': Why Italy'S Falling Birth Rate Is Causing Alarm." *CNN.Com,* 17 May 2023, www.cnn.com/2023/05/17/europe/italy-record-low-birth-rate-intl-cmd/index.html.

Nairaland. "The Origin Of AIDS: OPERATION MK-NAOMI." *Nairaland Forum,* www.nairaland.com/1158458/origin-aids-operation-mk-naomi. Accessed 15 Dec. 2023.

N.O.I. RESEARCH GROUP. "Ten Best Lies of Black History." *Final Call,* 29 Jan. 2013, www.finalcall.com/artman/publish/perspectives_1/article_9564.shtml.

Oxford Languages , Google. "Oxford Languages and Google." *Google,* 12 Sept. 2020, www.google.com/search?q=what+is+the+of+belief&sca_esv=579468707&rlz=. web, n.p, n.d.

Ottenburghs, Jente. "Why Do Some Humans Have Neanderthal DNA?" *Researchgate,* vol. 7, 2019, https://doi.org/Wageningen University & Research. Accessed 1 Aug. 2019 n.p.

Pakenham, Thomas . *The Scramble for Africa. Avon Books,* 1992.

"10 Pathological Liar Signs and How to Cope with a Habitual Liar." *Newport Institute*, www.newportinstitute.com/resources/co-occurring-disorders/pathological-liar-signs/.n.d.

Peltola, Larissa. "Rape and Sexual Violence Used As a Weapon of War and Genocide: An Examination of Historical and Contemporary Cases of Genocidal Rape and Prosecution of Rape in International Courts." *Claremont Colleges*, 1 Jan. 2018, core.ac.uk/download/pdf/159384976.pdf.

Population of Europe (2024) - Worldometer. www.worldometers.info/world-population/europe-population.

"Psychopath." Merriam-Webster.com Dictionary, Merriam-Webster, https://www.merriam-webster.com/dictionary/psychopath. Accessed 5 Nov. 2023.

Schmidt, Megan. "Neanderthals Were Just As Violent As Early Humans." *Www.Discovermagazine.Com › Planet Earth*, 17 July. 2023.

"10 Quotes From PowerNomics Pioneer Dr. Claud Anderson." *The Moguldom Nation*, moguldom.com/368243/10-quotes-from-powernomics-pioneer-dr-claud-anderson/. Accessed 1 Jan. 2023.

Reuters (2021, January 22). *Fact check: Biden's comments about 'doomed' United States taken out of context.* https://www.reuters.com/article/idUSKBN29R2BN/

Sáenz, Rogeli, and Kenneth M. Johnson. "White Deaths Exceed Births in a Majority of U.S. States." *Applied Population Lab*, apl.wisc.edu/data-briefs/natural-decrease.

Sanger, Margaret . *An Autobiography. W-W-NORTON & COMPANY Publishers*, 1935. p. p.366.

Savitt, Todd L. "The Use of Blacks for Medical Experimentation and Demonstration in the Old South." *The Journal of Southern History*, vol. 48, no. 3, 1982, pp. 331–48. *JSTOR*, https://doi.org/10.2307/2207450. Accessed 1 Dec. 2023.

"Scientists Discover A Girl With DNA From Two Different Species." *Explored Planet*, /www.exploredplanet.com/trending/scientists-discover-a-girl-with-dna-from-two-different-species/.

Shayne , Tasha . "Decoding the Actual Age of the Great Sphinx." *Gaia.Com*, 24 Dec. 2020, www.gaia.com/article/decoding-the-actual-age-of-the-great-sphinx.n.p.

Shockley, William , and Frances C. Welsing. "White or Black Superiority? A Controversial Debate : Dr. Francis Welsing Vs. Dr. William Shockley." *WorldCat*, 1 Jan. 1974, search.worldcat.org/title/white-or-black-superiority-a-controversial-debate-dr-francis-welsing-vs-dr-william-shockley/oclc/3522067.

Skinner, B. F. *SCIENCE AND HUMAN BEHAVIOR*. *Pearson Education, Inc.*, 2014. p. 182.

Sublette, Ned, and Constance Sublette. *"The American Slave Coast A History of the Slave-Breeding Industry"*. *Lawrence Hill Books*, 2015.

"Systemic Racism Pervades US Police and Justice Systems, UN Mechanism on Racial Justice in Law Enforcement Says in New Report Urging Reform." *United Nations*, 28 Sept. 2023, www.ohchr.org/en/press-releases/2023/09/systemic-racism-pervades-us-police-and-justice-systems-un-mechanism-racial.

The Week Staff. "Attacking the Grid." The Week, The Week, 26 Feb. 2023, theweek.com/crime-and-punishment/1021282/attacking-the-grid.

Totten, Samuel , and Paul R. Bartrop. *Dictionary of Genocide.* vol. 1 & 2, *Greenwood Press*, 2008.

Umeh, U. (2019, March 11). Mental Illness in Black Community,1700-2019: A Short History.BlackPast.org.https://www.blackpast.org/african-american-history/mental-illness-in-black-community-1700-2019-a-short-history/

"US Family of 11-year-old Shot by Police Vows to Seek Justice After Officer Gets No Charges." *The Guardian*, 15 Dec. 2023, www.theguardian.com/us-news/2023/dec/15/aderrien-murry-police-shot-911-family-vows-fight-justice.

Wadman, M. "Row erupts over child aggression study." Nature 392, 747 (1998). https://doi.org/10.1038/33760

Washington, H. A. Medical Apartheid: The Dark History of Medical Experimentation on Black Americans from Colonial Times to the Present. Anchor Books, 2007.

Welsing, Frances Cress. The Isis Papers: The Keys to the Colors. Chicago: Third World Press, 1991.

"What Does It Mean to Have Neanderthal or Denisovan DNA?" *MedlinePlus*, 2022, p. np,https://medlineplus.gov/genetics/understanding/dtcgenetictesting/neanderthaldna/.

"WHAT THEY ARE SAYING: HOMELAND MAJORITY'S FOURTH INTERIM REPORT ON THE FINANCIAL COST OF SECRETARY MAYORKAS' BORDER CRISIS." *HOMELAND SECURITY*, 16 Nov. 2023, homeland.house.gov/2023/11/16/what-they-are-saying-homeland-majoritys-fourth-interim-report-on-the-financial-cost-of-secretary-mayorkas-border-crisis.

Williams, Chancellor. The Destruction of Black Civilization: Great Issues of a Race Between 4500 B.C. and 2000 A.D. Third World Press, 1992.

Wilson, Amos N. The Falsification of Afrikan Consciousness: Eurocentric History, Psychiatry and the Politics of White Supremacy. Afrikan World Books, 1993.

Wolf, Cam. "The New Uniform of White Supremacy." *G.Q*, 17 Aug. 2017, www.gq.com/story/uniform-of-white-supremacy.

Woodard, V. The Delectable Negro: Human Consumption and Homoeroticism within US Slave Culture. NYU Press, 2014.

Woodson, Carter G. The Mis-Education of the Negro. Africa World Press, 2000. (Original work published 1933).

Wright, Bobby E. The Psychopathic Racial Personality and Other Essays. Third World Press, 1984.

Van Sertima, I. They Came Before Columbus: The African Presence in Ancient America. Random House 1976.

The Whiteness of Destruction: The Origins and Consequences of White Aggression

In "The Whiteness of Destruction," Dr. Mauray L. Tolbert embarks on a bold exploration of the origins and manifestations of white aggression, spanning over 200,000 years of European history. Through meticulous research and incisive analysis, Dr. Tolbert delves into the depths of human history to uncover the roots of white supremacy and its devastating consequences.

From the elusive missing link to the destruction of ancient civilizations like Kemet/Egypt, the scramble for Africa, and the genocide of indigenous peoples across the globe, Tolbert meticulously traces the trajectory of white aggression. He shines a piercing light on pivotal figures such as Christopher Columbus and the tyranny that spread to the Americas, leaving a trail of devastation in its wake.

With a scientific approach, Dr. Tolbert exposes the harrowing realities of American slavery, the insidious legacy of Jim Crow laws, and the ongoing struggle for Civil Rights in America. He elucidates the profound and enduring effects of systemic racism and colonization, unraveling the intricate web of power dynamics that continue to shape our world today.

"The Whiteness of Destruction" is a groundbreaking work that challenges readers to confront uncomfortable truths about the dark underbelly of human history. With compelling insights and thought-provoking analysis, Dr. Tolbert offers a comprehensive exploration of white aggression and its profound impact on society. This book is essential reading for anyone seeking a deeper understanding of the complexities of race, power, and oppression in our modern world.